THE MEN WHO WERE
THE BUSBY BABES

THE MEN WHO WERE
THE BUSBY BABES

TOM CLARE

Published in Great Britain in 2012 by The Derby Books Publishing Limited, 3 The Parker Centre, Mansfield Rd, Derby, DE21 4SZ

ISBN 978-1-78156-158-8

CONTENTS

The Phoenix

How they laughed, and loved, and played the game together
Played the game and gave it every ounce of life
And the crowds they thronged to see such free spirits
But, good God, there wasn't many coming home

The dice were cast, for some the last, the final challenge
On a snow bound ground in far off Serbia
The tie was won, the songs were sung, we sang together
But, good God, there won't be many coming home

Roger Byrne, Mark Jones, and Salford's Eddie Colman
Tommy Taylor, Geoffrey Bent, and David Pegg
Duncan Edwards, and Dublin's own boy Liam Whelan
My good God, there wasn't any who came home

Then Murphy picked the standard up
When all looks lost he made the cut
The fresh young flowers he'd fondly nourished
On a Munich runway had sadly perished

With aching heart he beat the gong
And told the world the Babes lived on
Then Best he came, he eased the pain
With Charlton, Law, and Crerand

The years between were cold and mean
They never had that feeling
Pretenders came and left again
There wasn't any healing

Then Fergie came and fanned the flames
With Eric's Gallic passion
He gave us Giggs, he gave us Scholes,
He gave us Butt and Beckham

He bought in Keane to lead the team
To even greater glory
My nightmares gone, my dream moves on
Again I see the Phoenix

There are those gone down that long, long road before us
Yet each morn we try and keep them in our sight
In memories eye, the Busby Babes are all immortal
The Red Devils spirit lives, it never died

By kind permission of Harry Gregg MBE

Foreword

There is no football club in the world that can compare to Manchester United.

Many can boast that their names are etched onto the European Cup, the Champions League trophy for the modern day students and followers of the game, more times than that of United, but none can conjure up the magic, the charisma or the world-wide following of the Old Trafford club.

For many of the seventy-five odd thousand who regularly fill the vast Old Trafford stadium it is the modern day United that has brought them to the ground. Players from the Premier League era like Beckham, Giggs, Cantona, Ronaldo and Rooney. Players who have created the modern day history of the club.

But the present, the Alex Ferguson years, create only a small corner of the vast canvas that is the history of Manchester United. Best, Law and Charlton from five decades ago are today enshrined in the match day experience with their prominent statues, but a goal kick away from the 'Trinity' is the memorial to the players who, for those of another generation, symbolise 'Manchester United'. The players who gave United to the world - the *Busby Babes*'.

Countless words have been written about those legendary individuals, the Flowers of Manchester, who perished at Munich on that cold February afternoon in 1958. I myself have penned many of those, with tributes to Roger Byrne and the colossus that was Duncan Edwards. But not having witnessed those two individuals, or their team-mates, in the flesh, I had to rely on the memories of their classmates, their friends and the newspapers of the time to recreate their story.

What you are about to read on Roger, Duncan and their team mates from that magnificent Matt Busby and Jimmy Murphy side of 1958, however, is written from the heart. There was little need for Tom Clare to search through piles of newspaper cuttings to discover the goals of Dennis Viollet and Tommy Taylor, the artistry of Eddie Colman or the magnificence of Duncan Edwards. He had simply to close his eyes and through the mists of time those red shirts would materialise and he would drift back to his beloved Manchester in the 1950's and his time with the Babes.

As the memories flowed and Tom's thoughts appeared on paper, there would also have been a hint of sadness, moments of reflection when the typing would come to a halt, as he recalled those wonderful players.

For those who were fortunate enough to have shared the Popular Side, or some other part of the vastly different than today Old Trafford with Tom, you will enjoy the memories. But for those who were not around at the time, this is your opportunity to learn about the men behind the images in the Munich Tunnel. Their lives before coming under the Busby/Murphy umbrella and how they helped create the legendary '*Busby Babes*'.

IAIN McCARTNEY
APRIL 2012.

Prologue

Writing this book has been very much a labour of love. Since my Grandfather started following Newton Heath Football Club in 1898, and then Manchester United from 1902 onwards, between the two of us, we have shared in every success, failure, and tragedy that is written in the Club's magnificent history.

As I am now in the twilight years of my life, the lineage in the Clare family is now coming to an end. It is because of this that I wanted to record the memories and experiences of my early life living in inner-city Manchester in the late 1940s, early 1950s, and of growing up alongside the emergence of the *Busby Babes*. That was achieved in my previous book *Forever a Babe*.

This book chronicles the stories of eighteen of the players from the squad that made up that wonderful *Busby Babes* team, and also of the man who really forged them into the players that they were; the legendary Jimmy Murphy. Jimmy's role is often understated in the development of those young players, but there is no doubt that without him, Sir Matt Busby could not have achieved the pinnacles which he did.

There are people who I need to recognize and thank for their never ending support in helping me to write this book. The triumvirate that is Barney Chilton who is editor of Red News, the oldest Manchester United fanzine; Tony Smith, and Iain McCartney, for all their help and advice whenever I have pestered them. All three have been there for me when needed and I am so proud to be able to call them my friends.

My grateful thanks to Tim Ashmore for producing the wonderful book cover.

I would also like to thank Steve Caron, and Nick Jones, at JMD Media for helping and enabling me to see this project into print.

Most of all I would like to thank my dear wife Cheryl who has worked so hard alongside me doing the proofing, listening to my moans, and putting up with my crankiness when things were not going so well. Without her love and total support, this work could never have been completed.

Tom Clare
Houston, Texas
April 2012

Preface

The word *nostalgia* is defined in the dictionary as; *a sentimental yearning for the past.* As we grow older, and move into our twilight years, nostalgia certainly plays more than a bit part in the remaining days of our lives. It is a natural thing to reflect on those days, times, events, and places, in times gone by, which are seated deep in the back-pocket of our memory. Nostalgia is a state of mind for which there is definitely no known cure. It dwells on all things past, but there is warmth of feeling which emanates from it and makes it seem like a next-door neighbor rather than a visitor from a far off distant place. There is so much to be said for it, and it has such a wondrous quality about it, that makes it unchallengeable! Like all beauty, it rests in the eye of the beholder.

Football is full of nostalgia. However, in this modern era, football nostalgia seems to begin with the advent of the Video Recorder, and also the DVD player. What went on in football prior to these machines becoming so freely available on the market is now left to old men like me passing on those stories and tales of yesteryear. Most people spontaneously reminisce when they are alone. Reminiscence can certainly motivate you. It can also give you a sense of meaning and purpose, especially in your later years.

My own nostalgia is seated in the early to late 1950s a period which I like to think was a golden era for soccer. It is amazing to think that since the inception of the Premier League, over three thousand foreign footballers have plied their trade at one time or another in English football. It is also peculiar to remember how instantly forgettable most of them have been. Contrast that with those 1950s years when there were many world class British footballers turning out for our football clubs week in, and week out.

The 1950s was a time when football club boardrooms were populated mainly by local men of trade – the butcher, the baker, and the candle stick maker. These were local businessmen who expected their investments to yield no greater return than that of a parochial celebrity – comfortable premises where they could booze, the right to annoy, pester, and question club managers with their ignorant opinions about playing matters. These were self important persons who were always happy to ignore the discomforts, indignities, and downright hazards suffered by the tens of thousands of working class spectators who poured into their grounds week in, and week out. These were also the same persons who never had any qualms about exploiting their own club's players when it came to wages. So few of them ever foresaw just how, in this so called modern electronic age, football would be exposed as a large fat goose just waiting to be plucked. In this modern era, the plucking really did gather pace, and it has become like an out of control juggernaut free-wheeling down a motorway.

There is certainly no doubt in my mind, that the lucky pluckers in football today are the owners and directors who wear the business suits. Football today now has such a massive coverage in all areas of the media that headlines about the game appear just as much on the front pages of the financial papers as they do on the back pages of the dailies. For those of us whose ties to football were forged long before the gargantuan television deals, sponsorships, and merchandising came to the fore, it is hard to accept the way in which the game is now being run and which has brought such exponential growth to its finances. That is not say that I am foolish enough to see this change with total condemnation – I do realize that this great tidal wave of money which has swept through the game during the last thirty years has brought some benefits as well as many problems.

Years ago, we the fans on the terraces had a huge stake in the game. But because of the love we had for our clubs and the game, we were more than happy to accept the conditions which prevailed in our football stadia at that time. There was conditions which could only ever be described as intolerable to cattle, and fans were in constant danger of having their trouser legs used as a piss-stone on a regular basis – and it was a reciprocal arrangement all the way down the terraces. As far as refreshments was concerned, there was nothing better to eat than the indigestible meat pie. As for beverage, you had a choice of either a lukewarm cup of tea, Oxo or Bovril. Today, fans are now accommodated in magnificent stadiums where the catering facilities are more likely to merit praise in the Egon Ronay or Michelin Food Guides. The risk these days of disasters on the scale of Burnden Park, Ibrox, Valley Parade or Hillsborough have been vastly reduced and almost totally eliminated. And yet for me, this so called bold new era has created a very deep unease, and brought me a fear about the widespread willingness to ensure that there is a material enrichment of football, even if the penalty is the impoverishment of its spirit.

I suppose that is why I am always so ready to return to the seat of my own nostalgia – the 1950s, Old Trafford, and my beloved Manchester United. Over sixty years has passed since I made my first visit to the old lady of a stadium which stood as the legacy of John Henry Davies' foresight back in the first decade of the Twentieth Century. Whenever I return to my home city of Manchester today, and visit the wonderful stadium that stands resplendent in its magnetic magnificence, the ghosts of my past, and particularly the years from 1950-58 return, and I am left with a myriad of warm memories.

Those years, and the events which happened in-between them, tied me to the umbilical cord of Manchester United. Whenever I sit in quiet reflection, the nostalgia floods back just like the ebb and flow of a tidal sequence. I experienced so much happiness during those years, particularly whenever I was at Old Trafford watching what I still believe to be, the greatest amalgam of young British football talent ever harnessed together at one time, at a football club. They were the flowers, the pollinators of British football at that time; they were the Flowers of Manchester.

Introduction - The Busby Babes

It says so much that even now, over fifty years since that terrible accident at the Riem Airport in Munich, Germany, that in football circles, the name of the Manchester United team which became known affectionately as the *Busby Babes*, crops up continuously in football conversation. Since that terrible day on 6 February 1958, when eight young men met their demise at the end of a Munich runway, so much has been written and reported about the players who made up that wonderful team. There was certainly an aura about them, and without doubt, compared to today's overpaid and overpriced players, they were certainly something special; not only as players, but also as people who embraced their adopted city and community.

With the passage of time, the number of persons who had the privilege of actually watching this team play is diminishing year by year. Fortunately, I am one of the few who did see them play, and on a regular basis, and my memories of all those young men have never faded. I was around as they emerged in the early 1950s, and then as they began to mature and take both English and European football, by storm. For just eight short years I shared in their triumphs, their disappointments, and ultimately, their tragedy.

In 1931, Mr. James W. Gibson was the benefactor who salvaged Manchester United Football club from almost certain extinction. For the second time in thirty years, the club had been floundering in a sea of financial trouble. The first time, in 1902, the club had been saved by five benefactors who had each put their hands deep into their pockets to keep it afloat. One of those men was Mr. John Henry Davies, a shrewd Manchester businessman. Davies became Chairman of the club, and under his guidance, just five short years later the club enjoyed its very first tangible success in winning the First Division championship in 1908. This was followed the next year by winning the FA Cup for the very first time, and in 1911, a second First Division title came home to their new stadium at Old Trafford. Previously, the club had played at a ramshackle stadium known as Bank Street, which was situated in the suburb of Clayton which is to the North side of Manchester, and it was surrounded by chemical and engineering factories. From the moment he took over as Chairman, Davies worked tirelessly to move the club to a brand new stadium, and this was finally achieved in 1910, when Old Trafford was built and completed, and was opened for the first time. Davies stayed as Chairman until his death in 1927 and from that moment on, the club began to falter once again.

James. W. Gibson could never have been called a football man. He was, like Davies, a shrewd Manchester businessman, and was a man with great foresight who was also a great leader, and a visionary. Together with two of the great stalwarts in Manchester United's history, (Louis Rocca, and Walter Crikmer) he began to put the club back on an even keel financially. It was a few years after he had taken over that he came up with a very far sighted idea for football during that period. At a board meeting, he happened to mention that many football clubs wasted far too much money in buying players from other clubs. The percentage of successful buys was found to be minimal in comparison to those that ended in failure. He put to the board that Manchester United should be producing their own players, and young players at that. Gibson's vision was for the United to build a team of talent scouts who would scour the local area looking for the best young football talent available. They would then be brought to Old Trafford and coached in what he termed as the Manchester United way.

It was a revolutionary idea and far ahead of its time. The majority of footballers in those times did not make it into the first team until they were into their middle twenties. There was no place in the game for young teenagers. Manchester United began to put Gibson's plan into action and they formed the Manchester United Junior Athletic Club (MUJAC) and began to pull in young players from the local and surrounding areas. In 1938, the first team finished in fourteenth position in Division One. But the signs were starting to show that the youth policy was beginning to bear fruit. In that same season, the Reserves won the Central League Championship for the first time in eighteen years; the A team won their Manchester League; and the Colts or MUJACs as they were known, romped away with the Chorlton Amateur league. At the club's Annual General meeting that year; Chairman Gibson was to enthuse:

"We have no intention of buying any more mediocrities. In years to come we will have a Manchester United composed of Manchester players."

Sadly, a little matter of World War Two was to put a halt to Gibson's visionary idea, and it would be six more years before the foundations could start to be built once more.

Immediately after the war, the club was at low ebb. They were without a manager and without a stadium. Louis Rocca wrote to Matt Busby telling him that there was a job for him at Old Trafford should he want it. Busby was a former Liverpool Football Club Captain and had been offered the chance to go onto the Anfield coaching staff once his military career had been completed. Rocca's letter excited him. However, what Busby saw when he arrived for his initial interview in Manchester, was a club that was virtually non-existent, and it is a wonder that Chairman Gibson, Rocca, and Crikmer, were able to persuade him to take on the job. No ground (Old Trafford was suffering from bomb damage incurred in World War Two), and with no money to buy players, the prospects did not look too bright. But when Busby met James Gibson at the Cornbrook Cold Storage facility in February 1945, they both outlined their ideas as to how each thought that Manchester United should be run. There was a mutual liking for the items and topics discussed during their conversation, and at the end of it, Busby walked away with a five years contract and a salary of £750 per year. It was to turn out to be the moment when the foundations of Manchester United started to become cemented, and the following twenty five years brought the most significant successes to the club, and also saw the most terrible tragedy ever to impact British sport.

Busby was a radical thinker where football was concerned. It was through him that the term track suit manager evolved. Prior to World War Two, football managers were *'suits'* and were never ever seen out on the training ground. Busby changed all that. He trained with the players, talked to them throughout practice games, and illustrated exactly how he wanted the game to be played. He also knew that he could not do everything himself and he enlisted the services of the genial Welshman, Jimmy Murphy, as his assistant. Murphy's work and contribution to Manchester United should never ever be forgotten, and he is without doubt the best assistant manager that the game of football has ever seen. Busby built his own team of trusted servants around him and trusted them implicitly to carry out the plans laid down for his, but most of all, James Gibson's vision.

The club's directors at that time were also responsible for team selection, but within a year of his appointment, he had wrested that responsibility from them, and he was also solely responsible for negotiating transfers, and for selling on players. In his own words:

"Call it confidence, conceit, arrogance, or ignorance, but I was unequivocal about it. At the advanced age of 35, I accepted the position only if they would let me have all my own way. As the manager, I wanted to manage — I would be the Boss."

In 1968, when talking to that doyen of sports writers, Arthur Hopcraft, Busby explained what his vision for the club had been when he took over in 1945:

I always wanted — let me get the right word for it — creative football. I wanted method. I wanted to manage the team as I felt players wanted to be managed. To begin with, I wanted a more humane approach than there was when I was playing. Sometimes lads were just left on their own. The first team hardly recognized the lads underneath. There never seemed to be enough interest taken in players. The manager was at his desk, and you saw him once a week. From the start, I tried to make even the smallest member think that they were part of the club.

Busby's reputation and that of Manchester United grew. He moulded his teams to his, and Jimmy's way of wanting the game to be played. His first team was mainly made up of players who had come back from serving their country in World War Two and had lost six years of their careers to that conflict. However, they became the most exciting team to watch during those post war years and in 1948, ended the club's thirty seven years wait for a major trophy when they were victorious in what is often described as one of the best Wembley FA Cup Finals ever as they beat Blackpool 4-2 at Wembley Stadium. They were also runners-up in Division One on four separate occasions before finally becoming League Champions in 1952 for the first time since 1911. That great team, although ageing, gave Busby the precious time which he needed to see the club's innovative youth policy come to fruition.

What followed was revolutionary, and his team of *Babes* would dominate English football for the next few years winning two First Division championships, and they came so close to winning what was then a glorious Treble. Busby was far sighted and had fought the Football League about Manchester United entering the new European Cup competition which had begun in 1955. He could see the benefits of his teams pitting their skills against the best football clubs in Europe. He could also see the financial benefits that would be brought to the club, but not only that, he coveted the prestige in Europe that Manchester United's name would bring. Where others had feared to tread, Busby had foraged forward, and with his calm, but firm political nous and manipulation, once again he won the day. If he had not, who is to say how long it would have taken for English clubs to have been allowed to compete in European competition?

Of course following the European dream, Busby, and the club, was to endure the horrific tragedy of Munich. It was a disaster which once again, threatened to destroy the future of the club. Fortunately, Jimmy Murphy was able to take over the mantle as manager and he did more than a remarkable job in keeping the club afloat. It is incredible that upon his recovery Busby was able to put together another great team and that just five years after the disaster had happened, they won another major trophy by lifting the FA Cup, and then went on to win two more First Division championships. Finally, in 1968, the Holy Grail was at last achieved when United became the first English team to win the coveted European Cup when they beat Portugal's magnificent Benfica team by 4-2 on a balmy evening in London's Wembley Stadium.

It was great testament to his character, will, and determination to keep Manchester United at the forefront of both English and European football. There had been battles along the way with both the FA, and the Football League, and there were several Chairmen at other First Division clubs who would have relished in the demise of Manchester United. He could be as hard as bell metal in his dealings with other clubs, or the legislators of the game, as well as with his own staff. However, never once did Busby lose his grip and he fought those battles in his quiet, dogged, but determined way. He was no push over as the authorities found out. His standing in the British game made him the patriarch of his time. As the sports writer Hugh McIlvanney wrote at the time of Sir Matt's passing in 1994:

Greatness does not gad about, reaching for people in handfuls. It settles deliberately on a blessed few, and Matt Busby was one of them. If Busby had stood dressed for the pit, and somebody alongside him in the room had worn ermine, there would have been no difficulty about deciding who was special. Granting him knighthood did not elevate him. It raised however briefly, the whole dubious phenomenon of the honours system.

Busby emanated presence, substance, the quality of strength without arrogance. No man in my experience ever exemplified better the ability to treat you as an equal while leaving you with the sure knowledge that you were less than he was. Such men do not have to be appointed leaders. Some democracy of the instincts of the blood elects them to be in charge.

That innate distinction was the source of his effect on footballers. He never had to bully. One glance from under those eloquent eyebrows was worth ten bellows from more limited natures. Players did not fear his wrath. They dreaded his disapproval. His judgment of the priorities of football was so sound, his authority so effortless, that a shake of his head inflicted an embarrassment from which the only rescue was recovery of his respect.

Using Shakespeare's words to praise somebody we knew is bound to be a rather wild risk but invoking Mark Anthony's lines about Brutus: 'His life was gentle, and the elements so mixed in him that nature might stand up and say to all the world - This was a man'.

Sadly, James W. Gibson never lived to see his vision fulfilled. He passed away in September 1951 and Harold Hardman, who had served Manchester United for over forty years, took over as Chairman. However, from 1952 onwards, the careful plans regarding the youth policy began to bear fruit as one by one young players were drafted into Manchester United's first team. By 1955, all of the old guard had gone and the team had an average age of just twenty two years. By the start of the 1955-56 season most had experienced first team football for the previous two seasons. They were fearless, and played a brand of open attacking football. They won the First Division title by an astonishing eleven points. Nobody could believe that a team so young could have achieved this. But it was certainly no fluke.

The following season they retained their First Division title, reached the FA Cup Final, and became the first English club to compete in the newly formed European Cup competition in which they reached the semi-finals before losing 5-3 on aggregate to the wonderful Spanish team, Real Madrid.

They were affectionately known as the *Busby Babes*, and wherever they played, the crowds would flock to see them. What was so special about them apart from the way that they played the game? Well, they were a wonderful group of young men who loved life, and had their feet firmly planted on the ground. There were no big egos, no prima donnas, and no pretentiousness. They were very much the boy-next-door types, but lived life to the full. You would never ever see them in the media for the wrong reason. They knew that they were special that's for sure, but it never affected them. These were young boys who would walk to the stadium before a game and willingly chat as they walked along to the fans who were going to pay to watch them that particular afternoon. Duncan Edwards used to cycle down to the stadium on match day and would leave his old Raleigh bicycle tied up to a drain pipe outside the Stadium Ticket Office where it would stay until he retrieved it after the game was over.

They were so accessible to the people and to the Manchester United fans. You would see them out and about during the week at the local parks watching the school children playing football. You would see them in the local shops, and at the local cinemas. They would do prize giving ceremonies for the local youth clubs. They certainly embraced the local community, and without doubt the local community embraced them. There is not a doubt that they were a remarkable bunch of young people, and they bonded with each other both on and off the field of play. They were a credit to Manchester United, to the different countries for which they played and represented, but most of all, they were a credit to themselves.

This book concentrates on just eighteen players, plus Assistant Manager, Jimmy Murphy. It has to be acknowledged, and recorded, that in addition to these players, there was more who were bona fide *Busby Babes* and who also played their part in the evolvement of that team. Jeff Whitefoot, a man who still holds the record to this day of being the youngest ever player (16 years and 105 days) to play for Manchester United in a Football League game, made 95 first team appearances between 1950 – 1956, winning a First Division Championship medal in 1955-1956. Just three months before the Munich tragedy, Whitefoot left Manchester United to join Grimsby Town, and just shortly after moved on to Nottingham Forest where he won an FA Cup winner's medal in 1959. Ian Greaves, John Doherty (who also left the club to join Leicester City in October 1957), and Colin Webster, all won First Division Championship medals in that same 1955-56 season. Freddie Goodwin (who also played County Cricket for the Lancashire County Cricket Club) had made 24 first team appearances before the tragedy happened, and went on to make another 83 appearances after it, before being sold to Leeds

United in 1960. Eddie Lewis made 24 appearances, and scored 11 goals, before being sold to Preston North End in December 1955.

Several young players made just the sporadic appearance like the two young goalkeepers, Gordon Clayton, and Tony Hawksworth. Jackie Scott, Noel MacFarlane, Peter Jones, Walter Whitehurst, Paddy Kennedy, Ronnie Cope, and Alex Dawson, were all players who came up from the Youth Team and made First Division appearances prior to Munich.

For those of us who watched the *Busby Babes* week in and week out, they gave us so much pleasure. It is a little difficult for fans today to understand just how aware we were of the players that populated the Youth team, the A and B teams, and also the Reserve team. Many fans did travel to away games, but that was always at the expense of missing out on watching the Reserve team play in their Central League fixtures. They played a high caliber of football and gates of 10,000 or more were not uncommon at their games played at Old Trafford. The Youth team was akin to the famous Real Madrid team of that era in that they were custodians of the FA Youth Cup for the first five years of its existence, just as the wonderful Spaniards had been with the European Cup. Even those youngsters were known to draw crowds of 25,000 and more to their games.

There was a potent exuberance of youth flowing throughout the club during the years 1950-58. It was this which formed the deep root of attachment to Manchester United which for those who were growing up at the same time of these talented young men, will carry to our graves. Reflecting all these years later, it is difficult to convince today's generations just how good the *Busby Babes* team was, both collectively, and individually. Does it matter? Not really because we did see them, and we saw their genius. We know that they were the greatest team that Britain has ever produced and their memory is imperishable. We followed and shared in their dream, and when they perished on that snow filled runway at Munich, they left a huge chasm in our lives that has never ever been filled. The following pages are written in the hope that the reader will understand just what a remarkable person each of those seventeen young players was, and why the aura of the *Busby Babes* is still as strong today, as it was all those years ago.

Jimmy Murphy – The Genial Welshman

I do not think that any chronicle which details the emergence and evolvement of the *Busby Babes* could be written without special mention of the part which Jimmy Murphy played in their development from junior players to first team stars. Although the team became known as the *Busby Babes;* without Jimmy Murphy's input, the plan and objectives which were formulated by Mr. James W. Gibson and Matt Busby back in 1945 could never have been implemented.

Although Matt went on to become a Knight of the Realm, without Jimmy by his side as his able lieutenant, it is almost certain that he would never have achieved the heights which he did at Manchester United. Busby was the blue collar worker, the architect who designed the master blueprint. Jimmy was the nuts-and-bolts worker who put it all together and finally handed over the finished product. Far too often, Jimmy Murphy's role at Manchester United is forgotten, and consigned to the distant past – cast away upon the winds of time.

It is sad that today, a large number of Manchester United's followers have little or even no idea or knowledge, as to who, or what, Jimmy Murphy was. It is also sad, that apart from a *Young Player of the Year* silver salver, presented annually to Manchester United's most outstanding junior player; and a small bronze head bust ensconced inside the Munich Room within the Manchester United Museum; that there is absolutely nothing inside or outside their magnificent stadium which recognizes Jimmy Murphy's eminent thirty five years of loyal service to the club. When one considers just how important Murphy was, especially during the weeks and months after the Munich tragedy, it is an oversight which surely needs rectifying.

Jimmy Murphy was born on 8 August, 1910 in the small Rhondda Valley town of Ton Pentre in South Wales. His father William was originally from Kilkenny in Ireland, but his Mother Florence was a local Ton Pentre girl. She had been married before but was a widow who had been left with six children to bring up. When she married for the second time to William, Jimmy would be the only child that they would be blessed with.

Jimmy's parents brought him up like most of the families in those Welsh valleys – hardworking, honest, loyal, and forthright. They also taught him a love for music and sent him to piano and organ lessons. He became an accomplished pianist and by the time that he was in his early teens, Jimmy was playing the organ in Treorchy Parish Church. But like most boys of his era, Jimmy loved to be outdoors and loved nothing more than to be kicking a ball around the streets of his village home. He developed into an extremely gifted schoolboy player and at inside forward he was not only a tigerish tackler, but also a wonderful passer of the ball with an eye for making openings for his other forwards. In 1924 he won a place in the Welsh Schoolboy international team. Years later he was to say:

"I came from a little Welsh village in the Rhondda Valley. I played for Wales as a schoolboy and they were unforgettable times for me, I was passionate and extremely proud to have been selected. Wales at schoolboy level at that time were really a nonentity, but in the year I played we beat England 3-2 in Cardiff and then drew 2-2 with Scotland at Hampden Park. Those results fired my imagination and brought me to the attention of English League clubs."

With a talent such as his, it was not a wonder that he started to attract the attention of the Football League club's scouts. West Bromwich Albion finally got his parents to agree to them signing him and at 14 years of age, Jimmy left the green valleys of the Rhondda for the industrialised area of Birmingham. It was a huge wrench for such a young boy and initially he suffered terribly from homesickness. But he had such an indomitable spirit and he fought and overcame his homesickness and eventually forced his way into the Albion first team.

"I was determined to make the grade as a professional footballer, said Jimmy. *After two years, I appeared to be getting nowhere when a stroke of luck fell upon me. All players need that little bit of luck at the start of their careers. I had run out of goals as an inside-forward and one day in a reserve game we had a player injured and I dropped back to the wing-half position and happened to play exceptionally well."*

He played so well that he kept this position and two weeks later, he was selected for his first team debut against Tottenham Hotspur at White Hart Lane. 'Spurs were top of the league table and West Brom drew 2-2 with them.

"Can you imagine how I felt?" asked Jimmy. *"I was a boy of 19 playing in front of over 60,000 people when I had only been used to appearing in front of a few hundred spectators in reserve matches."*

In 1933, Jimmy Murphy became the youngest player in the full Welsh international team aged just 21 years. He was a full international player for six short years, and he went on to captain his country, winning a total of 22 full caps. Murphy also went on to appear for Albion in the 1935 FA Cup Final at Wembley Stadium where they were beaten by Sheffield Wednesday by 4-2.

During their playing careers, both at club and international level, Jimmy Murphy and Matt Busby crossed paths on more than the odd occasion. Busby was a player with first Manchester City, and then Liverpool, and also Scotland. Their last meeting as players was in 1939 when Albion was playing Liverpool at Anfield. In his book *Matt, United, and Me* (Souvenir Press 1968) Murphy recalled:

Albion lost the match, and afterwards, as I passed the Liverpool dressing room I could see Matt, just in his shorts, talking to Tommy Cooper the Liverpool and England back.

Matt waved to me: 'Come in, Spud' he said, and then turning to Tommy with a smile he went on: 'You always need to wear two pairs of shin pads when you play against this chap'. We had a friendly chat, and then I walked out with these words: 'See you next year, Matt.'

There was no Liverpool-West Brom fixture the following year. Britain was at war and it was another six years before I met Matt Busby again.

Towards the end of those six years of conflict, Jimmy Murphy found himself in Bari, Italy. He was the Senior NCO in charge of a Services sports center. For all those troops that had been chased up and down the Western Desert by Rommel's Afrika Corps, Bari and the sports centre was Shangri-La. The Senior NCO that Murphy had taken over from was an over-zealous type and a stickler for the rules. He handed over an inventory that included every nut and bolt that was in the place. Jimmy got around all the paper work – he just tore it all up! He felt that the troops had had enough of red-tape and didn't need such rigorous regimentation. Soccer coaching clinics were organized, and also football matches, cricket matches, swimming lessons, donkey rides, and even cycle polo!

The job in Bari brought to Jimmy a lot of satisfaction, and he was so happy because the conditions were good, and he was bringing a smile to a lot of soldier's faces who had fought so many hard battles. He lived in opulence as well – a big white stucco residence that resembled a palace. Although the German POW's had built showers and dressing rooms, the Service lads preferred to use *Jimmy's Baronial Hall* as they nicknamed it – with good reason; it was there that he kept all the ice cold beer!

One day, in early 1945, Jimmy was out on the football field, and in his loud, voluble, and enthusiastic way, was talking about football to a group of Army lads. Standing on the periphery of the group listening, and taking in every word that Jimmy was spouting, was Matt Busby. When he had finished his narrative, Jimmy walked over to Matt and they shook hands. Busby then made him an offer which would change his life.

"If you fancy a job when you are demobbed Jimmy" said Busby, *"come and join me at Old Trafford."*

In a newspaper column in 1973, Sir Matt Busby wrote:

It was his attitude, his command, his enthusiasm and his whole driving, determined action and word power that caused me to say to myself, 'he's the man for me'. He was the man I needed to help in my overall plan for Manchester United… He was the man who would help me create a pattern that would run through the several teams of players from fifteen years of age upwards to the first team.

So began probably the most famous partnership in the history of British football.

Once at Old Trafford, Murphy like Busby embraced the youth philosophy of James W. Gibson. He immersed himself in his duties. Upon his arrival he was shocked to find how badly the ground had been decimated by the German bombing during those war years. There were no proper training facilities available, and the medical treatment room was a broken down old hut. The players which they inherited after the war contained a good few internationals and they had to hold their practice matches at the back of the old Stretford End, on the concrete and cinder path that ran between the wall at the Stretford End and the wall around the Glover's Cables sports field. In later years, those sessions behind the Stretford End became folklore, and many a seasoned professional player was toughened up mentally in those games which they affectionately named killer ball.

Eamon Dunphy, a former Manchester United junior player who became a celebrated journalist and author, stated in his book *A Strange Kind of Glory* (Heinemann London 1991):

Apart from Matt Busby, Jimmy Murphy was the most influential man at Old Trafford. He lived in Whalley Range. Every morning he was up first to make a coal fire in the kitchen and cook breakfast. His wife would get up after her morning cup of tea to get their six kids ready for school. Except for Sundays this was all the family ever saw of Jimmy. He worked long hours – a seventy or eighty hour week, initially with nothing to show for the time and effort invested.

Jimmy worked from nine in the morning until late at night. First with the full-time pros until lunchtime, and then in the afternoons on remedial teaching. At six o'clock on Tuesdays and Thursdays he'd be at the Cliff with the youths, part-time pros and amateurs. There was no going through the motions at nights. These youngsters were the future. Jimmy was as hard on them as the older pros. He liked to get to the pub for a couple of pints of ale before closing time. He smoked like a chimney. It would be eleven thirty when he got home to a silent house, the embers burning on his morning fire… football was his life, from day to day, hour to minute to minute….. He would laugh and joke, there was real warmth about him but whenever the subject changed from football he would switch it back.

Jimmy Murphy was dedicated to one cause, and one cause only, and that was Manchester United. The early years were tough going for Jimmy. Upon his arrival, Busby had told him: *"Jimmy, I want you to look after the Reserve team so that we have a constant flow into the first team."*

In their very first season together, the first team finished up as runners-up in Division One, but the Central League team won their championship. At the end of that season, Busby could see that there was something troubling the Welshman.

"What's wrong Jimmy? You don't look your normal happy-go-lucky self."

Murphy told him:
"Matt, there is not one reserve player who can step in and strengthen your League side."

"In that case" said Matt, *"we'll have to find and develop our own youngsters."*

Matt Busby believed passionately in the vision of a youth system that would bring young boys to Old Trafford, and would build a platform and a conveyor belt of talent that would feed through five different teams, eventually providing top class players for the first team. In his book *Matt Busby – My Story* (Souvenir Press 1957); Busby outlined his vision for the club when he took on the manager's role in 1945:

I wanted to build teams of world-class footballers and to do the job efficiently we had to get hold of them young - as soon as they were available, in fact.

All these youngsters would be coached by Murphy, Tom Curry, Bert Whalley, and the rest of the staff into playing a certain brand of football which was bright, attacking, and entertaining. But first, they had the task of finding these young players and persuading their parents to allow their sons to leave their homes to join Manchester United.

For the previous forty years or more, Louis Rocca had filled a multitude of posts for Manchester United, including that of Chief Scout. In 1945, Matt Busby was instrumental in making a staff appointment which was to prove so critical to the future of Manchester United. Joe Armstrong was a telephone engineer who worked for what was then termed the General Post Office. Before the war he had worked as a scout for Manchester City and it was as a City player that Busby had first met him. They became friends and through the years, had always kept in touch with each other. Matt persuaded him to join Manchester United immediately after the War, and Armstrong worked alongside Rocca, until Rocca passed away in 1950, and he then took on the mantle of Chief Scout himself.

Contrary to what a lot of people may believe today, Manchester United's scouting system in the late 1940's, and early 1950's was anything but the spider's web of contacts it seemed, and was presumed to be. The reality was that they employed just eight scouts, and of these, three were based in Ireland. The criteria laid down by Busby for these scouts, was to concentrate their efforts on schoolboy players and youth footballers.

Although the scouts reported to Armstrong, he also built up a considerable network of contacts within the local and national schoolboy football networks, including many, many, schoolteachers. He had a genial personality and endeared himself to the people with whom he came into contact with, especially the mothers of the players of whom he was targeting. Armstrong was a charmer to say the least, and that charm was responsible for tipping the scales in United's favour when it actually came to getting the desired signature from young players in the light of the stiff competition which they faced from other clubs. In a conversation that I had with Armstrong's son, Joe Junior (who still works as a scout for Manchester United) he told me:

"One of the key factors was that my father worked for the GPO. That gave him communication skills which were well advanced. Therefore, he could make good contacts and maintain those contacts. He was in his own way quite methodical, single minded - never a 'yes man'. He had an excellent memory. This helped him to identify the important things he needed to know. My father kept quite detailed reports on senior players. Schoolboy records were probably not quite as detailed although he probably kept some kind of record. My father would direct scouts to watch certain players in specific matches - he was the main link between the club and the scouts. The main contacts were the District Secretaries of the English FA who were themselves teachers, and then within that he had a lot of contacts in the Manchester area. He used to swear by the telephone because contacts were easily made by phone.

People used to write in to the club as well as the odd teacher. He found out what games were on and went to matches. Personal contact with individual teachers was important and he always seemed to do the right thing. For example, he would go through the proper channels whenever possible. Most of all he was trusted! The schoolboy structure was large and the best boys usually ended up playing for their Town, County, and then England Boys. My father thought the minor games, that is, Town games, were just as important as schoolboy internationals for scouting young talent. My father was adept at sorting out difficult addresses and venues for matches because of his telephone knowledge and contacts within the GPO. He was persuasive, good in company and always charmed the mothers - made a bee-line for the mother. He always recognised that the mother was the key figure to win over. He'd just be polite, interested in the family, a bit of a flatterer, a humorist but he was sincere, he did think about things. It wasn't just a front; he thought about what he'd promised. It used to hurt him if he felt he'd let somebody down. Running right through was the feeling that he was a religious man and because of that the family was important. The welfare of kids was seen to be important. Bobby Charlton referred to my mum and dad as Auntie Sally and Uncle Joe".

Quietly, Armstrong and his scouts started to recruit players, and by the early 1950's, the system was starting to produce results. On odd occasions, young players (in the case of Jeff Whitefoot just 16 years old) were starting to make their debuts in the first team. In April 1952, Manchester United finally won the First Division Championship for the first time since 1911.

However, by late October of the following season, United were down at the foot of the First Division. Not only were the supporters getting restless, but there was also concern in the Boardroom, and with the club's shareholders. Busby was annoyed and at the Shareholders meeting he was to tell them that the club had talent on the books that was worth £200,000 (an enormous sum in those days) and that they would soon be writing a new and glorious chapter in the history of Manchester United.

Jimmy Murphy was well aware that the bulk of the 1952 Championship winning team were 'over the top', and he knew that they would need a couple of seasons of patience and experiment before the first batch of youngsters came through and started to make their mark as First Division footballers. The signs were already there to see. The FA Youth Challenge Cup had been instituted in 1953, and Manchester United's youngsters romped away with it in the inaugural season by an aggregate of 9-2 against what was considered to be a very good Wolverhampton Wanderers team. United were to win that trophy for the first five years of its existence. That competition was always treated by Murphy as a major competition.

Things didn't happen overnight, but seven years of hard work by Murphy and his coaching staff slowly began to pay off as one by one, young players started to cement their places in the first team. By 1955-56, the nucleus of the first team squad was; Ray Wood (22), Bill Foulkes (22), Geoff Bent (23), Jeff Whitefoot (20), Mark Jones (20), Jackie Blanchflower (20), Duncan Edwards (18), Eddie Colman (18), Wilf McGuinness (18), Liam Whelan (19), Eddie Lewis (19) David Pegg (19), Albert Scanlon (19), Dennis Viollet (21), Tommy Taylor (22), Bobby Charlton (18), and John Doherty (19), in addition to the older members of the team, Johnny Berry (28), and club captain Roger Byrne (25).

In those days it was unheard of to have such a young team not only competing in the First Division, but winning it in 1956 by a record 11 point margin from their nearest challengers. They also reached the FA Cup Final losing to Aston Villa by 2-1 at Wembley. However, their task was made impossible after only six minutes of play, when an outrageous foul perpetrated by the Villa winger McParland on goalkeeper Ray Wood, fractured his cheekbone. There were no substitutes in those days, and although Wood did return to the field of play, he was nothing more than an onlooker and to all intents and purposes United played for 84 of that Final with ten men. Notwithstanding the disappointment at Wembley, it was a wonderful testament to all the hours and patience shown by Jimmy Murphy out on the training fields which had moulded all these wonderful young players into the caliber of players and the team which they turned out to be.

For three shorts years, these astonishing young players put Manchester United at the forefront of not only British football, but European football as well. The conveyor belt of talent that was emerging through their system was astonishing. At one time, the Reserve team contained six full international players. They pioneered the way for English teams to play in the European Cup, and in their very first home tie against Belgian champions Anderlecht RSC; they completely annihilated them by scoring 10 goals with none in reply. They reached the semi-final before falling to the wonderful Real Madrid team of the 1950's, but the experience was not lost on them.

The following season they were once again chasing the dream of a treble of trophies. They were looking to retain their First Division title for a third consecutive season, were still in the FA Cup, and once again had reached the quarter-finals of the European Cup. Although there had been a little stutter in their form in late 1957, Busby had freshened up the team up by leaving out Berry, Whelan, and Pegg, and had introduced Charlton, Scanlon, and the young Welsh winger Kenny Morgans, who was just eighteen years old, in their place. He also paid a world record fee for a goalkeeper when he signed Harry Gregg from Second Division Doncaster Rovers for £23,500, and he replaced Ray Wood.

The team then began to hit a rich vein of form in all competitions and won by some impressive scores, none more so than when they demolished their 'bogey' team, Lancashire neighbours Bolton Wanderers, by 7-2 at old Trafford. The *Babes* as they were now so affectionately called by the general public had reached the Fifth Round of the FA Cup, and also the Quarter Final of the European Cup. On Saturday February 1, 1958 they played Arsenal in a League game at Highbury. The game, which turned out to be their last on English soil, was an absolute classic with United securing a hard fought victory by 5-4. It set them up nicely for the second leg of their European Cup Quarter final tie in the Yugoslavian capital of Belgrade against Red Star, the following Wednesday, February 5.

At this time Jimmy Murphy was also the manager of the Welsh national team. On Wednesday February 5, they had a very important World Cup qualifying tie to play against Israel at Ninian Park, Cardiff. Because of this, Murphy could not travel to Belgrade with Manchester United. As the United players gathered at Old Trafford early on Monday morning, February 3, Jimmy was there to see them off. They were all in good spirits because they held a slender 2-1 advantage over the Slavs from the first-leg and they were confident of winning their way through to the semi-finals for the second successive season. They wanted nothing more than another crack at the wonderful Real Madrid team again.

It was a murky, foggy morning as the players arrived at the ground, and Jimmy was his normal ebullient self. There was banter between him and his young protégées as they waited for the big centre half, Mark Jones to arrive to make up the complete traveling party. Eventually he turned up some 15 minutes late because he had been tending to a sick budgerigar in his aviary at his home. Just after 8am the party finally boarded their coach and left for Ringway Airport, now Manchester International Airport. Jimmy stood on the Old Trafford forecourt waving them away shouting:

"*See you all on Thursday lads* ....*See that you do a good job.*"

With that they were gone, off into the mist, and Jimmy, because he did not drive, turned his attention to traveling down to Cardiff that afternoon to meet up with the Wales team.

Over the last 54 years, the events of the next few days in February 1958 have been well chronicled in books, and on several television documentaries and drama programmes. In an absorbing game played out in Belgrade, United quickly raced into a 3-0 lead. In the second half, Red Star pegged them back to 3-3, and those last few frenetic minutes of the game saw them hanging on to get the result that would take them into the semi-finals on a 5-4 aggregate score. The whole United party were ecstatic, as well as relieved, and they could now concentrate their thoughts on the vital league game at home to Wolves at Old Trafford on the following Saturday.

In Cardiff, Wales won their match against Israel by 1-0, and had qualified for the World Cup Finals to be played in Sweden later that summer. Jimmy Murphy left Cardiff by train in mid-morning on Thursday February 6, 1958, knowing that Wales had done a fine job, but even more, was buoyed by the fact that his young United team had done their job in Belgrade. He arrived at London Road Station (now Piccadilly) and hailed a taxi cab – not to go straight home, but to go straight to Old Trafford. He had with him a case of oranges that had been given to him as a present by the Israeli FA, and he got the taxi driver to secure them in the luggage compartment.

The team was due back at Old Trafford shortly after 6:30pm, and he could not wait to see their happy smiling faces. No doubt there would be plenty of banter, lots of back slapping, and also lots of fun poked at his Wales team. He was so close to all the young players. On the short journey to Old Trafford he engaged in small-talk with the taxi driver. When he arrived at the ground, he paid the cab fare and headed straight to his office.

In his book *Matt, United and Me,* he recalled:

I heard Alma George, the Boss's secretary calling me:

'Mr. Murphy....'

'Yes Dear' .... *I was anxious to get to my office and therefore a bit offhand with my reply.*

'Mr. Murphy, you don't understand.'

'Understand what dear?' *There was something in her tone which made me pause, and as I was nearly at the top of the stairs, I turned to look at the anguished face of the girl who had come to the club as Matt Busby's secretary and seen all our players arrive as mere boys.....*

'Mr. Murphy, please stop' she said. 'Haven't you heard the news? The United plane has crashed at Munich.'

My feet stopped. So did my heart. The fingers on the clock on the wall pointed to four o'clock ..... But time now meant nothing.

The numbing horror of that moment will live with me till I die. I dashed into my office and picked up the phone..... And put calls through to the Police..... The newspapers .... The BBC..... Asking for news. Then it started to come in.

Roger Byrne.....Eddie Colman..... Mark Jones.....Tommy Taylor..... Billy Whelan..... Geoff Bent..... And David Pegg were dead. Killed in a snow-storm at Munich airport. So was Bert Whalley, one of my closest friends and one of the greatest soccer coaches I ever met. Tom Curry, dear patient Tom the club trainer, and the club secretary Walter Crikmer, they too had been killed and Matt Busby was fighting for his life.

What happened over the next eighteen months brings nothing but credit to the man that Jimmy Murphy was, and explains why Manchester United still owe him and his memory such a debt, and why he is written into the very fabric and folklore of the club.

On 6 February, 2008 I was privileged to attend the Munich 50th Anniversary Commemorative Service held at Old Trafford. It did not surprise me, but maybe did a lot of the younger generations, that of all the tributes that day, the most heartening and emotional were those that were given in respect of Jimmy Murphy. He received more mentions and accolades from his peers, and from the media, than have been heard before, or since, at any anniversary of the Munich tragedy.

At that commemorative service, Jimmy's son, Jimmy Junior, gave a terrific eulogy about his father, and his father's record of quite remarkable achievements in 1958, and also of those that he achieved both before, and after that year. It is probably hard today for a lot of younger Manchester United fans to understand that we who knew Jimmy through what, and who he was, consider that there has never been enough recognition of his work, and influence, alongside Sir Matt Busby, which contributed in bringing all the recognition of, and successes to, Manchester United, during their stewardship of the club.

Manchester United was so very lucky that Jimmy Murphy was not on that fateful flight back in February 1958. As stated, fate decreed that he would be in Cardiff, managing the Welsh team in their World Cup qualifier against Israel. As those terrible, terrible events unfolded in Munich, it meant that there was somebody left behind at Old Trafford who was able to grasp the reins, and the metal, in order to keep the club going.

Jimmy Murphy was integral to United, not only at the time of Munich, but also before that when he was very instrumental in bringing all those wonderful young lads through the United system and who became known as the *Busby Babes*. That wasn't just the first team, but the teams below them as well. He was also an integral cog in the successes after Munich as well, which culminated in an FA Cup victory just five years after the tragedy; two more First Division Championship titles; and then on that never to be forgotten night at Wembley, in May 1968, just ten years after Munich, when the European cup was won for the very first time in Manchester United's history.

Jimmy's work at the club spanned an incredible thirty five years – a tremendous achievement in itself. Sir Matt Busby gets all the plaudits, but without doubt, without Jimmy by his side, he would never, ever, have been able to achieve what he did at during his tenure at Old Trafford. Former Manchester United player David Sadler, when talking to the Manchester United fanzine, *Red News*, a few years ago was to say:

Certainly, Jimmy Murphy was the one we saw a lot more of in the normal footballing week, than we did Matt, who we only got to see very occasionally between matches.

Jimmy was a very tough character, and didn't suffer any kind of fool within the football world. But if you look back to those accolades that were given out during that service in February 2008, it became more than abundantly clear that Jimmy Murphy had one love, one passion, and that was Manchester United, even to the detriment of his family. Jimmy Junior said on that day that his Dad had no hobbies, and that his job when he got up in the morning was to go down to Old Trafford and produce football players. He was a totally blinkered and driven man even before Munich.

David Sadler went on to say in that *Red News* interview that there were two definitive sides to Jimmy. The very hard, tough, shouting, cursing one, and on the other side, the softer, gentler, quiet spoken Welshman. Bobby Charlton recalled at the 2008 Memorial Service:

"I was sorry for Jimmy when the accident happened. He always figured himself as a Number Two, and then suddenly, he had to make a whole lot of important decisions, and he did a marvelous job. He was in love with the game more than he loved anything else, and that's a very difficult thing to say when his family are here present. He knew exactly how to make you a better player. I became a professional from an amateur, and that was down purely to Jimmy."

In a lot of ways, that drive, that commitment is obviously something which Manchester United fans and the general soccer follower can relate to today with Sir Alex Ferguson. Of course, it is the immediate aftermath of Munich that will always be brought up first whenever Jimmy Murphy is mentioned, and one should look at the huge task that he had in keeping Manchester United alive and at the forefront of English soccer.

In the days immediately after Munich, he had to try and find a team to put together, and play well enough to keep United in the First Division. Only two players came back from Munich supposedly fit enough to play football again – Harry Gregg, and Bill Foulkes. Others returned in the following weeks and months – Bobby Charlton, Kenny Morgans, and Dennis Viollet, but he had to make and mend with kids from the Reserve and A team, as well as two quick signings.

In the days after the tragedy he had to find time to see the families of those that had lost their loved ones, and also those that were still so seriously injured. He had to find time to attend the funerals of the boys who had been so close to him, and he also had to find the time to go over to Munich to see how those people who were still injured were progressing.

One of the saddest things that happened at that time, is that with all this going on around him, Jimmy was tapped up by some of the leading clubs in the First Division and was asked to leave United and join them. How very easy it would have been for him to just walk away from all the carnage that was going on around him? How reprehensible of those other clubs to make their approaches at such a time? But just like today, there was a lot of jealousy in the game, and there was more than a few club chairmen who would have been very happy to see the demise of Manchester United – two in particular – one in Lancashire and one in London.

This was a man who had just seen eight of his young players lose their lives, and three of his best friends (Bert Whalley, Tom Curry, and Walter Crikmer) lose theirs, and of course his boss was lying in the hospital critically injured. This is what Jimmy felt, and in his own words in his book *Matt, United, and Me*:

To the generation which has grown up since then, those players, and friends, may be just names. But to me they were Matt's boys. My boys! I had seen them come to Old Trafford as part of Matt's master plan to build the greatest team in Europe.....And now they were gone. Seven of the greatest players ever assembled in one club wiped out, and the greatest of them all, Duncan Edwards, fighting for his life. I was like a man living through a nightmare waiting to wake up. I locked the door, put my head on the desk, and wept like a child. Only last Monday I had waved cheerio to them: 'See you on Thursday lads..... See you do a good job.' They did. They had won through to the semi-final of the European Cup. Now they were gone. At the very moment when they had the world of soccer at their feet.

Jimmy learned of the accident at 4pm on the Thursday afternoon when he arrived back from Cardiff and had gone straight to Old Trafford. He never could recall what happened during the next twelve hours. It was 4am the following morning when he decided to go home. All he knew was that there had been a bottle of Scotch in his office cabinet, and when he went back to his office the following morning, it was on his desk – empty.

That same morning he flew to Munich with the families of those lost and injured. As they landed they had to endure the sight of the shattered remains of the stricken British European Airways (BEA) aircraft lying beyond the airport perimeter fence. It must have been heart rendering. Again, Jimmy recalled:

"I went to the hospital and Harry Gregg, Bill Foulkes, and Bobby Charlton, kept chattering non-stop about everything and anything that had happened. But what they were saying made no impact upon my brain. At any moment I expected to see Tommy Taylor's beaming face coming through the door; or Big Dunc creeping up behind me and giving me thwack in the back with a 'Hya! Jimmy.....'

Matt had been given the last rites, and close by lay the best player we ever had at Old Trafford, Duncan Edwards. Duncan's left thigh was a mess, and he had severe kidney damage, and had he lived, it was doubtful that he would have ever have played again. He lay dying, but nothing could ever quench the great spirit and courageous heart of this young boy."

The following story is often regarded as myth, or even urban legend, but I can assure you that it is not. Again, these are Jimmy's own words:

"But I knew. In one of his conscious moments the Boss waved a feeble hand for me to come to his side. I had to bend low over his bed to catch his words as his hand gripped my hand: 'Keep the flag flying Jimmy' he whispered. 'Keep things going till I get back.'

At that moment Matt didn't even know how many of his boys had been killed. I did. I stumbled out of the hospital into the snow which still lay as thick as a carpet over the city of Munich, I was in tears.

Yes..... I'll keep things going Matt .....But where am I going to find the players.....? Where am I going to find the players?

I traveled back with Foulkes and Gregg, and amid all the tragedy and sorrow, I had to get a team together from somewhere.....My heart ached for these two players ..... I don't mind admitting, I felt like crying.... Ten years of hard work and planning had been wiped out in a flash."

However did Jimmy Murphy cope in that first week after the tragedy? It does not bear thinking about the pressures that he must have felt, and been under:

"How can I describe what it was like? I was completely alone, isolated. There was no Matt Busby, no Bert Whalley. No one I could talk with on my level as far as the team was concerned. Then the coffins started to arrive at the ground. We put them in the old gymnasium. And there were all the funerals. And all the time I was wondering where I could get players. The League game against Wolves had been postponed, but things had to be done quickly. No one knows what I went through during that time."

But not only had Matt asked him to keep the red flag, and club, going, but Chairman, Harold Hardman spoke to him on his return:

"You have got to keep it going, Jimmy. Manchester United is bigger than you...bigger than me...bigger than Matt Busby. It is bigger than anybody. The club must go on".

And go on it did, almost entirely due to Jimmy Murphy. Out of almost nothing, he created a team which I always like to think of as *The Fourth Great Team*. People all recognize the three teams which were built by Busby and Murphy – the 1948, and 1952, Cup and Championship winning teams; the *Busby Babes;* and also, the team of the mid-sixties which won the FA Cup, two First Division Championships, and finally, the European Cup.

But the team that Murphy put together immediately after Munich deserves much more praise than it ever got, or gets. At the time, the press referred to them as *Murphy's Marvels;* and marvels they were. With just two players available from before the accident, Murphy had to mix and match with young reserve players, and players from the 'A' team, plus two quick signings, Ernie Taylor, from Blackpool, and Stan Crowther, from Aston Villa. How he ever moulded this team together, and inspired them to the heights which they scaled is beyond comprehension. But this he did.

I can recall being at the first game played by United after the disaster; a home FA Cup Fifth Round tie against Sheffield Wednesday. It was a cold, bitter February evening. Although the patched up United team won the game by 3-0, it wasn't really a football match. It was more a demonstration of grief so profound and resonant it still echoes today. Outside of Old Trafford that night, thousands who could not obtain entry into the ground massed in silence, muffled against the bitter cold, as if awaiting an announcement that there had been a terrible mistake and that the disaster had not happened. We could never have realized on that night that we were witnessing the start of a resurrection that had such consequences in creating the future juggernaut that is Manchester United today.

Amongst all the emotion, the heartbreak, the pain, and the sorrow, Jimmy Murphy took that team all the way to the FA Cup Final that season and kept them in the First Division.. That they lost to a tough, experienced 'bogey' team in Bolton Wanderers in the Final was no disgrace. Just five days after that Final, he sent out his young team out to play against the might of Italian champions, AC Milan, in the European Cup semi-final, first leg. Most pundits reckoned that United would be torn apart by the sophisticated Italian team. It did not happen. Again, against all the odds, United emerged victors by 2-1. They had to travel overland to Milan for the second leg, and this was no proper preparation for such an important game. There was no surprise when they were resoundingly beaten by 4-0.

Jimmy Murphy proudly leads out his Manchester United team for the FA Cup Final against Bolton Wanderers at Wembley Stadium on Saturday, May 3rd, 1958. The players behind him going left to right are; Bill Foulkes, Stan Crowther, Harry Gregg, Colin Webster, Ian Greaves, Ronnie Cope, Alex Dawson, Bobby Charlton, Dennis Viollet, Ernie Taylor, and Freddie Goodwin.

The following season, beyond all expectations United finished runners-up to Wolves in the race for the First Division title. In the process they scored a staggering 103 goals. This was just a year after the disaster. It was incomprehensible that this patched up team could achieve what it did. Former United defender Bill Foulkes in his autobiography *United in Triumph and Tragedy* (Know The Score Books 1968) said:

Much is made, and quite justly, of the post-Munich Red Devils' astonishing achievement in reaching the 1958 FA Cup Final, but I believe that an even more Herculean feat tends to be almost criminally underestimated. In 1958-59 we finished as runners-up in the Championship race with a side which was, with all due respects, little more than an emergency combination, stitched together hastily in the aftermath of the crash.

With Matt Busby on the mend, but still far from fully functional at the start of the campaign, it was the heroic Jimmy Murphy who set the tone once more, preaching, a non-stop sermon of togetherness. 'Defend in strength, attack in strength' was Jimmy's motto, and we followed it to the letter. However, I have to admit that while the rearguard did its bit, with Harry Gregg constantly showing the form that had earned him recognition as the outstanding goalkeeper of the 1958 World Cup Finals, it was our forward line of Warren Bradley, Albert Quixall, Dennis Viollet, Bobby Charlton, and Albert Scanlon which made us special that term. We scored more than a century of league goals and played some of the most dazzlingly attractive, free-flowing fast-moving football it has ever been my pleasure to witness.

That success did come at some expense though. Between 19 February 1958, and April 25 1959, Manchester United used 24 players in their first team. Of those, Hunter, and Heron, played just once. By 1962, those two, plus Greaves, Goodwin, Cope, Crowther, Webster, Taylor, Dawson, Pearson, Harrop, Scanlon, Wood, Bradley, and Carolan, had all left the club. For some, there was a big psychological effect upon them, and their superlative effort in helping Murphy keep the club alive took its toll. However, those efforts must never be underestimated and it gave the club time to breathe, and instill new life within it.

Busby and Murphy were able to rebuild another great team, winning the FA Cup in 1963, the First Division championship in 1965, and 1967, and the European Cup in 1968. They also once again won Murphy's beloved FA Youth Cup in 1964 for a record sixth time. They bought wisely, Albert Quixall, Tony Dunne, Noel Cantwell, Pat Crerand, Maurice Setters, Dennis Law, David Herd, John Connelly, and Alex Stepney. But they also brought through some wonderful players from the youth ranks; Nobby Stiles, David Sadler, John Fitzpatrick, Bobby Noble, John Aston, Jimmy Rimmer, Francis Burns Brian Kidd, and the mercurial George Best. Of the team which beat Portugal's mighty Benfica at Wembley in 1968, eight of the eleven were products of Manchester United's youth policy, the outsiders being Stepney, Dunne and Crerand.

In 1969, Matt Busby was knighted, and he decided to retire. He was growing old, and the toll of the previous ten years took a toll upon his health. Initially, the reins were handed over to Wilf McGuinness, and Jimmy continued scouting and assisting with the kids. For Wilf McGuinness, it didn't work out and in 1971 Busby had to take over the reins once again. Frank O'Farrell was appointed manager during that summer and Busby once again stepped down.

For Jimmy Murphy it was sad what happened to him. He retired in 1971 when the Club pensioned him off when Busby stood down. Nick Murphy (Jimmy's son) explained that he still went down there to the ground every day:

"It was his whole life. Manchester United was his whole life. He loved the place, loved going there, he couldn't keep away."

In his book *A Strange Kind of Glory,* former United reserve team player Eamon Dunphy was to say:
Once Busby retired and Frank O'Farrell took over, Jimmy's role at United was clarified. After a long wait he was given £25,000 as a retirement settlement, and a scouting job at £25 a week. The scouting job was really a sinecure during the Busby / McGuinness era. In football terms he'd been pushed to the margins of the club he loved. He was almost a non-person. This uncomfortable existence was made worse by the decisions taken by the Board which Jimmy knew was really Sir Matt. He'd never driven a car. For several years he'd made the journey from Whalley Range to Old Trafford in a black cab provided at the club's expense. The fare was £3 each way. Jimmy received a letter from Les Olive informing him that the arrangement was being discontinued. He was also informed that United would no longer pay his telephone bills.

Nicky Murphy recalls his father's hurt:

"My dad was never interested in money, but the football side of things meant everything to him. He never ever said anything against Sir Matt or the club, but he was very hurt. He couldn't understand it. He had a lot to contribute. He turned to British Rail, and it was funny really. I know that it sounds unbelievable, but for years afterwards, when Dad made the journey by rail, he'd make the journey without a ticket. The railway guards knew him so they never ever asked to see his ticket. He'd just wave and walk through the barrier!"

After O'Farrell's acrimonious departure from Manchester United, Tommy Docherty did bring Jimmy back into the fold. He scouted for Docherty and it is a little known fact about what Jimmy achieved in those last years. He found that classic pair of wingers Steve Coppell, and Gordon Hill, he spotted Peter Beardsley playing for Carlisle. He also spotted Paul Parker (who eventually joined United). Stuart *'Pancho'* Pearson was spotted, as were Gary McAllister, and Ray Houghton who went to other clubs. Tommy Docherty would tell you – he never even saw Coppell play before he signed him. Sadly the jewel that United missed was a young reserve team striker at Leicester City. Jimmy advised United to sign him at the earliest opportunity, but his advice was ignored. The player in question was a young Gary Lineker. Nick Murphy recalls Jimmy talking about Beardsley:

"My dad saw him first playing as an out and out striker. He wasn't impressed. He thought that Beardsley should play as a sort of advanced midfield player."

One night during a conversation with his son in the *Throstle's Nest* pub close to his home, he exclaimed to Nicky:

"Why should I bother my arse going down there, nobody listens?"

Ex-Manchester United player Norman Whiteside remembers his early days:

"If I ever saw Busby or Murphy, around Old Trafford, they were wonderfully encouraging and complimentary. I wouldn't have thought they would have bothered giving someone potentially so insignificant the time of day, but whenever I bumped into them they would say: 'I hear you're doing well' and 'keep going', building me up all the time."

Paddy Crerand in his recent autobiography *Never Turn the Other Cheek (Harper Collins UK 2007)* explained Murphy's time - about the man who loved a few pints talking football and life, with a smoke, who called everyone *'son'* and admitted:

I found it hard to make out with the small talk. Munich didn't just destroy Jimmy's life in seconds; he lost his great friends including Whalley. He virtually ran the club during Matt's recovery in hospital, re-arranging fixtures and signing players. A proud Welshman from a little village in the Rhondda Valley, he still took Wales to the quarter-finals of the World Cup in the summer of 1958. He stayed loyal to United despite lucrative offers from Arsenal, Juventus, and the Brazilian national team. High profile jobs were never for Jimmy, he was far happier teaching youngsters.

On Murphy's treatment, Crerand added:

Jimmy was cut out, and clearly very upset at his diminishing role at the club. It seems that no-one at United gave much thought to what Jimmy would do and while he stayed on at Old Trafford, he didn't really have a role. He should have been treated better by a club he had served so well. Jimmy had even camped outside players' houses, refusing to leave until their parents signed United's forms.

Bobby Charlton:

"My whole career from the age of 15 was linked with Jimmy Murphy. He was so intense he used to frighten me. He was hell to work for and at times I used to hate him but I owe more to Jimmy than any other single person in football. Everything he did was for a purpose and I am grateful to him. The success of Manchester United is a testimony to his work."

Alex Dawson is too much of a gentleman to repeat in print the swear words Murphy aired at the time but I loved this tale in an interview with *Red News* about the FA Cup game against West Bromwich Albion in 1958:

I don't know what came over the West Brom manager, Vic Buckingham, saying things like: 'We're sorry for what happened to United. But we won't stop at 10 goals' before the game. Jimmy was right up! He gave us this team talk, well the words, 'effing' this, he was really going, Jim! 'Now I've told you how to beat them and when we do, I'll go in there and I'll piss all over them'. You never saw Matt really angry, but you knew, you knew he wouldn't show it but underneath he was annoyed. Jimmy gave us team talks, and when the game was finished he'd say: 'Well done, I tell you, that's how to do it.'

Then of course at the 2008, 50th Anniversary Commemoration, where mentions of Murphy littered the Memorial Service, Harry Gregg stole the show, with his description that Murphy's tongue could cut teeth and the coaching set up was described thus by Murphy's son Jimmy Junior: *"Matt was the architect, my Dad the master builder, who went out to get the materials, with Bert Whalley laying the foundation."*

David Meek who reported United's games for the *Manchester Evening News* later that week admitted:

"*I don't think he was appreciated enough after Munich. There was a real danger of the club going out of existence.*"

And Paul McGuinness, the Director of the Manchester United Youth Academy talked of Murphy's legacy:

"*Jimmy's special one was the Youth Cup, winning five in a row, Jimmy's legacy is the way United (youth to senior) play now*".

Gregg ended with a tale that had everyone smiling:

"*I owe Jimmy a lot. He could laugh with you, cry with you, and fight with you. Jimmy and Matt were like hand and glove, wonderful people. I hadn't a clue what they were talking about though! Matt would say 'Up together, back together,' Jimmy would say, 'Attack in strength and defend in depth.'*"

But of course it will always be to 1958 where Murphy is identified for his inspiration at work. On turning down the chance to manage elsewhere including Arsenal and Juventus:

"*My heart was at Old Trafford. I wanted to help Matt pick up all the pieces and start all over again. Just like we did in 1946.*"

Murphy was at the ground when fans flocked to it upon hearing news of the tragedy:

"*Thousands hurried down to the ground to see if they could help; the police threw a protective cordon around relatives and friends who had lost their loved ones. Those of us left at the ground did our best to calm and console the grief stricken. But what word of sympathy could I find to comfort the bereaved. There was nothing to lift the blanket of despair.*"

On his return to Manchester from what must have been a heartbreaking trip to Munich:

"*I have seen the boys. Limbs and hearts may be broken, but the spirit remains. Their message is that the club is not dead — Manchester United lives on.*"

Charlton explained the toll that it must have taken on Murphy:

"*Jimmy, typically, was the strongest presence in those days when the Old Man was surviving only with the help of an oxygen tent. He said that we had to fight for our existence — and the memory of the teammates we had lost. He had been through a war when men had to live with the loss of so many comrades, had to fight on through the suffering and live with what was left to them. It was the same now at Manchester*

United, Jimmy insisted. But later I heard that it was just a front that Jimmy put on. One day he was discovered in a back corridor of the hospital, sobbing his heart out in pain at the loss of so many young players."

Bill Foulkes:
"The doctors told me that I should go away and have a long holiday away from it all, but how could I? I couldn't stop thinking of poor Jimmy Murphy on his own at Old Trafford".

Murphy admitted:
"I suffered. I said cheerio to Tommy Taylor, Duncan (Edwards) and all the lads in the gym and told them I would see them on Thursday... when they came back they were in coffins."

It is testimony to Murphy that so many participants of the era suggest without him United wouldn't be who they are today. The late Colin Webster former Manchester United player:
"If Murphy had not been at Old Trafford, the 'Busby Babes' would never have existed. He brought in 80 percent of them – I don't think Matt Busy could have done it on his own."

The late Albert Scanlon on his inspiration:
"I woke up again later in Munich to hear a voice saying: 'Albert Scanlon will never play football again.' Jimmy Murphy came in and I was crying and I told him what I had heard. He said: 'that's not true, Albert, you are all right.' Given that it came from Jimmy, it was enough for me."

Frank Taylor – the only journalist to survive the disaster:
"Three men saved Manchester United from oblivion. They are Jimmy Murphy, Bobby Charlton and Matt Busby. But Murphy was the key figure."

Bill Foulkes:
"Jimmy handed the reins back to Matt, he resumed his role as his able, faithful lieutenant. He had been a tower of strength throughout the post-Munich period and it saddens me to say that I don't think the club ever fully appreciated the extent of his input, or what it took out of him both physically, and mentally. His loyalty was illustrated shortly afterwards when he spurned the chance of managing Arsenal to continue working alongside Matt at Old Trafford, and while his sheer quality was never in doubt, he emphasised it spectacularly by leading Wales to the quarter-finals of the World Cup only a few short months after the air crash. Manchester United should understand, and never lose sight of the fact, that Jimmy Murphy, who died

in 1989, goes down as one of the most loyal, dedicated, and inspirational contributors to their cause in their entire history. His memory deserves to be honoured like few others."

Again, the journalist, the late Frank Taylor:

"Jimmy Murphy worked night and day to prevent Manchester united becoming just another struggling league club. He gave the club back its pride. He forced the players and the supporters to realise that Manchester United could become great again.

Let no one doubt Jimmy Murphy's contribution to his club. In a sense, he was born to be a backroom boy, at his best with young players in the dressing room, rather than exchanging small talk in the Board Room. In his time, he had plenty of chances of moving up the ladder to become a fully fledged manager himself. He wasn't interested, not even when he was offered the managership of Liverpool, before Bill Shankly took it on.

Once he had signed for Manchester United, to help Matt Busby build his dream club, Jimmy Murphy decided that this would be his mission in life.

An emotional, warm-hearted man to those who know him, fate decreed that Murphy would be the man to start the rebuilding of the club at a time when Busby was fighting for his life. He would not claim any credit because he was not that sort of man.

British sport would be richer if we had more people like Jimmy Murphy around. A loyal servant, a soccer expert in his own right, and yet content to be a No 2 to a man he always rated as No 1 in the game."

Matt Busby recalled his Assistant as:

"A kindred spirit. Together we have shared the triumphs as well as the heartache and tears of Munich. When all seemed lost, Jimmy took over the reins and not only kept the club going, but took it to the 1958 Cup Final. Jimmy's superhuman efforts then were typical of the man, who shuns the spotlight of publicity...his unflagging efforts and optimism in those dark and tragic weeks concealed his heartbreak over the loss of such wonderful boys, and gave us the time and opportunity to rebuild Manchester United again until by the 1960s we were once more a power in the game."

And Murphy ended his own book:

I know in my heart I made the right decision those many years ago in Bari. And if it were possible to turn back the clock I would still give the same answer: 'Sure Matt...I'll be happy to join you'. That's what Matt and United have meant to me. I would do it all over again.

In an interview a few years after Munich, he was also to say:

People have always wondered why I turned down some of the top jobs in football to stay with Matt, but our

Jimmy Murphy on the extreme right of picture waits to be introduced to HRH the Duke of Edinburgh prior to the start of the 1958 FA Cup Final. The players from left to right are; Freddie Goodwin, Ernie Taylor, Dennis Viollet, Bobby Charlton, Alex Dawson, Ronnie Cope. Behind the Duke is United captain, Bill Foulkes. Harry Gregg and Stan Crowther can be seen behind Foulkes.

association is founded on mutual respect. Matt respects everybody with whom he has dealings, all the way down from the boardroom to the ground and laundry staff. That is just one of his qualities. The others include wonderful intuition and extreme patience. His foresight was proved when he led English clubs into Europe and when he broke up the 1948 team to give youth its fling. My greatest reward was at Wembley in 1958, when the Boss came back from Munich, still a sick man. He said, 'Thank you Jimmy, you've done a wonderful job. I'm proud of you.'

Murphy's son, Jimmy, will never stop beating the drum for his father:

"My job is to keep my family memories alive. He deserves credit for what he did. I've got a list of people I'm going to write to who have got things wrong recently in the press and those that (also) got it right"

Four years ago, the Association of Former Manchester United Players, approached the club and asked for the North Stand to be renamed, *'The Jimmy Murphy Stand'*. They were turned down unequivocally for a number of nonsensical reasons. However, now a precedent has been set with the naming of that stand 'The Sir Alex Ferguson Stand'. Surely, the club should now reconsider, and name one of the other stands after this great servant who served the club so loyally and with great dignity? If that can't happen then a statue should be erected at the stadium next to the man he served so loyally. These men, who built Manchester United into a dynasty, who kept it going after the disaster, is a partnership that should be seen - on permanent display – as the crucial dual relationship that it so clearly was. As Matt said:

"It must have been a terrible time for Jimmy and everyone at the club after the crash. It needed someone who, though feeling the heartbreak of the situation, could still keep his head and keep the job going. Jimmy was that man."

In 1968, Matt, looking back, described bumping into his old friend Murphy and seeing him coach some army lads in Bari in 1945, said:

"It was one of the most fortunate things that has ever happened to me. This was the man for me! And for nearly 23 years we have marched shoulder to shoulder as comrades in sport, working for a common ideal: to make Manchester United the finest club in Britain, in Europe, and the best in the world."

That they did, and shoulder to shoulder is where both should be hailed for all to see at Old Trafford in lasting legacy.

Roger Byrne –
The Original Captain Marvel

Captain Marvel, Captain Fantastic, Captain Reliable. All accolades which over the years have been given to various Club Captains of Manchester United. United have had some truly great Captains at the club down through the years and they have all left their own legacy on the club's history. Roger Byrne is certainly up there with the best of them, and he led by example on the field, and with quiet effective authority off it. He was certainly the buffer between the dressing room and the manager's office.

Roger Byrne came into this world on February 8, 1929 born to parents William, and Jessie. They lived in a small terraced house at 13, Beech Street, in the East Manchester suburb of Gorton. They were an everyday working class family. Initially, young Roger was educated at Abbey Hey Junior School, before moving on to Burnage Grammar School after having passed the 11-Plus Examination. Like most boys, Roger loved the outdoors and loved sports. However, during those early formative years, there was nothing in his make up to suggest that he would go on to be a professional footballer. If anything, his chosen sport seemed to be leaning towards cricket and he fared reasonably well for the club which he joined, Denton West Cricket Club, where he played mostly in the Second XI.

Joining Denton West at the same time as Roger was another young man destined to become an iconic figure in the cricket world. That person was a certain J.B. *'George'* Statham who was to find fame and glory as a fast bowler with the Lancashire County Cricket Club, and England. Brian Statham was also a very good footballer who played in the outside-left position. During the winter months both Byrne, and Statham, played soccer for the Ryder Brow Boys Club, who ran several teams. Roger played at inside left and they both played in the first team which played in the Lancashire Amateur League.

In the spring of 1948, Manchester United was made aware of the two promising young players who were turning out on the left side of the Ryder Brow's forward line. United sent their scouts to have a look at the two youngsters, and the reports were so favourable that both of them were quickly offered the opportunity to sign amateur forms for the club. Roger Byrne accepted, but Brian Statham decided not to accept the offer, choosing instead to pursue a career in cricket. It was a decision which he was never to regret.

Roger's progress was halted after just a few months as he had to complete his two years National Service and he was conscripted into the Royal Air Force. It was quite amazing to find out that during his two years service time, he was considered as not being good enough to play in the Station football team and so ended up having to play rugby for the duration of his service! Once his National Service was completed, he returned to Old Trafford and it was then that his career began to progress.

He as a deceptive type of player and many outside of Old Trafford came to the conclusion that there would be no place for him in regular First Division football. There is a record of a scout's report produced after one of Roger's performances for the Manchester United Reserve team which read as follows:

Heading — Poor; Tackling — Ordinary; Right Foot — Fair; Left Foot — Non-Existent; Overall Impression — Disillusioned.

The scout could not have got it more wrong, and fortunately for the staff at Old Trafford, they saw the real qualities in him and were able to bring those to the fore as he started to mature as a player. One of the things which they did was to move him from playing outside-left, to the defensive position of left full-back, and it was in this position which he found his niche.

It was early in his career, and although he did not know it, Roger very nearly left Old Trafford for Oldham Athletic. It seemed that United were willing to part with him for the princely sum of just £1,000. Bill Wooton, who was Oldham's manager at that time had been tipped off that United were willing to let Roger go. The papers were all prepared, and the deal was supposed to be concluded after a Lancashire Cup match at Peel Park, against Accrington Stanley. Byrne was down to play outside left, but on the way to Accrington, the United left back fell ill, and Jimmy Murphy moved Roger into the full back position. He played a blinder that evening, and the watching Wooton knew that any chance of securing Roger Byrne's signature was destroyed by his performance during that game. When he approached Jimmy Murphy after the game was over and asked if he could speak with Roger, he was met with any icy stare and Jimmy told him:

"He's not going anywhere. So don't bother."

Roger progressed from then on as a full-back, and he became a regular selection for the Central League team. He did not have to wait too long before he had his first chance of senior football and this came on 25 April, 1951, when he was selected to play at left back in a friendly testimonial match against Reading at the Berkshire club's Elm Park ground. Also having his first taste of first team football that evening was a young Mancunian named Dennis Viollet who was selected in the outside-right position. Considering that it was a testimonial game for two

Reading players, it turned out to be a quite lively affair which finished in a draw, 4-4, and had been played out in front of 13,268 spectators.

Roger started the 1951-52 season in the Central League team but his form was good and he was pushing hard for a first team place. His chance came on 24, November 1952 when he made his Football League debut in the game at Anfield against Liverpool which finished in a 0-0 draw. Also making his League debut in the same game that afternoon was an 18 years old boy from Northern Ireland by the name of Jackie Blanchflower, and he occupied the right-half position. The team that day read:

Crompton; Carey, Byrne; Blanchflower, Chilton, Cockburn; Berry, Pearson, Rowley, Downie, Bond.

Roger was to be ever present from then on until the end of that season, and he was a member of the first Manchester United Championship winning team since they had lifted the trophy back in 1911. Byrne made a major contribution to the team that season playing in twenty four League games as well as making one appearance in the FA Cup. However, for the last six games of that season, Matt Busby moved him back to his old outside-left position, and it was a move which worked because Roger scored seven goals in those six games.

Although the 1951-52 season finished with him winning a First Division Championship medal, the following season saw him become discontented. His form in the opening months of the 1952-53 season deserted him. He played in the first nine league fixtures, and also in the FA Charity Shield victory against Newcastle United at Old Trafford in late September. After the game against Sunderland on 27 September 1952, he was left out of the team to play Wolverhampton Wanderers at Molyneux the following Saturday.

To some people they saw him as arrogant, with a big ego. Without doubt, Roger Byrne was very singe minded even to the point of being stubborn. His stubbornness had almost led to him being sent home from the club's summer tour to the USA, when he clashed with Busby about a sending off he received in a friendly game against Mexican team Atlas in Los Angeles, and his reluctance to follow Busby's orders during that game. In his book *Soccer at the Top (Weidenfield & Nicolson 1973)* Matt Busby recalled:

Atlas were a rough lot. Seeing how things were going, I told Johnny Carey to instruct the team to keep their heads. He did this, but Roger defied him and was sent off. I did not like my players to be sent off abroad, where club and national reputations suffer more. Nor did I like mine or my captain's instructions to be forgotten, even allowing for provocation. So I had to make my point once more — we would do it my way. I told Roger he must apologise to Johnny Carey, or I would send him home the next day. I would give him two hours to do it in. No more than 15 minutes later, Johnny came to see me to say, 'Roger has been to apologise.' So Roger rose in my estimation, high in it though he already was. I knew it was only a lapse into a headstrong state that had caused his dismissal. Now he had shown he was big enough to apologise.

However, when the 1952-53 league campaign began, the frustration and main cause of his discontent was the fact that he didn't like being played in the outside left position. He pointed out to Matt Busby that he was more at home playing in a defensive role and that he preferred the left full back berth. Busby unhesitatingly told him that he would play in whatever position that he was selected to play in, and that there would be no negotiating about it.

Frustration welled up in him during the days which followed, and at a training session later on in the week, Busby shouted out some instructions to him from the touchline. Once again Roger's response was quite dismissive and he used factory floor language in his retort. It took Busby aback, and he retired to his office pondering what he should do about the situation. Never one to shirk his responsibilities, the manager, after deciding that there could be no challenge from any player to his authority, shocked everybody when he placed Roger Byrne on the transfer list.

Johnny Carey was the Club Captain at the time and he took Roger to task about the situation as did Allenby Chilton, and Jack Rowley. They all pointed out that something new and exciting was about to be unleashed on British football from within Old Trafford. The three elder statesman explained to Roger that they were nearing the end of their careers and that a defensive position would be his for cementing if he buckled down to it, and that the young players that were beginning to emerge within the club from the junior teams would make Manchester United the team of the future.

Busby had a famous saying – *"That's not United"* when he thought that a player's behavior had fallen below the standards expected by the club. There was little doubt that Roger's challenge to his authority fell within those parameters. However, Busby knew that Roger Byrne was something special, and that he would have to make a compromise if he really wanted to keep him. So compromise was reached because Byrne was a rare leader and would be a vital factor in captaining and leading the future *'Babes'* team. In less than two weeks the situation was resolved, and Busby put him straight back into the team – at full back, and he was to stay there until fate curtailed his career.

Johnny Carey retired in summer 1953, and Allenby Chilton was made the Club Captain. Busby's man management skills showed when he made Byrne the team's vice-captain. There was no doubt that in the two years that followed, Byrne learned much from Chilton's leadership, and also from Busby's management skills even though the former was very autocratic. He bridged the gap between those young players in the dressing room and Chilton, and he was also their bridge to the manager. He truly blossomed as a full back and it wasn't too long before he began to catch the eye of the international selectors with his displays.

Byrne was extremely quick, and was never one for diving into the tackle. He was slightly built for a full back but had a very good tactical brain. It was unusual that he played in that left back role because his stronger foot was his right foot, but it never seemed to deter him. He would "jockey" wingers into positions where he wanted them to be, and he was so adept at "nicking" the ball away from them. He was masterful at reading the game and had an uncanny sense of anticipating danger which was often seen when he came across to the middle of the pitch, covering behind the centre half whenever the situation was needed. Jimmy Armfield was given the tag of the first full back to start the "overlapping full back" ploy. This is completely untrue. Roger Byrne was the first full back to be seen to do this regularly in games. As a player with the experience of having played in the outside-left position, he was always very comfortable at getting forward and supporting attacking play.

Even by today's standards, Roger Byrne is probably one of the quickest defenders that I have ever seen. His recovery speed was phenomenal, and many was the time as I watched games, wingers would have thought that they had "skinned" him, only to find that he was there back in front of them again. On April 3rd 1954, he made his debut for England against Scotland in the cauldron that was Hampden Park with 134,000 watching, and he played well enough in an England victory won by 4-2. This began a run of 33 consecutive international games for his country. Quite phenomenal back then when players were in and out of the international team at the whim of selectors. Billy Wright, the blue eyed golden haired man from Wolverhampton Wanderers was the England skipper, but I'm sure that Byrne would have succeeded him in that role. To be honest, in my opinion, Wright was past his sell by date from the mid-fifties onwards, and was very fortunate indeed to amass 100 caps, given the quality of many other centre-halves plying their trade in the First Division during those years.

At United, the *Babes* were starting to emerge. In 1955 Chilton retired and Busby appointed Byrne as the Club Captain. It was the only choice because Roger was a born leader. Extremely intelligent, utterly straight, and radiating with self-confidence without being arrogant, he was forthright in his views, and many of the young players were wary of his sharp tongue. He kept the "kids" in check and was never afraid to take them aside and have a "quiet word" if he thought that they were transgressing or that their off the field activities were beginning to affect their form. He was not as autocratic as Chilton had been, but he had this quiet, calm, confident manner, which the players respected, and his authority never came into question. His relationship with Busby deepened and I am sure that in Roger Byrne, Busby saw a man who would eventually one day take over the mantle from him as Manager of Manchester United.

On taking over the captaincy from Chilton, in an article he wrote for a local newspaper, Roger said:

Following in the footsteps of Johnny Carey, Stan Pearson, and Allenby Chilton was an honour. Playing under the captaincy of such players, you cannot fail to learn and improve. Obviously the captaincy is not just a case of running out and tossing a coin. I remember on my first tour with United in Denmark, we were playing a combined Copenhagen XI, which included five of the Denmark side. They were awarded a free-kick two yards in front of our goal and being so inexperienced I did not have a clue what was expected. Johnny Carey calmly walked to the ball and directed the rest of us onto the line – and we prevented a goal from the resulting free-kick.

After the game I made a point of asking quite a few of the team what they would have done if they had been captain and they surprised me by answering that they did not know. From then on I paid special attention to the captain's role just in case the honour ever came my way.

The *Babes* were a wonderful set of young men led by an exceptional Captain. The younger players were different in that they were all big friends even away from the playing side of their lives. It's not that Roger hung around with them because he had his own life away from football. Roger had plans for the future when he would no longer be playing football. At that time, he himself had no aspirations to progress his football career into football management. He enrolled into a physiotherapist's course at Salford University and Salford Royal Hospital. It was while he was pursuing his studies that he met his future wife who was then Joy Cooper. Joy was on the same course and their relationship blossomed as the course progressed. Whilst at the hospital, whenever staff or patients wanted to talk to him about football, he was always very reluctant to get involved. He would reiterate to them, in a nice way, that football just happened to be part of his life, and when he was at the hospital, he expected to be treated not as a local celebrity, but just like everybody else.

He was the only Manchester United player at that time to own a car, not that he was a prolific driver! Shortly after he had obtained a permanent driving licence, Busby was at home in King's Road, Chorlton cum Hardy one evening, when there was an almighty crash outside of his home. On going out to investigate, he was confronted by the sight of Roger in his car half way down his front lawn after having crashed through the Busby's garden wall! There was also a tale told by Ray Wood, the Manchester United goalkeeper, about the day he and Bill Foulkes were given a ride into Manchester's city centre by their skipper. It turned out to be the last time they ever got into his vehicle, and they described the short journey to their destination as being a white knuckle ride!

Roger Byrne (on the right) shakes hands with Real Madrid captain Miguel Munoz before the start of the European Cup Semi-Final second leg at Old Trafford, Manchester on Thursday, April 25th, 1957.

Success came to the *Babes* in that 1955-56 season when they won the First Division Championship with the youngest team ever, and by the largest difference in points from the team finishing second. I can recall racing across the Old Trafford pitch from the "Glover's Side" at the conclusion of their last home game of that season against Portsmouth on April 21st 1956, to see them presented with that wonderful old Championship Trophy. The crowd was huge in front of the old main stand and the player's tunnel as Roger led his young team up a makeshift stairway and podium, to be handed the trophy by Joe Richards, the Football League Chairman. Those young boys mounted the platform at the top of the stairway, and their smiles and exuberance told such a story. As Byrne brought the trophy and his team down the stairway, they were happy to talk to the fans, show their medals and allow fans to touch the trophy before they disappeared up that tunnel and into the sanctity of the dressing room. No laps of honour back in those days!

The following season, Roger led his *Babes* into Europe, and his performances were inspirational. He led from the front and on the field he could also be a minder to some of the younger players. I can recall a game against Aston Villa at Old Trafford in September of 1957, when the Villa left half, Stan Crowther (who was to join United later that season on the night of that first game after Munich against Sheffield Wednesday) was giving Billy Whelan a turgid time physically – in fact Crowther was lucky to stay on the field. Byrne had a word with him and got no real response. He bided his time and it came in the form of a long high ball dropping towards him as Crowther moved to close him down. Roger was quite deliberate in what he did and he met the ball full on the volley with his right foot. It went with the speed of a bullet and Crowther could not get out of the way as the ball hit him full in the face knocking him out. He was taken off the field with concussion and

never returned to the game. Roger let no one take liberties with his young charges.

On 5 June, 1957, Roger and Joy were married in St. Mary's Church

Roger Byrne leads out his Busby Babes in a home match at Old Trafford in March 1957. Behind him can be seen Jackie Blanchflower.

in Droylsden. They settled down to a life together in a Manchester United club house at 20, Edale Avenue, in Flixton, an area which is just outside Manchester. Life was good apart from the away trips into Europe which kept them apart. United retained their title in 1956-57 and narrowly failed in their first European quest, as well as falling valiantly to Aston Villa in the F.A. Cup Final. Despite being on the end of the most violent premeditated act of violence that I have ever witnessed on a football pitch which left his team a man short for most of the game, the mark of Roger Byrne the man, was shown after the final whistle to end the match had blown. Despite the bitter disappointment of losing at Wembley in the FA Cup Final, and despite the circumstances which alluded to that loss, Roger Byrne gathered his young team mates around him, and as Johnny Dixon, the Aston Villa Captain, arrived at the top of the Royal Box, Byrne led his young charges in applause for the victors of the day, as they received the famous old trophy. I could never envisage anything happening like that in this modern era. I will always recall a newspaper headline from the morning after that Final which said: *Villa Get the Cup but United Get the Glory* – never were truer words ever written.

At the end of that 1956-57 soccer season, the popular magazine *Charles Buchan's Football Monthly* made Roger Byrne the recipient of the magazine's annual *Player of the Year* award. Buchan certainly knew his football having been a player with Arsenal, and Sunderland, as well as having won six full international caps for England. Upon retiring from the game he carried on a career as a journalist with the *Daily News* which later became the *News Chronicle*. He was responsible for writing one of the first ever soccer coaching manuals, and was also founder of the *Football Writers' Association*. In September 1951, he started and edited his *Football Monthly* magazine. Writing in the August 1957 edition of his magazine he was to say:

At the end of each season, Football Monthly selects a Player of the Year. I have no hesitation, this time, in awarding the honour to Roger Byrne, Manchester United left-back.

Not only has he played in every England international, but he has led his side to victory in the League championship for the second year running, to the final of the FA Cup, and to the semi-final of the European Cup.,

Though the fame of John Charles, Wales and Leeds United centre-half transferred to Italian club Juventus, and the exploits of Tom Finney, Preston North End's centre-forward discovery, have commanded a lot of attention, there can be no denying the wonderful stimulus given by Byrne to both England and Manchester United teams.

His cool, calculated work at left-back, either when his men are in winning mood or fighting to avoid defeat, have been an inspiration. He rarely plays a poor game.

Of course, Byrne has his detractors who assert that he is too inclined to take risks and prone to lose his balance at times.

But one of the reasons why Byrne is undoubtedly the best full-back in the country today is his confidence in his own ability. What appear to be risks — and would be risks to the ordinary player — are part and parcel of Byrne's immaculate style.

The square back pass from the bye-line to his goalkeeper and the bold dash forward to assist the attack come naturally to Byrne, who started his career as a forward and has complete command of the ball.

And if Byrne occasionally resents the attention paid to him and his colleagues, it is because he is so wholeheartedly immersed in the game. That he is the captain of United proves that these rare moments are insignificant.

Byrne is still comparatively young, 27 years of age. The longer he plays, the better he will become. He has the brains to make the best use of his great skill.

Born in Manchester, he has been a United man first and foremost. He has played a conspicuous part in their many successes.

Byrne is not only a quick thinker but very fast on the run. He has the speed to cope with the fastest of modern wing forwards. And the positional sense to limit their activities.

Most important of all, Byrne always uses the ball to advantage. His well-timed clearances have started many England and United attacks from within their own quarters.

With either foot, Byrne places the ball from his full-back position, straight to the feet of his forwards. It is a relic of his youthful days when he puts across many accurate centres from outside-left.

Byrne is busy, too, planning for the future. He is training hard to qualify as a physiotherapist and I have no doubt he will become as skilled in this art as he is on the soccer field. C.B.

The following season, 1957-58 was looked forward to so much. The word *treble* was now in the football vocabulary, and this was United's aim that season. They started out brightly enough but had a mid-season blip and going into February of 1958 they were second in the League table just six points behind Wolves, who were scheduled to play at Old Trafford on February 8th. After losing a League game to Chelsea on December 14th 1957 by 1-0, Busby decided to freshen up the team. He went out and bought Goalkeeper Harry Gregg from Doncaster Rovers for a world record transfer fee for a goalkeeper of £23,500. For the game against Leicester City on December 21st at Old Trafford, he left out Wood and introduced Gregg, and also left out Berry, Whelan, and Pegg, introducing Morgans, Charlton and Scanlon. The team hit a rich vein of form in the next 11 games which led up to that fateful afternoon in Munich. In those eleven games in all competitions, they won seven, and drew four, scoring thirty four goals, and conceding sixteen in the process. They were back on track led by their inspirational Captain.

Roger picked up a slight thigh injury in the game against Arsenal, at Highbury, in London, on the afternoon of 1 February 1958. This was to be the last time that he played upon English soil and the match was a fitting tribute to both him, and his young team mates. In a classic encounter with the *Gunners,* United prevailed by 5-4. It is a game that is still talked about by the older generation of both Arsenal, and Manchester United fans even today.

When the team left Manchester's Ringway Airport for Belgrade on Monday, 3 February, 1958, there was a lingering doubt as to whether Roger would be able to play in the game against the Red Star team which was just two days hence. As a precaution, Matt Busby had drafted young reserve-team full-back, Geoff Bent into the traveling party as cover for him.

On arriving in Belgrade, United went to the Majestic Hotel. Trainer Tom Curry worked long and hard on Roger's injury using a heat lamp and a poultice. At a training session the following day, he put himself through his paces during a rigorous fitness test and much to Matt Busby's relief, declared himself fit to play the following day.

The game against Red Star the following afternoon opened dramatically. United held a slender 2-1 lead from the first leg, but in only the third minute of the game, Dennis Viollet took advantage of a defensive mix-up in the 'Slav's goal-area and fired the ball home. Things got even better for the Mancunians when just on the half-hour mark, youngster Bobby Charlton fired in two more goals. At this point, United held a 5-1 lead on aggregate. To all intents and purposes, the game and the tie, was well and truly over. It did not work out like that however. Immediately after half-time the 'Slav's pulled a goal back to make the score 3-1. The Referee became overly fussy and continuously penalized United for tackles that were almost innocuous. It was no surprise when he awarded the home team a penalty kick when the decision should have been a free-kick to United for a foul on Foulkes. The penalty was converted to make it 3-2, and then with time running out, another bad decision gave Red Star another free-kick on the edge of United's penalty area. Kostic, the Red Star inside-forward, who had been a thorn in United's side all through the second-half, fired the ball at the wall of defenders lined up just ten paces away. It took a deflection off Dennis Viollet's shoulder and evaded Harry Gregg's dive and clawing hands. It was now 3-3 and the aggregate was 5-4 – for those last few minutes United hung on grimly and were relieved when the final whistle blew. They were through to the semi-finals of the European cup for the second successive year.

In Belgrade in the evening after the game against Red Star, spirits were high at the reception in the Majestic Hotel where both team's management and players mixed together. Formal speeches were made and Byrne led the players in a rendition of Vera Lynne's famous old wartime song of *We'll Meet Again.* Sadly that was never to be. He again showed what a leader he was when some of the younger players grew restless, and impatient, as midnight approached. They wanted to leave and visit a watering hole. Roger wrote a message on a napkin and passed it up to the top table where Busby was sat. The message on that napkin read:

You promised the boys that they could leave once formalities were over. Permission to go?

A simple nod of the Manager's head acquiesced to the request, and the young guns were away to enjoy themselves on what was left for some, the last night of their young lives.

We all know the tragedy that was Munich, and at what cost it came. Roger died instantly in the carnage of the disaster and Harry Gregg found him on the tarmac with not a mark upon him and with his eyes wide open. Even today, Harry sadly regrets not closing his eyes. Roger was just two days short of his 29th birthday. The biggest sadness was that he was not to know that Joy, his wife, was pregnant, and that he was never to see his son, Roger junior. Roger's body, together with those of his colleagues was flown home to Manchester and they rested initially in the gymnasium underneath the main stand at Old Trafford. The young policeman who had the duty of guarding the gymnasium door that night recalled that it was the longest and saddest night, of his career. After a funeral service at St. Michael's Church in Flixton, Roger was cremated at the Manchester Crematorium.

United lost not only a great skipper that sad day, but also a man of great integrity, a born leader. He was certainly a man that exuded class and was full of charisma, whose sense of fair play and leadership, gained him the respect of not only his team mates, but everybody who came into contact with him. His tongue could be sharp at times, but those young kids accepted him and his discipline without question. He was simply their Captain.

Rest on in your peace Roger. I can still see you even today, leading those "Babes" out of the tunnel, tapping the ball up twice into your hands then kicking it up into the air towards the Scoreboard End goal. We were left with so many memories of not only a wonderful player and captain, but also of a wonderful human being.

Roger Byrne played 277 games for Manchester United scoring 19 goals.

He also made 33 consecutive appearances at international level for England.

Ray Wood – The Affable Young Geordie

Ray Wood is a name which is often forgotten whenever the *Busby Babes* are mentioned. The signing of Harry Gregg in December 1957 seemed to signal the end of Ray's career at Old Trafford. However, at the time of the tragedy he was still too good a goalkeeper not to have bounced back, even though it may well have been with another club. What is not in dispute is the integral part which this likeable young Geordie played in the evolvement of the *Busby Babes.* Ray Wood was born on 11 June 1931, in Hebburn, County Durham. As a youngster Ray always traveled to St. James' Park to watch at least one Newcastle United game a season. It was always the game when Manchester City would be the visitors. He would arrive early at the stadium to make sure that he could take up a position behind one of the goal areas. Then he would wait anxiously for the teams to run out – and for only one player in particular, the big City goalkeeper, green-sweatered Frank Swift. The dark haired 'keeper was Ray Wood's boyhood hero. Ray was in awe of him and he would stare at him wide-eyed, and wonder if he too, could ever be like him.

Wood began his career in football as an amateur with Newcastle United, but after failing to make his mark at St. James's Park, in 1949 he moved on to Darlington, where he signed on as a professional. His stay at Feethams was short – just three months in duration. However, during that three month period, his performances for Darlington were such, that he came to the attention of Manchester United. Playing for Darlington at Crewe Alexandra in a FA Cup tie, Ray had a tremendous performance. Watching that afternoon was none other than Louis Rocca, Manchester United's chief scout. He recommended that United should sign him as soon as possible.

One Friday evening in October 1949, he was at home when there was a message arrived from the Darlington manager Billy Forrest. It asked him to report to Feethams immediately as he wanted to speak to him about a transfer. It worried Ray, so his father went along to the stadium with him. When he arrived there, Ray was shocked to find himself face-to-face with Manchester United Manager Matt Busby. Terms were agreed and United secured his signature for a £5,000 fee. For the affable young Geordie it was a dream move. The following morning he found himself in a car bound for Manchester United. United had bought him with more of an eye on the future, but because of injuries he was immediately pitched into the fray in a First Division game against, of all teams, Newcastle United at Old Trafford on December 3rd 1949. Was it a dream debut for the 18 years old youngster? He told the *Charles Buchan's Football Monthly* magazine in 1955:

A nightmare is the only way that I can describe the game. Before I went out onto the field, Mr. Busby told me not to worry, that I need not think that I had to be any better because I was in a First Division team. That sounded fine inside the dressing room, but out on the pitch it was no consolation.

After twenty minutes, Newcastle right winger Tommy Walker put one past me, and although that was the only goal that I let in – and we drew – I was a very unhappy youngster. Despondent I left the ground.....To be cheered a little by my parents, but wondering miserably, if I had not been too ambitious in switching to the First Division.

My confidence was shaken and it did not surprise me when I was dropped for the rest of the season.

He went back to the junior teams after that, and began learning his trade as understudy to Jack Crompton, and Reg Allen. There was not much chance for him to progress his ambitions over the next few years and it was not until the 1952-53 season that he started to see more first team opportunities due initially to Allen's retirement through illness, and Crompton's intermittent form. Ray was a versatile sort of player, and as was the want back then, there did at times seem to be some strange team selections when junior players were shuffled about in the 'A' and 'B' teams as the coaches worked out which position they were best suited for. He was even given a run at centre forward in the A team for three games, and he raised some eyebrows when he scored six goals in those few appearances! He was extremely quick off the mark and he surprised a number of opposing attackers with his pace. What they did not know was that in earlier days, he had been a professional sprinter up in Northumberland, amongst the various pit villages where he 'dashed for cash.' His speed was an asset with his goalkeeping and he was probably the quickest goalkeeper of his era when it came to moving off his goal line.

He finally cemented his place in the first team in the 1953-54 season and his performances began to make the England Selectors take note. He was certainly in line for nomination to the England World Cup squad of 1954 but sadly for him, a broken wrist towards the end of that

season put paid to his international chances. England came back from that World Cup in Switzerland with their tails between their legs. However, just a few months into the new 1954-55 season, Ray was selected for the first home international against Northern Ireland at Windsor Park, Belfast, in October 1954, and it ended in a 2-0 victory for the English. It was a feather in his cap really as at that time there was so many good English goalkeepers around – Merrick of

Ray Wood makes a flying save during a game at Old Trafford in 1956.

Birmingham, Ditchburn of 'Spurs, Williams of Wolves; all great goalkeepers in their own right.

Wood continued to play exceptionally well for United. He was as I said, exceptionally quick off his line and had great anticipation and a safe pair of hands. His bravery was unquestioned and he was a terrific shot-stopper. If he did have a fault, it was coming for crosses and sometimes he could be found to be hesitant. However, his strengths outweighed his weaknesses and he was integral to that great team which developed, and won, two consecutive championships in 1956, and 1957.

I suppose that the thing Ray will most be remembered for was the 1957 FA Cup Final against Aston Villa when he was on the receiving end of the most horrific, premeditated, and violent assault, that I have ever seen perpetrated upon a football pitch. Just six minutes into the game, in a Final of which United were red hot favourites to win, McParland, the Villa left wing, headed a ball tamely into Wood's hands. The ball was already safe in Ray's capable hands, but McParland continued to charge through, launching himself through the air and connecting with his head into Wood's face, shattering his cheekbone. He took no real part in the game after that even though he wandered around for a while on the right wing as a little nuisance value.

At half time, with the score 0-0, Matt Busby sent physiotherapist Ted Dalton outside of the stadium with Ray, the object being to throw a ball at him a number of times to see how he reacted. They went out onto the grass verge, and Dalton began throwing the ball to him – poor Ray hardly saw any of them. As they

Top right: Ray Wood holds the ball in his hands just seconds before Aston Villa's Peter McParland charges into him and fractures his cheekbone.

Bottom right: Ray Wood being attended by the Manchester United Trainer, Tom Curry, during the FA Cup Final in 1957. Wood had been the victim of a horrendous shoulder charge by Aston Villa's Peter McParland and suffered a depressed fracture of the cheek. Notice, the despite his injury, he still has the ball between his knees! Roger Byrne is the player wearing the number 3 shirt, and Jackie Blanchflower is wearing the number 5. The other players are on the left, Liam 'Billy Whelan, and Bobby Charlton. The Referee in the pictures is Arthur Coultas.

finished this little exercise, a young boy who had been playing football with his friends on the grass verge just a short distance away from them, meandered over and said:

"Mister, you can come and join me and my mates in our game if you'd like to!"

Just yards away, 100,000 spectators were all waiting to see if Wood could rejoin the Manchester United team, and play in goal for the second half of the FA Cup Final. Unbeknown to them, here he was being offered a game in a kid's football kick-about! Ray did go back out onto the field but not in goal. United fell behind by 2-0, ironically to two goals scored by McParland. However with eight minutes to go, Taylor pulled a goal back from an Edwards's corner, and Wood returned back between the sticks as United went all out on the attack to try and pull back the one goal deficit. Great effort though it was, it was all to no avail and United lost that final by 2-1.

Wood was back for the start of the next season, and by United's standards, they weren't firing on all cylinders. In December, after a couple of results that hadn't gone their way, Busby acted by first signing Harry Gregg, and then for the game against Leicester City on December 21st, he dropped Ray together with Johnny Berry, Liam Whelan, and David Pegg. There was a story that Busby thought that Wood had lost his nerve a little after the injury received in the FA Cup Final.

In the week leading up to the signing of Gregg, Manchester had been full of rumour about his imminent arrival. It was reported that Busby was willing to pay as much as £35 thousand for the young Irishman's signature. Naturally all this talk unsettled Ray and he did make a statement to the press that in the event of Gregg being signed, he would hand in a transfer request. His reasoning was that if United signed Gregg, then they would be undermining both his confidence and ability. He told Bob Pennington of the *Daily Express*:

"If Gregg signs for United, I shall want a transfer. It would show a lack of confidence in me. I know we have dropped points lately, but I don't think that I am responsible. I'm a married man with responsibilities. Reserve team football would be no good to me. I've nothing against Harry Gregg, but I must consider my own future."

Busby did sign Gregg, but although United had to pay Doncaster Rovers a world record fee for a goalkeeper, it was nowhere near the figures being bandied about in the press. Both clubs finally agreed on a fee of £23,500.

It was a blow to the likeable young Geordie, and he gave the situation a lot of thought. In the second week of January 1958, he handed in a transfer request to the club. United had five goalkeepers on their books at the time; Gregg, Wood, Clayton, Hawksworth, and young David

Gaskell. Clayton had only two senior appearances to his credit, and Hawksworth only one. Gaskell who had leaped ahead of them in the pecking order was only 17 years old, and he too only had two senior appearances to his name. With United chasing three major trophies, the League, the FA Cup, and the European Cup; Busby felt that there was a distinct lack of experience where the three other young goalkeepers were concerned. Wood's transfer request was rejected out of hand.

Ray Wood was on the aircraft that fateful day in Munich and did suffer bad injuries to his head, leg and hip. His leg was actually broken by his rescuers as they pulled him from the wreckage. One of the aircraft wheels was lying on top of Ray, and the rescuers had to use a crowbar to lever it off him. Unfortunately in doing so they also put pressure on his leg and broke it. He returned back to Manchester after convalescence and tried to pick up his career at United. Sadly it wasn't to be, and he was never the goalkeeper that he had once been.

In December 1958, the legendary Bill Shankly took him over the Pennines to Huddersfield Town. It seemed to me personally that it was an obscenely short time between the disaster and his release from Old Trafford and one that in later time he came to be bitter about. He was to serve Huddersfield for the next four years and I can recall in March 1963 seeing him return to Old Trafford to play against United in an FA Cup 3rd round tie. 1963 was a bad winter and the tie had been postponed since the January. Unfortunately for Ray, although it gave the United fans one last chance to see one of their former heroes, it was a bad night for him personally as United romped away with the game 5-0, Denis Law scoring a hat-trick aided by goals from Albert Quixall and Johnny Giles. It's hard to imagine what his feelings were as he left the pitch that he had graced so well just a few short years before.

He left Huddersfield in 1965 and played for short periods with Bradford City, and Barnsley, before retiring from the game in 1968 – ironically the year that United lifted the European Cup. He spent most of his time abroad from then on, coaching in places like Ireland, USA, Zambia, Canada, Kenya, Greece, Kuwait and Cyprus. He went through a very bad time in his personal life and his first wife Elizabeth certainly blames the part that the tragedy played in their lives and led to their eventual break-up. It was Elizabeth who campaigned so vehemently on behalf of the families, and it was those efforts and Ray's, which finally got the club to allow a testimonial match to be played at Old Trafford in 1998 for those families.

It is sad to note that she was one of the many of the families to fall on hard times. Just prior to the staging of that benefit match in 1998 she had written to Martin Edwards because she was overdrawn at the bank and was having difficulties even meeting her train fare to attend the game. She had asked for an advance against her share of the game's payout only to receive a reply from him being told that; *'it was against Club policy'*. Hard to take when here was a woman that had witnessed the horrors of the aftermath of that tragedy; who had stayed by her husband's side in the hospital for almost eight weeks and watched as close, personal friends fought for their lives. She pointed out that it was British European Airways who had flown the families of the survivors out to Munich immediately after the disaster, and that it was they, and not the Club, who made sure that they had daily expenses. Ray was also bitter about the treatment that the families received from the club afterwards, and in his own words not too long before he passed away, felt that they had all been shafted.

I can recall him so well. He was so soft spoken and never one for the limelight. As I said at the beginning, Ray Wood's name is one that hardly ever gets mentioned in regards to the *Busby Babes*, but there is no doubt that as the last line of defence in over 200 games for Manchester United, the likeable young Geordie played more than a passing part.

Ray passed away at Bexhill on Sea on 7 July 2002, at the age of 71 years. Rest on in Peace Ray and thanks for all the memories.

Ray Wood played in 208 games in all competitions for Manchester United

He won 3 full international caps for England.

Harry Gregg – Man of Courage

On 1 October 2008, the recipients of the Pride of Britain awards received their awards at a glittering ceremony at a well known hotel in Central London. One of the categories of the award was that of *Special Recognition*. Included in the line of recipients was a 76 years old, Northern Irishman and he was being recognised for his courage in a disaster that happened on an airfield in a foreign country over fifty years ago. That man was Harry Gregg, the former Manchester United, and Northern Ireland goalkeeper.

Harry Gregg is one of the greatest goalkeepers to have ever pulled on the green jersey, be it for Doncaster Rovers, Manchester United, in his two games for Stoke City, or for his beloved Northern Ireland. Gregg first came to my notice November 1957 when he played for Northern Ireland against England in a Home International match at Wembley Stadium, when England was surprisingly beaten by 3-2. The single most reason that England suffered defeat that day was because of Harry Gregg's superlative goalkeeping performance. It was one of the finest goalkeeping displays that you could ever wish to see and I just wish that there was still footage of that game around for people today to see it. One save that I will always remember is a twenty five yard blockbuster from Duncan Edwards that looked destined for the top corner of the net. That is, until there was a blur of movement, and flying through the air like a swallow to his left, Harry punched the ball away. The *'Big Fella'* stood there hands on hips looking at Harry in admiration.

When the final whistle went and victory had been achieved, the Irish fans clambered over the Wembley walls which surrounded the pitch, raced onto the field, and Harry, along with the other players, was hoisted high and chaired all the way back to that famous old tunnel which led to the dressing rooms. It is my opinion that it was his performance in that game which persuaded Sir Matt Busby to sign Harry, and also to pay a world record fee for a goalkeeper at that time.

Harry Gregg was born on October 27th 1932 in the small Northern Ireland town of Tobermore, in County Derry. As a young boy, Harry was sports mad, but his favourite game was always football. In an interview with the Irish radio station, Radio Kerry, in 2001, he said: *I lived for football, but as a young boy in those days, I was capped for my country as a schoolboy international. I was captain of the Under-14 international team. In that same team was the great, Jackie Blanchflower. Sadly, the late, great, Jackie Blanchflower. I went like all boys did in those days to the local YMCA. I did a fair bit of boxing. I got to the semi-final of the Northern Ireland Boxing Championships, got a bye from the semi-final into the final, and I was so proud and big-headed. When I got into the ring for the final, a fellow from Ruffle Street battered the head off me, and so I gave up the boxing! I was also a very good gymnast and used to give exhibitions. However, the heart of it all, I was a left-back playing football in those days, but they thought that I was a little too rough at school so they put me in goal, and I played for the next thirty years and I hated every minute of being a goalkeeper because it was like being in a cage. I wasn't allowed outside the 18 yard line.*

Gregg started his playing career with Windsor Park Swifts, the reserve team of Linfield, before signing for his local club, semi-professional, Coleraine. At the age of 18, he was spotted by a Doncaster Rovers scout, and the Yorkshire club paid Coleraine a fee of £2,000, to take him across the Irish Sea and into League Football in England. Doncaster was then playing its football in the old Football League Division Two and was under the astute leadership of one of football's legendary greats – the wonderful Irishman, Peter Doherty. Doherty had a big influence upon Harry Gregg's early career in England, and he watched his progression at Belle Vue.

Although he was at what could be termed as an unfashionable Second Division club, Gregg's performances brought him to the attention of the Northern Ireland selectors. On 21 March, 1954 he made his first appearance at full international level when he kept goal against Wales in a World Cup Qualifying match at Ninian Park, Cardiff, where Northern Ireland were the victors by 2-1. He was to win seven more full international caps whilst at Doncaster, and the last one was in that game at Wembley on 6 November 1957, against England. The performance of Gregg in that game was the catalyst to the start of several First Division clubs looking to sign him. First Sheffield Wednesday made a firm bid for him, but their valuation, and that of the Doncaster Board, was miles apart, so the transfer never even got to the negotiating stage.

At this time, Manchester United was beginning to drop a few points in their 1957-58 League campaign. From the 30th November until the 14th December 1957, they only took one point from a possible six. Busby decided to act. He was of the opinion that Ray Wood had lost a little confidence, and so he went after Harry Gregg. At first there were rumours that Doncaster Rovers wanted a mammoth £35,000 for him, but this eventually turned out to be untrue. However, the initial negotiations proved hard going. In the Kerry radio interview, Gregg recalled:

I was never really involved in the financial side of things. Sheffield Wednesday had made a bid of £18,000 about a month before but Doncaster Rovers said that I wasn't going anywhere. Then out of the blue, I had no knowledge of it at all, I was told to report after training to the medical room at Belle Vue at two o'clock, and then when I got there I had to get into a car and put a blanket over my head. I was driven to the manager Peter Doherty's house, a place that I had never been to before. I went and met with Peter Doherty and he told me, 'Manchester United want to sign you. Matt Busby is coming over to sign you.' I said to the manager, 'Boss, I've had a wonderful time at Doncaster Rovers – do I get anything out of it?' Doherty said, 'No, No, No, we'd rather keep you' and with that I thought, 'What the hell am I doing here in your house then?'

There was a knock on the door and in came Matt Busby and Jimmy Murphy whom I had never met before. I'd watched them and heard of them, but had never met them. Peter Doherty turned to Matt Busby and said, 'Matt – the boy is ready to go', to which Busby replied 'No, No, No Peter, I want to speak to the boy.' So that immediately created an impression with me and I was getting sold down the river like a side of beef, and here the buyer was saying, ' no, no, no, I want to talk to the boy.' Matt Busby turned to me and said, 'Do you want to join Manchester United?' and I immediately and too quickly, said 'yes'. Busby responded 'Hold on, we don't pay any money – do you still want to join Manchester United?' Because I believe that you back yourself in life, I told him, 'I still want to join Manchester United.'

I signed the forms there and then and Doncaster Rovers got £23,500, and I got what was called 'accrued share of benefit' - £37!!! But I would do it all again and for less! It was the happiest day of my life. The only reason I did it was to better myself and for security for my wife and daughter who was two months old. However, I did want to join what I considered then to be the Hollywood of football, and even though all these years have passed since, I've yet to be proved wrong.

He was signed on Wednesday the 18 December 1957, and what a great early Christmas present that must have been for him. He joined a dear old friend of his at Old Trafford, Jackie Blanchflower, whom he had known since schoolboy days when they had both played in the same Northern Ireland schoolboy international team. Harry was leaving a struggling of Second Division team at that time. It is interesting to note that amongst the team mates that he was leaving behind at *Donny* was a certain centre half by the name of Charlie Williams, who was later to find fame on ITV's *Comedians* television show. For the big, likeable Ulsterman, his move to United to join the now famous *Busby Babes* was a dream come true.

Harry made his debut for United just a few days later against Leicester City, on Saturday, December 21st, 1957. I attended that game and stood behind the goal at the Scoreboard End. That was the end that the *Babes* always came out to when they emerged from the old player's tunnel. I just wanted to see our new goalkeeper. In those days I was a budding young goalkeeper myself, and my idol (after Edwards of course!) was Bert Trautmann who played for Manchester City. On the day of the game against Leicester, the teams came out and this big twine toed fellow started his jog towards the Scoreboard End goal. I was mesmerized just

Harry Gregg leaves the Wembley pitch after his superlative display against England on 6 November 1957. Against all the odds, Northern Ireland had inflicted a 3-2 defeat upon the host nation.

watching him! He had such presence. He took his place in the goal as the forwards started firing balls at him.

In 1957 United had a young mascot who could have been no more than six or seven years old, (I always wonder what ever happened to that young boy) and he would go around the players during their five minute warm up and hand to them a stick of chewing gum. As he approached Harry, he stopped dead, as though frightened, and on seeing this, Roger Byrne, United's captain, took the boy by the hand, and took him on to Harry who took the stick of gum, knelt in front of the youngster, said a few words, and then ruffled his hair. It's just a little thing that sticks in my memory. The game began and very early on a high cross was floated into the area and underneath it was Edwards and Byrne, but out off his line came Gregg, soaring into the air, knocking both Edwards and Byrne out of the way as he did it. He caught the ball cleanly and quickly bowled the ball out to Eddie Colman, setting United on the attack. The look on both Edwards and Byrne's faces was as if to say; *"He'll do for me!"* United won easily that day by the emphatic score line of 4 -0.

Harry's first game also caused a little bit of wide eyed astonishment with the fans. When play was at the other end of the field, he would wander outside of his area and could be found mid way between the edge of the eighteen yard line and the half-way line. Back in those days, goalkeepers just did not do that, and it caused a lot of comment. The match report (written by *Old International* - a pen name used by sports writer Don Davies) in the *Manchester Guardian* on Monday 23 December 1957 contained the following passage:

Gregg, a most modest man on whom the burden of financial transaction rests lightly, was the first to admit that he had not a great deal to do. He was fortunate that Leicester could give him little more than a training gallop but, nevertheless, his quality was evident from the start and he will give great confidence. Everything he did was incisive, his cutting out of cross balls was a joy to behold, and if occasionally he seemed over eager, almost to the point of madness, this was understandable enough on his first appearance at Old Trafford In addition his accurate throwing out and goal kicks should be the start of many United attacks in the future. There are not many goalkeepers who kick a ball far enough to put one of their forwards offside.

The next game was against Luton Town at Old Trafford on Christmas Day 1957, and again I was there behind that Scoreboard End goal, and again, he didn't concede as United ran out easy winners by 3-0. The following day, Boxing Day was the return fixture at Kennilworth Road and he conceded his first goals as the game was a tight fought 2-2 draw. Kennilworth Road was a ground that he would come to remember in later years for an entirely different reason!

Just two days later, on 28 December he faced his first *derby* game against Manchester City at Maine Road. City was also going well that season and once more, it was a game that I attended. Over 70,000 packed into the ground that afternoon, and I was stood on what came to be known as the *Kippax* in later years. Back then it was a large arcing, open Spion Kop of a terrace. The game was a ding-dong affair and no quarter was asked or given and it ended all-square at 2-2. It was in this game that the sports writers of the time took Harry to task for his habit of wandering outside of his area when play was at the other end, and he got a fair bit of criticism for it. In my eyes it was unwarranted and I suppose that Sir Matt felt the same way as he never chose to discourage him.

I saw his first ever European game against Red Star Belgrade at Old Trafford on January 14th 1958. I say that I saw it - but not too much of it! Today I doubt if that game would ever have been started. It was thick with fog that night, and for most of the game, you couldn't see across the far side of the pitch! United won 2-1 but I have to be honest; I could not see either of the goals that Bobby Charlton or Eddie Colman scored as United won 2-1.

The following Saturday they destroyed a team that used to be their nemesis - Bolton Wanderers, and by an astonishing score line of 7-2! Bolton was always a big bogey team to United, but that day, they were just steamrollered. The last time that I saw Harry play with the *Babes* was in their last home game, a 4th Round F.A. Cup tie against Ipswich Town which was won at a stroll by 2-0, and Harry had little to do. The week after he took part in that famous last game on home soil, the 5-4 win at Highbury, and then it was on to Belgrade.

He performed heroically in the 3-3 draw against Red Star, particularly in that second half when Red Star threw the kitchen sink at United. His performance that afternoon often gets overlooked, but he produced some vital saves that were critical to United getting the 3-3 draw. After the after-match banquet at the Majestic Hotel, he retired with others to a room where they played poker until 3a.m.

We all know what happened later that day, 6 February, 1958, and the part that Harry Gregg played which can never ever be allowed to be forgotten. What that man did was above and beyond the call of what any man could, or should have done. That he saved lives is beyond dispute. Cometh the hour, cometh the man, and that man was Harry Gregg. He doesn't like being called a hero, but that undoubtedly is what he is. The courage he showed that day was phenomenal to say the least.

Once back from Munich, he totally immersed himself into training, and playing football once again, and helping Jimmy Murphy to keep the flag flying. His goalkeeping displays were tremendous and he was a pivotal figure in helping Manchester United reach the FA Cup Final again. Sadly, there was to be no winner's medal for him as United was defeated by 2-0 by local neighbours, Bolton Wanderers. For the second season running controversy surrounded the FA Cup Final. Although Bolton was leading 1-0 at the time, and the game was deep into the second half, the second goal caused a massive dispute. Parrying a shot from Dennis Stevens (Duncan Edwards's cousin) the Bolton inside-forward, Gregg could only push the ball straight up and into the air. He turned to watch the flight of the ball and as he waited to catch it, in the final moments of the ball's descent, Nat Lofthouse came charging in, barging both Harry and the ball over the goal line. Incredulously, the referee, Yorkshireman Jack Sherlock, awarded a goal as Harry lay prostrate on the Wembley turf. Although Bolton had been the much better team on the day, the incident soured the game.

After the disappointment of the FA Cup Final, there were two games in the semi-final of the European Cup against the might of AC Milan to be navigated. Not many people outside of Manchester gave United any kind of a chance. However, in the first game played at Old Trafford, United came from behind to win by 2-1. It did give the fans a false hope of the team reaching the European Cup Final; however the preparation for the second leg in Milan could only be described as far from ideal. The team had to travel overland by train from Manchester to Milan. It was a long, tiring journey. In the cauldron that was Milan's San Siro Stadium that evening, United were soundly beaten by 4-0. For most of the players it was the end of the season, but not for Harry Gregg.

In the summer of 1958, the World Cup Finals were held in the month of June in Sweden. Incredibly, all four British home nations qualified. Six small counties from the North of Ireland went to that World Cup and surprised everybody by reaching the quarter finals. When the Finals were over, the European press named their selected team from all the nations which had taken part. Harry Gregg's name was the first on their list — he had received the accolade of being the World's best goalkeeper.

I recall some of his performances in the early years after the tragedy, and particularly one at Preston's Deepdale in a 0-0 draw. Again, his performance was incredible, and for a big man, his agility had to be seen to be believed. Two saves in

Harry Gregg makes a save during a match in 1959.

67

particular I remember that afternoon were to shots that he really had no right to get near to, but he flew through the air with all the grace of an eagle, and beat them away with his fists. It is something that I wish modern day goalkeeper's would take note of - technique - today they just seem to allow the ball to hit them - Harry beat the ball away and it would more often than not, would fly away out of danger. It was also at Deepdale that afternoon that I first heard him get involved with somebody in the crowd at the back of the goal. Somebody was giving him stick, and Harry left the guy in no uncertain terms what he would do to him if he got his hands on him! It became a recurring thing with him - particularly at away grounds!

He played such a huge part in the rebuilding of Manchester United and that part should also never be forgotten. Sadly, injuries took their toll on him and it is my opinion that the first shoulder injury which started the injury sequence off, happened against Tottenham Hotspur at Old Trafford on Wednesday, 14th January, 1961. 'Spurs were all conquering at that time and were on a roll. This was the season in which they became the first winners of the famous *Double* in the 20th Century. They had trounced United in the previous three league encounters between them, and 'Spurs were expected to walk over a United side that was still trying to rebuild after the disaster. 'Spurs had a star studded line up which was brim full of international players — Brown, Mackay, and White, from Scotland; Blanchflower from Northern Ireland; Medwin, and Jones, from Wales; Baker, Norman and Smith, from England. They were an exceptional team.

It was a typical bitterly cold January evening and Old Trafford was packed with over 65,000 fans. The pitch had a cover of sand upon it and the surface underneath was rock hard. United took to the field with the following line up; Gregg; Brennan, Cantwell; Setters, Foulkes, Nicholson; Quixall, Stiles, Dawson, Pearson and Charlton. From the off, United were in a determined mood and started to harry, and hustle 'Spurs out of their rhythm and stride. One thing that I will always recall from that match was a young Nobby Stiles playing at inside right, getting in his first tackle on the elegant Danny Blanchflower very early in the game. I can still see it now - the ball was there to be won - the wizened elegant international player on one side, and the young upstart of a sprog on the other. Nobby's fierce determination and will-to-win was there for all to see as he took about ten yards of turf, the ball, and Danny Blanchflower, all in one flowing sweeping movement. Danny shot up in the air like a coconut being tossed at a fairground, and he hit the ground like a falling sack of coal. He was never the same again throughout the rest of the match and obviously, he had one eye on Nobby as he tried to avoid him whenever he could!

The game was competitive and 'Spurs elegant style was ruffled. So much so, that United took the lead with a goal scored by none other than that little inside forward, so dangerous from two yards, Nobby Stiles. Midway through the first half Harry Gregg dislocated his shoulder diving into a ruck of players as they scrambled for the ball just on his six yards line. Alex Dawson took over in goal and Harry went to centre forward - his shoulder and arm strapped up in a sling! United were able to hold on to their lead until the interval, and as the players left the field, the consensus of opinion from the fans was that Gregg would not return for the second half. We should have known better!

Harry made a continued nuisance of himself as he dashed about harassing the 'Spurs defenders. However, as the game wore on, 'Spurs were getting the upper hand. With about ten minutes left United managed an attack going towards Old Trafford's Scoreboard End. Harry made a diagonal run from right to left towards the goal. His run took the 'Spurs towering centre half, Maurice Norman, with him. It created a couple of yards of space into which ghosted young Mark Pearson coming from left to right, and behind Norman. The ball came through at pace to Harry, and with the deftest of back heels, he played young inside-forward Pearson in, and he smashed the ball past Bill Brown the 'Spurs goalkeeper and into the net. 2-0 and the 65,000 fans inside Old Trafford erupted. Harry was engulfed by his team mates, and he had to fight them off for fear that his shoulder would take another battering. Sadly, that shoulder injury was to plague him for the rest of his career. That goal knocked the stuffing out of the 'Spurs team and United were good value for their 2-0 win when the final whistle blew. It is a game that I will always remember because although the club was still rebuilding, that indomitable Manchester United fighting spirit was there for all to see.

In 1963 Harry Gregg played in every round of the F.A. Cup up to the semi-final. Sadly, a run of mediocre results leading up to that semi - final resulted in Harry losing his place. Nobby Stiles also missed out on a place in the Final as well. It was sad really, because if ever there was a man who deserved some silverware in his career at United, it was Harry Gregg.

For the next few years he was in and out of the team and he vied with David Gaskell and Pat Dunne, for the number one 'keeper's spot. His real swan song at Old Trafford was during the 1965-66 season when he was the number one choice for the majority of games played. There were some very memorable games in that season, and it may surprise a few people when I make mention of them. United were drawn against Portugal's Benfica, in the Quarter Final of the European Cup. The first tie was at home and was so closely fought with Bill Foulkes scoring what turned out to be the winning goal in a 3-2 victory. The away tie which was played in Benfica's magnificent Stadium of Light, is well known to United's supporters. This was the night that a young George Best ran amok, and tore the Portugese team of stars apart. United won 5-1, catapulting the young Irishman into super star status. But in both those games, Harry Gregg was the Manchester United goalkeeper! He also played in both of the European Cup semi-final legs against Yugoslavia's Partizan, from Belgrade – a place that held so many, many, memories for him. That Manchester United should have gone on to the European Cup Final that year is beyond doubt, but a combination of injuries, and missed chances saw them lose 2-0 in Belgrade, and win 1-0 at Old Trafford. It was such a major disappointment for players and fans alike - so near, yet so far. United also reached the semi-final of the F.A. Cup that season, but they also lost to Everton by 1-0 - again so near yet oh! so far.

Harry Gregg played his last game for United on 7 September, 1966 in a 3-0 defeat at the Victoria Grounds in Stoke. His contribution to Manchester United can never be underestimated. What he did can never be looked at in terms of medals or trophies won. That he doesn't have a cabinet full of them is a travesty in my eyes. However what he does have is so many, many, wonderful memories, especially of those eleven games in which he played with probably, and I make no bones about saying this, the finest young team that Manchester United has ever produced. You cannot get much better than that.

Just a few years before Jackie Blanchflower passed away I had the honour of sitting with him at a former player's re-union dinner. He spoke so wonderfully well of his great mate, team mate, and comrade. He told me a story about Harry when he was staying with the Blanchflowers just after he had signed for United. Apparently Jean and Jackie had been out one night, and when they came home, they could hear somebody mooching about at the back of the house. Jackie thought that they had burglars and so picked up a stone from the garden. He tiptoed around the back of the house ready to pounce on the would-be burglar only to find Harry sat there shivering - he'd lost the key which they had given to him! He also told me about Hurry's first day at Old Trafford when the lads wanted him to play snooker and he was very reticent. Eventually he relented and they couldn't understand some of the shots that he was trying to play. All came to light later as he told Jackie that he had a hole in the sole of his shoe and didn't want the lads to think that the world's costliest goalkeeper could not afford a decent pair of shoes!

He was a volatile character and never suffered fools. He had a love-hate relationship with little Johnny Giles and erupted one time when the team was away on tour, chasing the little Dubliner all around the hotel, before Giles finally barricaded himself in a room. At Luton Town's Kenilworth Road ground, a fan ran onto the field at the end of a match and made a bee line for Harry. He had not the faintest idea of who this fan was, and the sweetest of right hooks saw the fan ending up flat on his back in the mud. Nobody ever took liberties with Harry

Gregg, and there was a lot of barnstorming, hard, centre forwards around back in those days who would intimidate goalkeepers whenever they could. It never worked with Harry, and on a number of occasions, especially in goal mouth melees, some of them would be suddenly found face down in the mud almost comatose - and nobody ever saw a thing!

His life has suffered a lot more than its share of tragedy and he's always had mountains to climb throughout. It says so much for the man that he has faced life's challenges head on - just as he faced those fearless centre forwards of his day. He never ever shirked those challenges, and he always rose above them. It says so much for the courage, determination, and tenacity of the man, but it also tells of his great modesty and the wonderful love of his family that he has.

In 1993 Harry was awarded the MBE (Member of the British Empire). In his own words:

"One morning in 1993 when we had the hotel in Portstewart, my wife came up to me and told me that there was an envelope for me out at the front. I told her that it would be somebody wanting autographs and asked her to check it out and I would sign them. However, she was persistent and told me that she wanted me to come out and see it. So after being pestered, I went up and it was from Buckingham Palace asking me if I would accept an MBE if it was offered. I said to my wife, 'I'll think about it.'

And I did think about it. To be honest with you I could have had one years before, it wasn't something that I wanted, and eventually I decided yes, provided I could take it in honour of two things;

In honour of the greatest Irish footballer that ever played, Peter Doherty; and in honour of the boys who didn't make it at Munich.

I accepted the MBE under those circumstances.

I went to Buckingham Palace and I met His Royal Highness Prince Charles. Afterwards, when I came out with three members of my family, there was lines of photographers charging £40 a head to have your picture taken with your MBE, and wearing your top hat and tails. I wasn't having any of that so I walked across the courtyard, hailed a taxi, got the family in, and cleared off home."

With Harry, what you see is what you get, and that is the way that he is. The word legend is banded about today all too frequently, and it is bestowed upon people who, in my honest opinion, are not fit to wipe Harry Gregg's boots. He didn't win much in the way of medals during his time at Manchester United, but what he did do was to win his place in the love, and affection, of all of us who were so privileged to see him in his prime. A legend? There is never any doubt about that - but a real legend in the truest sense of the word.

Live long and happy Harry and thanks for all the memories.

Harry Gregg made 247 appearances for Manchester United.

He was capped 25 times for his native Northern Ireland.

Bill Foulkes – The Man of Granite

Football used to be described as *'a man's game'*. In this so called modern era, I often wonder whether or not this phrase is still true. The game has altered so much over the last twenty five years as far as the physical aspect goes. Sadly, I think that it has lost some of the attraction that it once had because of the fact that the physical side of football has been slowly eroded down the years. Yes, we can all eulogize about the great players in the game today, but I'll guarantee that most of the players placed in that bracket are either forwards or midfielders. It used to be that when going to the match, your appetite would be whetted by looking forward to the confrontations of full back against winger; inside forward against wing half; goalkeeper and centre half against centre forward. It was a joy to see those defenders who had mastered the art of the tackle, whether it is of the sliding type; the block type; or the full blooded *'come into the office'* type! It also gave the spectator a chance to see something about the character of the players that these defenders were marking, and would also allow them to see whether or not they had the heart, the courage, and that little bit of devil not to be intimidated by them, but to also give it back.

All players need the skill to make the top echelon in the game, but skill alone will not see them prevail. They have to have the temperament to survive and progress, and that comes from attitude, character, courage, strength of mind, the will to compete and win, and having a great pride in the shirt that they wear. Unfortunately today, in my own honest opinion, I see a lot of players that lack those extras to make themselves truly great players. Those that do attain greatness certainly do have that mix.

I got to thinking about some of the great defenders that I have seen during my lifetime, and wondered just how long they would last out on the pitch if they were playing the game today. The conclusion that I came up with was, for no more than ten minutes! The rough and tumble, and physical aspect, was all part and parcel of football back then, and it was accepted without rancour. Players had to come to terms with it or they would disappear into oblivion - and believe me, many of them did!

Bill Foulkes pictured during a training session at Old Trafford in 1957

People today will argue that the game back in the past was brutal, and that something had to be done to clean it up. I disagree with what I hear. Yes, the tackle from behind had to be outlawed, but I see far more brutal assaults on players in this modern era than I ever did back then. Today's brutality is more often than not cynical, cowardly, and also downright dangerous. The art of tackling has all but disappeared. This certainly does not surprise me given the edicts handed down by FIFA and our own FA, and also the various governing football bodies Referee's Committees around the world. There has also been a great change in referee's personalities from the moment that they became professional - some of them have egos bigger than today's star players. As Bill Shankly once said:

"The trouble with Referees is that they know the rules, but they don't know the game!"

Never has that statement been as true as it is in this modern era! There is such an inconsistency with referees in the game today. Many terrific legitimate tackles that win the ball fairly, more often than not see the tackler receiving a yellow card. I have seen brutal, cynical challenges that cause injury, go unpunished.

The term, hard men, is often heard, and I got to thinking about what that term really means. What constitutes a hard man? Is it somebody who just kicks and intimidates opponents? Is it a player who takes the kicks without retaliating? To me, the epitome of the hard man is the player who has an abundance of skill, be it a defender or a forward, who has the physical and mental strength to meet the challenge, who gives and takes without question, is honest in his endeavours, and who gives his all for the shirt that he wears, and who, at the end of the day, fans grudgingly admire with the greatest of respect. Players from yesteryear whom I would place in this bracket would be Jimmy Scoular, Peter Farrell, Roy Paul, Stan Willemse, Roy Warhurst, Trevor Daniel, Tommy Banks, Roy Hartle, Tommy Docherty, Tommy Cummings, Brian Miller, Alex Forbes, Maurice Norman, Dave Mackay, Dave Hickson, Trevor Ford, Tommy Smith, Ron Flowers, Tony Kay, and Dennis Smith. That's twenty without thinking too hard!

If I look at today's players, I struggle to come up with very many. Where are today's real hard men? All of those players that I mentioned were players that opposing fans grudgingly respected and would not have hesitated to have had them in their own teams. Manchester United have had more than their fair share down the years, even going back as far as the first decade of the 20th Century when the famous United half-back line of Duckworth, Roberts and Bell, sprang to prominence. Charlie Roberts was as hard as they came, and in the Twenties, nobody in the game had a more fearsome reputation than a United centre half by the name of Frank Barson.

Busby's first team after he became manager had another rock hard centre half in Allenby Chilton, a player who gave, nor asked, any quarter. He was followed by Mark Jones, Duncan Edwards, and then came Stan Crowther, Wilf McGuinness, Maurice Setters, Nobby Stiles, John Fitzpatrick, Jim Holton, Kevin Moran, Bryan Robson, Paul Ince, Roy Keane, and Jaap Stam, and today, Nemanja Vidic. From the forwards, players I would bracket as hard men were Jack Rowley, Dennis Law, George Best, Joe Jordan, Norman Whiteside, Mark Hughes, Eric Cantona, and Wayne Rooney.

One player's name is missing though, and to me he is one of, if not the, biggest, unsung hero in Manchester United's United's great history - and he would, without doubt in my opinion, be classed as a hard man. He made 688 appearances in the red shirt over a period of nineteen years, but his career took in eras of both a glorious and tragic part of United's history. Manchester United very nearly missed out on signing him because he was courted fastidiously by Bolton Wanderers. Although he had been given trials by United, he did not hear from them for a while, and he was on the verge of signing for the 'Trotters'. However, being fair minded, he did let United know what he was about to do, and they immediately sent for him, and got him down to Old Trafford to put pen to paper and sign part-time professional forms.

Prior to this he had been playing his football for St. Helens Town, for whom his father had kept goal for a number of years beforehand. He was also working down the pit at the time that he signed for United, and did so for four years afterwards, even after he had won a place in the first team. His debut game in the first team came at the age of twenty years and eleven months, at Anfield, against Liverpool, wearing the number two shirt, on the 13 December 1952, in a 2-0 victory. The player concerned is of course, Bill Foulkes.

If you look back at the 50s and 60s, and think of United's glories throughout those years, the names that immediately spring to mind are of Carey, Rowley, Aston, Pearson, Byrne, Colman, Edwards, Taylor, Viollet, Pegg, Charlton, Law, Best, Stiles, Crerand. Yet look a little deeper and one man really did play more than his part in those glories. That man was Bill Foulkes. Unfashionable, unassuming, never the player to really catch the eye, he was certainly effective. Initially as a right full-back, and then as a centre-half, Foulkes was a fitness fanatic, and it says a great deal about his physical dedication that he was able to stay part time for four years, only training at United on a Tuesday, and Thursday evening, throughout the early part of his career.

One thing that a lot of United fans do not realize is that just prior to United signing Tommy Taylor, Busby had been giving thought to playing Foulkes in the first team at centre forward! Jimmy Murphy had experimented with Foulkes by playing him up front in the reserve team, and it had met with quite some success. Foulkes scored a bagful of goals in just a small number of games. In fact in one game against Newcastle Reserves at St. James's Park, he scored four times. He was earmarked for a run out in the first team against Stoke City, but turned an ankle in training in the mid-week before that game, and he was ruled out. The following week Tommy Taylor was signed from Barnsley.

The 1952 Championship winning team was slowly being broken up as Busby's youth policy started to bear fruit. With only training twice a week, most of his work was done with the young players from the junior teams at The Cliff. Foulkes was only too well aware of the task that confronted him in trying to break through into United's first team. He had made his debut at Liverpool in the latter part of 1952, but his chances in the immediacy after that were few and far between. Roger Byrne had cemented his place at left back, and the right back berth was a choice between Johnny Carey, Johnny Aston, and Tommy McNulty. Plus Billy Redman was also in contention. Carey was almost at the end of his career as was Aston, and McNulty did himself no favours with Matt Busby due to his off the field activities. In the 1953-54 season, Busby slowly began introducing his young players. However, he was a wise manager in that he kept two of his old guard in the team, namely Allenby Chilton, and Jack Rowley.

Upon Carey's retirement from the game, Chilton was made Club Captain. He was a very feisty character and wasn't averse to handing out a few backhanders to the younger players if he felt that they had stepped out of line. Jack Rowley was also a player who could look after himself, but in my opinion, Busby kept these two old stalwarts in his team to look after, and mind, the youngsters. In the middle autumn of 1953, Foulkes got his chance again, and for the next sixteen seasons was hardly out of the team. It was a tribute to his dedication and fitness, that even as a part timer, he managed to force his way into the first team. He played so well over the next twelve months that on 2nd October 1954, he appeared in the England team that beat Northern Ireland 2-0 at Windsor Park, Belfast. Again, no mean feat for a part timer. It's sad to reflect today that little was he to know that day, that it would turn out to be his one and only appearance for his country.

Matt Busby had been badgering him to turn full time professional from the day he got into the first team. But Foulkes was married, earned more from working down a coal mine than he did from football, and was more secure in financial terms than most full time players. However, he was still ambitious as far as his football was concerned, but there was another reason holding him back from signing on as a full time pro - a thing called National Service. As a miner, he was in a category that fell under the term of, protected trade, and as such, he was ineligible for the mandatory two years of military service. However, his call up for the full England team in October 1954 was the spur that he needed to take the plunge into the full time professional ranks, and in January of 1955, he pleased his manager by signing a full-time professional contract.

Busby's youth policy had now started to bear fruit, and the team was now being affectionately referred to as the *Babes*. By the Easter of 1955, Chilton, and Rowley, had departed - Chilton as player-manager to Grimsby Town, and Rowley as player-manager to Plymouth Argyle. Busby's team of youngsters was now starting to take the First Division of the Football League by storm, playing an enterprising attacking style of football. They were precocious, effervescent, and even audacious. For the players, once they had made their mark in the first team, they did not want to be left out. There was so much brilliant young talent around Old Trafford, that if they did lose their place, they found that it was so difficult to regain it once more. The two oldest players in the team in 1955, were Johnny Berry 27, and Roger Byrne, both 26; Foulkes was 24, Whitefoot 21, Jones 22, Edwards 18, Whelan 19, Taylor 23, Viollet 23, Pegg 20, McGuinness 18, Doherty 20, Bent 19, Goodwin 20, Lewis 20, Scanlon 20, Webster 22, Wood 22, Blanchflower 21. There was a conveyor belt of youngsters on the way up as well, with players like eighteen years old Bobby Charlton, and Eddie Colman, to name just two. So to hold down a first team spot was essential as far as the player was concerned. Foulkes had to be on his game each and every week.

He played in the last game of the 1954-55 season, and then sure enough, his Call Up papers dropped through the letterbox of his home in early May, 1955. Not only was he Called Up, but a number of other United players also received their beckoning not too long afterwards - Duncan Edwards, Bobby Charlton, Eddie Colman, all being to the fore. Foulkes was conscripted into the Royal Army Service Corps, and was initially stationed down in Aldershot. Busby talked to Foulkes before he left to start his army service. He made a statement that would leave most people with lockjaw had it been heard today! Busby told Foulkes that as he was stationed so far away, if he wanted to keep his place in the first team, he would have to make his own arrangements for getting to the games - the Club could not help him! He promised Foulkes that if he arrived at the various grounds in good time, he would play! Whether or not this was a tongue-in-cheek statement, or whether or not Busby was testing Foulkes' resolve is hard to say - only Busby had the answer. Nonetheless, for a player who had not long cemented his first team place down, and had won his call up to the full England team as well, it was a rather disturbing thing to hear. I also wonder if he told the other players who were doing their National Service, the same thing. I have my doubts.

Nonetheless, on 20 August 1955, Foulkes turned up at the St. Andrews ground in Birmingham, for the opening game of the 1955-56 season against Birmingham City. The story goes that Ian Greaves, the young reserve team full back, was already in the dressing room getting ready to get changed and play at right back in that game. Foulkes arrival put Busby in a predicament given his statement to Foulkes just before he had departed for military service. True to his promise, he told Foulkes to get changed and Greaves had to hand over the number two shirt! How long this arrangement went on for, only Bill Foulkes can tell!

After basic training, life in the Army for Foulkes was not so bad. There was plenty of football and he captained an Army team that would have held its own against any team in any competition. Footballers from most clubs in both the Football, and Scottish Leagues, were also doing their National Service and, the Army XI regularly contained as many as eight or nine international players. In November of 1956, I can recall going to Maine Road to watch the Army XI play against an FA XI, and Manchester United supplied four players for the Army team - Foulkes, Colman, Edwards, and Charlton. Also as team mates they had Alan Hodgkinson, and Graham Shaw from Sheffield United, Jimmy Melia from Liverpool, David Dunmore and Cliff Jones from 'Spurs. The Army won 4-1 as I recall and there was an attendance of over 50,000!

With all the football, Foulkes had no problem with his fitness. He played week in and week out, and thanks to an understanding Commanding Officer, was always allowed to get away to play for Manchester United. He had endeared himself to the United fans and had earned himself the nickname of *Cowboy,* because of his bandy legs! Foulkes was an uncompromising, no nonsense, type of full back who had done well against the myriad of talented wingers who plied their trade in the First Division. In those bygone days, every club played with two wingers, and they were excellent at what they did. Oh! That this was the case today! To hold his place down, first as a part timer, and then whilst doing his National Service, was a very big compliment to Foulkes' skill, fitness, ambition and attitude.

He was virtually ever present in United's team from the start of the 1955-56 season, until just after the turn of the year. United suffered a disastrous exit at Bristol Rovers in the third round of the FA Cup in the January of 1956, losing 4-0 at the Eastville ground. 14 days later, at Deepdale, against Preston North End, United were again beaten, this time by 3-1. Bill had a torrid time that day against Tom Finney - but how many full backs did not during that era? It was a game that I attended with a number of my school mates and I can recall that it rained heavily throughout the game, and the pitch was turned into a quagmire!

Busby decided to leave Foulkes out for the next game in favour of young Ian Greaves, and he was never to regain his place again during that season. This was the break-through season for the young *Babes* and they finished as League Champions by the massive distance of eleven points in front of their rivals, with a young team of which the average age was just twenty two years!

Foulkes had played more than the requisite number of first team games to qualify for a winners medal that season, as had a young, cheeky, fresh faced wing-half, by the name of Wilf McGuinness. That Championship win really did make the British football public sit up and take note. No team had ever won the Championship before with such a young average age.

At the start of the 1956-57 season, Busby restored Foulkes to the right back position for the opening game, which again, was against Birmingham City at St. Andrew's. From that moment on, he made sure that he wasn't going to be left out again. This was the season that United first entered European competition and the Army authorities were more than generous in allowing him leave for the away legs in Europe. United played fifty seven matches that season and Foulkes played in fifty four of them. The three games that he missed were because, twice the Army required him to play in Kentish Cup matches against the Belgian Army, and then the week before the F.A. Cup Final in the final League game of the season, Busby rested several regular first team players. It was another Championship winning season for United, and they also reached the F.A. Cup Final.

Foulkes was definitely the first choice full back and just before the start of the 1957-58 season, the day that he had been looking forward to, arrived - *demob day!* He could now go home to his wife, and also concentrate fully on his Manchester United career. United began that season well winning five and drawing one of the opening six fixtures. But they then lost to Bolton Wanderers at Burnden Park by 4-0. This began a run of three straight defeats, the other two being against Blackpool, and Wolverhampton Wanderers. By United's standards of the previous two seasons, they were suffering a stutter, and three more defeats followed during the next few months. It left them six points adrift of Wolves by mid-December, so Busby decided to act. He bought in goalkeeper Harry Gregg from Doncaster Rovers, and he dropped Ray Wood. He also dropped Johnny Berry, Billy Whelan and David Pegg and brought in a young winger named Kenny Morgans who was not long out of the youth team, Bobby Charlton, and Albert Scanlon. At that time, making changes like this was considered drastic, but it had the desired effect. From then on until February 6th 1958, the team never lost, winning seven games and drawing four, and in that period trounced their bogey team, Bolton Wanderers, by 7-2!

Foulkes was playing well, but little was he to know that his life was about to change forever. We all know the happenings of 6 February 1958, and we know the part that Bill Foulkes had to play in that tragic event. That United were able to put a team out just thirteen days later in an FA Cup tie, was little short of a miracle. When you consider what had happened, even more of a miracle was the fact that both Bill Foulkes, and Harry Gregg, were able to play in that FA Cup tie. They had lost seven of their closest friends (and were to lose one more just thirty hours after that FA Cup tie took place) and several more were still lying injured. No trauma counseling back in those days for them. Jimmy Murphy made Foulkes Club Captain, and given the circumstances, that was a tremendous burden and responsibility for him to have to carry, given the state the club found itself in.

The first team was all of a sudden a mixture of reserve team, and youth team players, plus two buys, Ernie Taylor from Blackpool, and Stan Crowther from Aston Villa. As well as playing his own game, Foulkes had to lead from the front and help carry a lot of players who were not only scarred by the tragedy, but also before their time as far as playing in the first team was concerned.

Somehow, that team fought their way to the FA Cup Final, eventually losing to Bolton Wanderers at Wembley. They also performed heroically in the European Cup semi-final against AC Milan, winning 2-1 at Old Trafford. The team had to make the long overland journey to Milan by rail, and this was no preparation for the second leg. Tired, the team lost 4-0. We all know that Busby created three great teams, but for me, Jimmy Murphy's team from February 1958 until the end of the 1958-59 season, stands right up there alongside them all. I always refer to that team as the '*fourth great team*', because although it never won any silverware, what they achieved in carrying the club forward, and finishing as runners-up in the First Division just over a year after the tragedy, was nothing short of a phenomenal effort.

Foulkes' character, like that of the other survivors, changed after the tragedy. He also, became very introverted, moody, and was difficult to get inside of and kept his distance. The younger players christened him *Popular Bill* or *PB* for short. It was a reference to his moodiness. As Club Captain, he had carried that enormous responsibility on his shoulders. The pressures on Foulkes were obviously, at some time or another, going to eventually tell, and so it was that his form became a little erratic. The burden had proved a little too much for him - and that in my own honest opinion, was perfectly understandable.

In the early part of 1959, Busby decided to leave Foulkes out of the team, and the Club Captaincy was handed over to Dennis Viollet. Foulkes needed that rest. On Easter Saturday, in April 1959, young Ronnie Cope, the United centre-half, was injured in a game at Turf Moor, Burnley, which United lost by 4-2. There was no adequate cover available and so, for the fixture at Portsmouth on the Easter Monday, Busby drafted Bill Foulkes back into the team, only this time at centre half. He stayed there in the team until Cope was fit again in the following September of the new 1959-60 season, but was then reverted back to his right back position and was not left out of the team for the rest of the season.

The centre half position was becoming problematical and the 1960-61 season saw Ronnie Cope, and young Frank Haydock, battling it out for the shirt. Both of them never really made

Bill Foulkes, on the left, tries in vain to stop Jimmy Greaves scoring a goal for Tottenham Hotspur in the 1962 FA Cup Semi-Final, which was played at Hillsborough in Sheffield.

it. I think that it would be true to say that Busby had been impressed with Foulkes' performances during his run at centre-half, and so it was, that in the middle of the 1960-61 season, he made centre half Foulkes' permanent position.

For the next 8 years, Foulkes was virtually an ever present in the Manchester United team. He shared in the glory of the FA Cup win against Leicester City in 1963. He won another two First Division Championship medals in 1965, and 1967, and of course he was in the team that triumphed against Benfica in the European Cup Final at Wembley in May of 1968. I suppose that it was also such a fitting script, that Foulkes should score the goal against Real Madrid in the Bernabeau, which took United to that European Final. He was by this time, almost thirty eight years of age.

Without doubt Bill Foulkes had played his part in the Club's history. No player plays 688 games for Manchester United, and for a manager like Sir Matt Busby, without being more than a half decent player. Foulkes was as tough as granite, and in my opinion, was as hard as anybody that has ever played the game. Nobody took any kind of liberties with him. Even in training he neither gave, nor asked any quarter. As a full back, he played against some of the greatest wingers in the game; as a centre-half, he also mixed it with the toughest and the best of centre-forwards of his era, and in both cases, the number of times that he came off second best could be counted on one hand.

He was almost never out of the team through injury, and there was a solid consistency in his play. He was a rock at the heart of the United defence. He was the minder for ball playing colleagues who were of a more delicate disposition than he was. Foulkes was very destructive in the tackle, and relentless in pursuit of the man he had been assigned to mark. In his minder's role, I recall that sunny afternoon in Madrid, in April 1957, when the great Alfredo Di Stefano had kicked young Eddie Colman to the ground in his frustration of being man marked so effectively. It was both a cruel, cowardly act, and one that should have brought the great man an early bath. Foulkes was on Di Stefano in an instant, grabbing him by the front of the shirt. The great Alfredo paled visibly, and uttered the words; *"oikay Foulksay - no more!"* as he feared for his own wellbeing! On another occasion, in a league game at Preston's Deepdale, I saw Tommy

Docherty cynically kick him, off the ball. He had picked the wrong guy to be cynical with - Foulkes was on him like lightning and picked him up with one hand. He hurled Docherty into the Deepdale mud like a rag doll! Unpretentious, unassuming, solid, dependable, consistent, that was Bill Foulkes. He was never one to court the limelight, or to be in the news for the wrong reasons.

Age finally did catch up with him just a year after that wonderful European Cup win. At the start of the 1969-70 season, after just three games, and a heavy home defeat against Southampton by 4-1. Ron Davies, the big Welsh centre-forward scored, all four Southampton goals that day, and it was to prove to be Bill Foulkes' last game for Manchester United. It was sad that he had to end his playing career on that low note, but the march of time had caught up with him, and it was there for all to see.

As I said earlier, the mention of the 1950s and 1960s teams immediately brings to the tongue the names of some of United's greatest ever heroes. Sadly in my opinion, Bill Foulkes hardly ever gets a mention. Yet he was a tremendous servant of Manchester United both as a player, and a man, and he never ever let them down. He had the mental toughness to overcome adversity, tragedy, and the physical toughness to survive in what was back then, a very, very, tough era.

After retirement, he went into coaching, and had spells in Norway, USA, and Japan. Sadly, he found it necessary to secure his family's future by selling his hard won football medals and his cap. I am glad in a way that he never donated this memorabilia to the United Museum, as I find it insulting that former player's families have to pay for the privilege of seeing their loved one's pieces of Manchester United's history. Others with less conspicuous records than Foulkes' have been honoured by club and fans alike - in my opinion, it is about time that this situation was remedied.

Sadly, today, Bill Foulkes now suffers from Alzheimer's disease and is looked after in a local area nursing facility in Manchester.

Bill Foulkes made 688 appearances for Manchester United and scored 9 goals.

Foulkes was capped only one time for the England senior team.

Eddie Colman – Snake Hips

Cheeky, precocious, exuberant, effervescent, bubbly, exciting; all those words could be used to describe Eddie Colman. But as far as football is concerned, you could only ever describe him as supremely gifted and talented. He was certainly one of those players that left an indelible imprint on your memory with his own style of playing the game. He was definitely different from his contemporaries of that era – in many ways – but more of that later.

Eddie Colman was born and bred a Salford lad, and entered this world on 1 November 1936 – just one calendar month later than the indomitable Duncan Edwards. He was born at number 9, Archie Street, Ordsall, a really tough area that lies close to what is now Salford Quays, but back in those days was simply known as the Docks. Like most of Manchester's inner city areas, Ordsall was an area of industrial buildings and streets made up of murky, dark bricked, two – up, two – down, terraced houses, situated in cobbled stoned streets, and this was where the local people were housed. The original opening frames of the long running soap opera *Coronation Street* showing back to back terraced houses divided by an entry were of Eddie's birthplace – Archie Street.

They were all honest, (well some of them!) hard working, God fearing people who lived there – but tough as granite and you had to be able to look after yourself to survive in those parts. He was born a few years before the outbreak of World War Two, and during those hostilities, with both the Manchester and Salford Docks, and Ordsall's industrial buildings being an obvious target for the German Luftwaffe, the area saw a lot of devastation. Many of those terraced houses were blitzed and there were many casualties. This was the initial environment that the young Eddie grew up in.

Ordsall lies virtually alongside Old Trafford, and it's no surprise then that the local kids grew up supporting Manchester United. If they were not at school, kids back then spent most of their time outside, and for the boys, it was always football through the autumn, winter, and spring, and cricket through the summer. Very few working class families owned television sets back then and computers were virtually unheard of – so kids did not have the distractions that they have today, and tended

Eddie Colman pictured at Old Trafford in 1957.

to expend their energies outdoors. It was unusual to find a boy who wasn't interested in football. Games of football would take place in those cobbled stoned streets and on the *"crofts"* where houses had been demolished as a result of the bomb damage. The matches would go on for hours, and if a youngster had a ball, no matter what size (although usually tennis balls were the norm), then there was a game.

This was how the young Eddie initially honed his footballing skills. Academically, he was an average boy. He attended Ordsall School, the same school which was later attended by Alan Clarke, and Graham Nash who formed the pop band *The Hollies*. Physically, Eddie was small in stature with a tiny frame, blonde hair, and a cherubic face. But that was misleading to say the least. To look at him, he was the angelic boy-next-door, but Eddie had an impish streak and was a born practical joker, which often got him into trouble both at home, and at school. However, he shone on the sports field and had great abilities both playing football and cricket. His size never deterred him on the football field and he was never ever afraid to get stuck in and mix it with boys that were physically more mature than him, and in most cases, older.

In the immediate post–war years, he began to develop and it was no surprise therefore that he started to attract attention as first he starred in his school team, and then made selection for the Salford City Boys team, a year earlier than was normal. Eddie was a United fan, and after playing school football on a Saturday morning, he would walk the short journey with his mates, along Trafford Road and across the Swing Bridge, to watch United. Busby's team at that time was the team to watch, but it was also at this time that he was starting to implement his youth policy, gathering the best young talent available, and bringing them to Old Trafford.

Although there was a multitude of football scouts queuing up at the Colman household's front and back doors, there was only ever going to be just one club which Eddie would sign for – and that was Manchester United. When Joe Armstrong, Manchester United's chief scout, first watched him play, he reported to Matt Busby cryptically:

"Put a grass skirt on him and you have a hula-hula-dancer!"

When both Busby, and his assistant, Jimmy Murphy, went to watch him play, they did not have to think twice. Both thought Eddie was natural and had a great future ahead of him.

He joined United in 1952, and immediately settled in trying to establish himself alongside a multitude of talented youngsters – many of them had been schoolboy internationals. But this never ever deterred young Eddie, and he had absolute belief in himself, and a temperament that was mature beyond his years. There was a lot of competition amongst the youngsters back then, but Eddie never shirked that challenge, and although still small, he put in some sterling performances for United's juniors in his first year, playing in matches against teams where the opposition players were mostly adults. Being amongst United's exalted young stars, he never at any time felt inferior to them, and indeed, relished the challenge which they presented.

Eddie's personality was impish but to see this side of him, you really had to know him. His team mates soon found out that Eddie was the complete prankster! It got him into a few scrapes, particularly with Jimmy Murphy, but I'm sure that Jimmy, after his initial annoyance, sat down and laughed also. Eddie was very popular amongst his team mates, and as he moved up through the B and A teams, that popularity never diminished. He captained a very successful Youth team for the first three years that the FA Youth Cup was competed for, and amongst those teams were the likes of Duncan Edwards, Billy Whelan, Bobby Charlton, Wilf McGuinness, and Shay Brennan. His style of play from the right-half position was different from the normal wing-half of his day. , wing-half's back in those days could be likened to enforcers – they were normally well built, and most were destroyers. Eddie, because of his size and stature, was full of guile and craft, and he had a quick footballing brain. He was an exquisite passer of the ball and could thread it through the eye of a needle. He could also tackle, a fact that a lot of pundits of the time failed to see. But he had developed this wonderful body swerve, the likes of which people had never ever seen, and has not been seen since.

Jimmy Murphy in his book *'Matt, United, and Me'*, said:

Eddie was an original. No matter how I search my memory, I cannot recall another player with his particular flair or personality or that cheeky wiggle of his hips as he swept past opponents.

In modern football, which shrieks for the personality player, little Eddie would have shone like the North Star. The press boys took him to their hearts and dubbed him 'Swivel hips, the player with the wiggle like Marilyn Monroe.'

Just eleven days after his nineteenth birthday, on 12 November 1955, he made his first team debut in 1-3 defeat at Burnden Park, against Bolton Wanderers. At 5'7" and just 9 stones 2 lbs., against such a physical team that Bolton was back then, you would have feared for young Eddie's safety! Not a bit of it – he was in amongst the '*Trotters*' like a Jack Russell hanging on to a trouser leg! This was the first time that his trade mark body swerve had been seen at the top level of the game in England. The man on the receiving end was none other than Nat Lofthouse, the Lion of Vienna. Lofthouse was the typical old fashioned centre forward, tough as teak, and no-holds-barred, and was also a seasoned international player. He was very, very physical.

As young Eddie carried the ball away from danger just beyond the eighteen yards line of United's goalmouth, Lofthouse made track for him. It was a David and Goliath situation. There was this young, blond, angel faced kid, making his debut, and was just about to be introduced to the tough professional game of First Division football, by the old wizened master of his craft. As Lofthouse moved in for the kill, the youngster made an exaggerated movement with his hips and arse - it was as though he was on the dance floor doing a rumba! It mesmerized Lofthouse into taking the movement and with just another little swift movement of those hips and arse – Eddie was off in the opposite direction with the ball, leaving Lofthouse in no-man's land! Not only did that dummy confuse Loft house, but it also confused most of the people inside Burnden Park that afternoon, particularly those sitting in the Manchester Road Stand, for there was a murmur went out like you had never heard before. Eddie Colman had arrived.

He was to remain a permanent fixture in the team after that, and he played a huge part in the *Babes* winning their first title in that 1955-56 season.

The fans took to him as one of their favourite sons, and they christened him '*Snake Hips – the boy with the Marilyn Monroe wiggle.*' It was a follow up to the phrase that the press boys had used in their earlier columns.

Colman was the perfect foil for Edwards in the middle of United's midfield. They complimented each other so well – were so precocious, and feared nobody, and certainly no reputation. They were a formidable partnership together. Eddie was never amongst the goals and only twice scored at first team level. His first came just two weeks after his debut when he scrambled the ball home from close range at White Hart Lane against 'Spurs in November 1956. His second was all important, when again he forced the ball home from close range at Old Trafford, in the against Red Star on that dark, January foggy night, in 1958, which gave United a 2-1 lead to take with them on that ill-fated trip to Belgrade. His sense of humor was to the fore when Henry Rose, the Daily Express journalist, asked him after that European game, what it felt like to score such an important goal. Eddie responded:

"You know me Henry; I'm the most dangerous player in the world from two yards!"

Just a year earlier, when United had flown to Spain for the European Cup Quarter Final first leg game against Bilbao; upon landing in the Basque capital, he was one of the first players to alight from the aircraft. Instead of being met by glorious sunshine, it was sleeting heavily, and bitterly cold. Eddie was heard to remark:

"Caramba! Just like Salford!"

For all his skill on the ball, few people realized that there was no better tackler in the game at that time. Edwards had the power and the physique to make him a formidable opponent when challenging for the ball, but Eddie was so beautifully balanced and mobile that when the time came for United to play Real Madrid in the European Cup, everyone was surprised to find that Eddie Colman was given the job of marking the great Alfredo di Stefano. A peseta millionaire, all airs and graces, policed by a humble, but nevertheless, highly mobile and brilliant, footballer from Salford, which was never the most wealthy or salubrious of places. There can be no greater tribute to his skill than that.

It was true to say that Eddie was now an established and integral member of the *Babes* and once again, he picked up another Championship winner's medal as well as playing in the FA Cup Final, in the following 1956 – 57 season. I have no doubts at all in my own mind that he would have gone on to win full England international honours had fate not decreed otherwise. He was in superb form at the time of the tragedy, and together with the established English internationals of Byrne, Edwards, and Tommy Taylor, I also think that Eddie, Mark Jones, and David Pegg would have made the World Cup squad that went to Sweden in 1958, and that they would probably have been the backbone of the England team for years to come.

Off the field Eddie just loved life. If anybody was going to leap up onto the stage and sing, then it would be the ebullient little fellow from Salford. His impish sense of humour was so infectious, and he became very close to Bill Foulkes, and Foulkes' wife, Theresa. Bill was a hulking brute alongside the diminutive little Eddie, but if United were going away for a match, he would tell Theresa:

"Don't worry about Bill, I won't let anybody touch him, I'll take care of him for you."

Wilf McGuinness told me:

"I never ever met anybody with such a lovely personality as Eddie. He was a bubbly type of character, just so full of life. When the Teddy Boy outfits first came out, Eddie had one, drainpipe trousers, suede shoes with the big crepe soles, and he was a real jiver. I never once saw Eddie lose his temper. On the pitch he was really quick and he had that amazing body-swerve and jink, and his control of the ball and vision was first class."

He was very fashion conscious and in the middle fifties when drain pipes, winkle pickers, and three-quarter-length jackets became the style, Eddie was one of the first to be seen wearing that garb. Eddie's best friend as I recall was a little guy called Johnny Moore, who years later became a well known comedian on the night-club circuit in the North of England. They were inseparable and there was no show without '*Punch*' – where you would find one, you would always find the other! They could both be seen around the local dance halls at weekends, but

Eddie would never let on to the girls that he met, what he did for a living. Whenever they asked he would just tell them:

"I work in Trafford Park" or *"I'm a painter and decorator"*.

He loved a pint, and going out with the lads for a drink and a sing song. There was numerous times that Eddie, Wilf, Bobby, Tommy, David, Billy, would gather down at a pub in Sale. Eddie idolized Sinatra and fancied himself as a pianist/crooner. He used to do his party piece in the singing room — *Pennies from Heaven* — much to the delight of the locals. He also loved music and took his portable record player with him wherever he went. He loved Louis Armstrong, and Billy Daniels, but most of all, he adored Frank Sinatra. The late Albert Scanlon recalled a funny tale from the evening before the famous game which was played against Arsenal in London on 1 February, 1958. The team had traveled down to the capital on the Friday afternoon before, and in the evening Albert accompanied Eddie to the cinema, the Odeon, at Marble Arch:

"Frank Sinatra, Rita Hayworth, and Kim Novak were showing in a film there, so I trooped along with Eddie. Half way through the film, Frank Sinatra sang the song 'The Lady is a Tramp' and when he had finished, Eddie stood up in the middle of the cinema and started clapping for almost ten minutes! He was a fanatic was Eddie."

His liking for a pint did lead to some trouble for him, and it came from none other than Roger Byrne, the United captain. No doubt the exuberance of youth was the main culprit, but on a couple of occasions Eddie did let his standards drop a little and once or twice turned up late for training. It does have to be said that Eddie was not the best of trainers — he just wanted the ball all the time. The occasion of Byrne's intervention was after one of the famous "killer ball" games that the players used to play on the gravel at the back of the Stretford End. The players were stood around when it had finished and Roger barked at him that he wanted a word. He took him out of earshot of everybody and when their conversation was over, Eddie was white-faced. It transpired that Roger had certainly left him in no doubts that if he did not pull his socks up and get a grip on his lifestyle, then there was no doubt that he would be on his way out of Old Trafford. That he heeded Roger's advice was to his good. Shortly after this, Eddie met a wonderful young girl named Marjorie, and he was smitten.

Eddie was another of the *Babes* who was idolized by thousands of young kids of that era. Again, like most of those boys that he played alongside, there was no airs and graces with him — just a plain little Salford lad who happened to play football for the club that he adored. Nothing flash, no pretentiousness. It was a common sight to see him walking off home after

The white Italian marble statuette that used to stand on Eddie Colman's resting place. Sadly, because it was vandalized, it is no longer there today.

playing in a match at Old Trafford, chatting to fans as he went. My last sight of him was after the FA Cup Fourth Round tie against Ipswich Town at Old Trafford on 25 January, 1958. United had strolled through the game to win 2-0. About an hour after the game had finished, he came out of the main entrance wearing his big black duffle coat with wooden buttons, and was immediately surrounded by kids. He signed away smiling and laughing, and then joined some friends, and they walked away down past the old ticket office, into the darkness, and out of sight.

After the disaster, I would often play *wag* (truant) from school, and walk from my home in Chorlton-upon-Medlock, through Hulme and on to Regent Road in Salford. I would trek up into Weaste, and then into Weaste Cemetery. Eddie was buried at the top of the main drive on the right hand side, on the corner, just in front of the church. His family had a beautiful statue made of him passing the ball. It was carved and sculpted in Italian, white marble. The statue stood about three feet tall and was so beautiful to look at. I spent many an hour stood there in front of his resting place, and also that statue, reliving old memories, and shedding many a tear. Unfortunately, the statue was vandalized many years later and is no longer there upon his resting place. It is a very sad indictment of the times which we live in today.

Each year, when I am over in England, I always try to find time to visit Eddie's resting place. Nobody who watched him, or knew him, could ever forget the wonderful young boy with the amazing body-swerve, and the larger-than-life character, who just epitomized the spirit of those wonderful young men known as — *The Busby Babes.*

Rest on in Peace Eddie, you are never forgotten.

Eddie Colman made just 107 appearances in all competitions for Manchester United and scored 2 goals.

Mark Jones – The Gentle Giant

That the *Busby Babes* were the glamour team of their era is beyond doubt. Matt Busby had quietly introduced his youngsters into First Division football between the 1952-53, 1953-54, and 1954-55 seasons. It had taken three years to assemble this array of mercurial young talent, and there had been some setbacks along the way as his young apprentices came to terms with First Division football. By the start of the 1955-56 season, his young team had an average age of around twenty two years – unheard of in those times. Talk to people about the *Babes* today, and they will automatically come up with the names of Edwards, Taylor, Byrne, Colman, and Pegg. But just as there have been more than a few unsung heroes in all of Sir Alex Ferguson's past and present Manchester United teams, so it was with the *Babes*. The man I am going to write a few lines about was certainly an unsung hero, but he was as essential to the *Babes* team as have been Vidic, Ferdinand, Stam, Bruce, Pallister, McGrath, McQueen, Buchan, Holton, Ure, and Sadler, who played in the United teams which followed afterwards.

To meet Mark Jones was an absolute pleasure. He was so quiet, unassuming, and modest, down-to- earth, and could even be termed shy. He was born in Barnsley, Yorkshire, on June 15th 1933 and once again, details of early childhood are buried in the mists of time. What is known though, is that he developed into an outstanding young schoolboy footballer. A no-nonsense type of centre half. He was so good, that he captained not only his school team, but also his City Boys team, Yorkshire Schoolboys, the North of England Schoolboys and finally, England Schoolboys. Mark was capped four times as a schoolboy international, and each time he played, it was in a different position. Also in that same England schoolboys team was Dennis Viollet who would also join Mark at Manchester United.

It was no wonder then that he had come to the attention of many of the top clubs in England. However, he had only thoughts of joining Manchester United because his idol was Allenby Chilton, the United centre half. I think that it is true to say, that Mark was certainly one of the original *Busby Babes* when he signed amateur forms for United in the summer of 1948.

He would travel over from Barnsley twice a week to train with the juniors at the Cliff. It must have been a tiring experience for him because after leaving school, he also apprenticed as a bricklayer – hard work in a time when Britain had started to rebuild immediately after the war years. The work helped Mark fill out physically and before too long, here was this big strapping young teenager, standing over six feet tall and weighing around thirteen stones that had the physique of a heavyweight boxer! He progressed through the junior teams and in the summer of 1950, finally signed professional forms for United. In the autumn of that year, 7th October, to be precise, the day that he had dreamed about arrived when he was selected to make his first team debut against Sheffield Wednesday at Old Trafford in a team that read;

Allen; Carey, Redman; Gibson, Jones, McGlen; Delaney, Downie, Rowley, Pearson, and McShane.

United won 3-1 that day and it is interesting to note that Harry McShane, (actor Ian McShane's father) was amongst the goal scorers. Mark was to play a further three more games that season and was never on the losing side, defeating Everton 4-1 at Goodison, Arsenal 3-1 at Old Trafford, and the return fixture against Wednesday at Hillsborough 4-0. It was a terrific start to his football career at top level. He was to play a further three games in season 1951-52, Manchester United's first Championship winning season since 1911, and again, he never finished on the losing side. Unfortunately, those three appearances did not qualify him for a winner's medal. In 1952-53, he played in two games, only this time, he tasted defeat for the first time in both games.

It was in early 1953 that he was called up to do his National Service. However, the Medical Officer at the military recruiting station declared that he had flat feet, and as such, he was declared unfit to serve in the forces! Notwithstanding this, Mark was never to figure in any first team games again until in early 1955. That he had been kept out of the first team by his boyhood hero Allenby Chilton, must have been of little consolation to him, but Chilton's remarkable consistency of form and fitness over a period of four years, when he was well into his thirties, was of tremendous credit to the older player. It has to be stressed that Chilton had a great effect on shaping the player that Mark was to become as he honed him into the centre half that Manchester United needed.

It became something of a dressing room joke at Old Trafford when the players used to assemble during the week for training. Each morning Mark would look for Allenby and ask him:

"How do you feel today?" Bright and breezy, Chilton would reply; *"Champion, just champion, I can go on for another two or three years yet."*

Chilton's days came to an end in early 1955 after some bad defeats – two of which were in games which I watched against Manchester City. I had attended my first ever Manchester derby game at Maine Road in late September 1954 when City won 3-2. On February 12th 1955, I watched my first derby game at Old Trafford, but it was a disaster for me, and United, as City went nap, winning 5-0. The following week, on February 19th, United were away to City again in the fourth round of the FA Cup. Once again, City triumphed by 2-0 in a game that United really dominated, but suffered because of their wastefulness in front of goal. It was also a game that saw Chilton sent off for using foul and abusive language to the referee – how would the referees cope in today's modern game! What an introduction for me to derby matches! Chilton's last game for United was at Wolves the week after that Cup tie, and once again United lost by 4-2. For the next game, because of Chilton's suspension, Mark played his first game at senior level for two years and was to make the position his own from then on.

There were certainly no frills where Mark Jones was concerned. He was a bone crunching tackler, and majestic in the air, and after he had won the ball, there was no just hoofing it up field as many of the centre-halves back then were want to do. He was quite content to play it simple and give the ball to Colman, Edwards, Viollet, or Whelan, who could use the ball much better than he could. He was certainly a stopper, and he was very adept at it. He had buckets of determination when going for the ball. For a former bricklayer, he became the rock, the cornerstone of the defensive stonewall!

There is a little bit of a myth that abounds in United's history that the centre-half position was complicated by a continual battle between Mark, and Jackie Blanchflower, for the number five shirt. This simply is not true. Mark was virtually ever present during the 1955-56 season, when the *Babes* secured their first Championship win. He was also almost ever present in the 1956- 57 season, until a knee injury in the sixth round FA Cup tie at Bournemouth, in March of 1957, kept him out of the team. Jackie Blanchflower had played most of his career at inside-right for United, but he was very versatile player, and Busby had experimented with him at centre-half once or twice in the Reserves. Ronnie Cope was normally Mark's deputy, but after the Bournemouth game, Busby went with Blanchflower, who it has to be said, played so superbly that he couldn't leave him out. Blanchflower played for the rest of the season winning a championship medal, and also playing in the FA Cup Final, and he also played into the November of the following season, when a dip in his form allowed Mark to reclaim the number five shirt, which he kept until the time of the tragedy.

Before Mark married his childhood sweetheart June, in 1955, he was in digs at Mrs. Watson's boarding house on Birch Avenue, in Old Trafford. It was just a short walk away from the Old Trafford stadium. He shared the digs with several other players, notably Jackie Blanchflower, David Pegg, Tommy Taylor, Billy Whelan, Bobby Charlton, and Duncan Edwards. Mark took on the job of looking after the younger boys. There was many an evening when he would round them all up, and they would all walk from Old Trafford, down to the Manchester city centre, to catch a movie at one of the many cinemas that were around in that area. They would never catch a bus because it was considered by them to be too boring.

After he and June married, they had to spend three weeks living in Mrs. Watson's boarding house until they settled down to married life in the Chorlton –cum- Hardy area of Manchester. Their club house was on King's Road, (they had to wait for Jack Crompton and his family to vacate it) just a short way up that road from Matt Busby's home. It was well known back then that Mark Jones, and Jackie Blanchflower, was close friends. So much so that Jackie was best man at Mark and June's wedding. Jones was never a man for the bright lights and after a game it was commonplace to see him emerge out of the main entrance wearing his trilby hat, smoking a pipe, and the gabardine raincoat. The pipe smoking was the point of a lot of banter from his young team mates who christened him with the nickname *Dan Archer* after the character in the famous *Archers,* BBC radio programme.

Off the field he was such a mild mannered person. He was quiet, and loved nothing better than to get off home to June, and his newborn baby son, Gary. His hobby was shooting, and together with his canine companion *Rick,* he liked nothing more than to go off to a Cheshire farm and shoot. Mark also had a passion for breeding budgerigars and canaries, and he built an aviary for them at his home. However, this often led to other bouts of mickey taking from his young mates. But he took it all in his stride. *The Gentle Giant* was a nickname given to the late, great, John Charles, back then, but it was also a name that would describe Mark Jones so aptly.

He put in some tremendous games for his beloved club and none more aptly than that glorious night at Maine Road when Manchester United triumphed over Bilbao, in the European Cup. The Spaniards threw everything they could at United that evening, but they could not breach the defence of which he was the central lynchpin. He faced some of the toughest and hardest centre forwards of his era, but none ever baulked him – household names of the time like Lofthouse, Ford, Hickson, Milburn, Revie, Swinbourne, Allen, Wayman, Bentley, and Smith. Unfortunately fate decreed that he would never ever realize his ambition of playing for his country. He was called up into an England party and he was named as a reserve, but that was as far as it went – no subs or place on the bench back then. That dream would, I am certain, have been realized, as he was certainly knocking on the door at the time of the tragedy. I also believe that had he lived, Billy Wright would not have reached the figure of 105 caps for England.

My own experience of meeting Mark came on a couple of occasions through schoolboy football. In 1957 my school team had reached the final of a knockout competition, and it was played at Newton Heath Loco, in the Newton Heath, area of Manchester. For us kids on that evening, it was like the experience of professionals reaching Wembley. An enclosed ground, nets, referee and linesmen, a large crowd (we played before the start of a game between

Mark Jones pictured at Highbury when playing for Manchester United against Arsenal on 1 February 1958. It was to be the last time that he would play on English soil. The other Manchester United players pictured are Kenny Morgans on the left, and Duncan Edwards on the right. The Arsenal player is David Herd who was to join United just three years later.

Manchester Catholic Boys and Liverpool Catholic Boys) and we were all so starry eyed. My school team lost that Final by 4-2, and although I was disappointed at losing, I had played fairly well. It was great consolation to me that the medals were presented by Mark, and that for me was just thrill enough. I couldn't wait to receive mine and as I did, he handed me the medal and ruffled my hair saying in his thick Yorkshire accent; *"well played young 'un."*

In November of 1957, he again did the presentations for a school's five-a-side competition which was held at The Proctor's Gymnasium and Hulme Lad's Club in Hulme, which my school side won. That night he had the Labrador dog *Rick* with him, and it just sat at his side as he spent time with all the kids, signing every bit of paper that was put in front of him. Here was an established Manchester United player, giving of his free time to schoolboy football in the Manchester area. He was such a very gentle man off the field.

Mark Jones gave a lot of his spare time to other people. He would attend a lot of charity functions, knock over piles of pennies that were collected in local pubs for different charities, he would open fetes. He was the pleasant charming young man who would carry an old lady's shopping basket. Mark was often seen on match days helping supporters who had arrived in invalid carriages. The Jones's were blissfully happy and contented, in their life in Manchester. They socialized with the other players and their families. Sometimes, when out for a drink with their friends, Mark and the little impish Eddie Colman, would do a duet together on stage singing *Frankie and Johnny*. Mark had a fear of flying, and although he loved playing in the big European games, he was never happy with the long hours of air travel.

June, his wife, was five months pregnant with their daughter, Lynn, at the time of the disaster. After it happened, his brother Tom took *Rick* the Labrador dog, but it pined for Mark so badly, and died just a few short months later. His wife gave away the fifty four birds which he had kept in the aviary. She put an advertisement in a local paper, and there were scores of local children that came to the house to take one of them. Harry Gregg brought home Mark's belongings from Munich and handed them over to June. He had his trilby hat which he asked June if he could keep.

I have great memories of him playing for Manchester United, and as I said at the beginning, he really was one of the unsung heroes. The doughty stopper, the uncompromising centre half, the archetypal pivot, the seam of Yorkshire granite. Most of all, I remember a man who loved his family, loved his club, and was indeed a very gentle giant.

Sleep on in peace Mark – never forgotten.

Mark played in 121 games in all competitions scoring just 1 goal.

Jackie Blanchflower – Mr. Versatility

On a cold, winter evening, back in 1994, I had the pleasure of sitting with Jackie Blanchflower at an Association of Former Manchester United Players dinner, which was held in one of the executive suites underneath the South Stand, at the Old Trafford stadium. It is an evening that I will always remember with such fondness and one which gave me so much pleasure.

Jackie by this time had passed his sixty first birthday. He was portly, and red faced, and a far different figure to the slim young man that I had first watched play for Manchester United Reserves back in the early 1950s. So much water had passed under the bridge since Jackie's halcyon days as both a Manchester United player, and an established Northern Ireland international. But on that evening, he was the life and soul of the party, and it was such a great pleasure to sit and listen to him, and also for me, to know that I was in the presence of man who, but for tragedy, would certainly have gone on to be one of the greats in British and European football. Jackie Blanchflower was that good.

He was born in Belfast on the 7th March, 1933. Like most youngsters of his age he developed the love of playing the game of football in Belfast's streets and schools. Initially he was a forward, and had developed great skills with his two feet, and was an impeccable timer of the ball both on the ground, and in the air. He rose to prominence in local schools football, and eventually reached the pinnacle, by playing for Northern Ireland Schoolboys. His performances alerted Manchester United, and he was eventually signed from the Belfast junior club, Boyland, in May, 1949, and he joined the first batch of the famous *Busby Babes.*

On 21 November 1951, Jackie's dream came true when he made his First Division league debut against Liverpool, at Anfield, in a game that finished 0-0. He came in at right half for

another youngster, Don Gibson (who later married Matt Busby's daughter Sheena) who was out with a knee injury. For Jackie, it was a long wait for his next first team appearance – two years in fact. On 31 October 1953, Jackie was one of the youngsters who were introduced in the League game against Huddersfield Town, at Leeds Road, which became known as the game when the team was christened the *Busby Babes,* He was ever present through the remainder of that season playing in twenty seven League games (13 goals) and one FA Cup game (1 goal) –

Jackie Blanchflower pictured before the start of the 1954-55 season.

a really consistent, and creditable beginning by any standards. His form was such that on 21 March1954, Jackie won his first cap for Northern Ireland, in a World Cup Qualifying match against Wales, which they won by 2-1.

The following season 1954-55, he played in thirty of the first thirty one games that were played, and he contributed nine goals. Unfortunately, in February of 1955, after two disastrous defeats to Manchester City (5-0 at Old Trafford in the League, and 2-0 at Maine Road in an FA Cup Fourth Round tie) Jackie was one of the players left out of the team for the following game against Wolverhampton Wanderers. It was not until the last three games of the season that he was able to get back into the team, and he scored another two goals. Emerging out of the Reserve team was another youngster from Ireland, who was named Liam Whelan, and he became the real threat to Jackie's place in the team, even though John Doherty was still around.

There had been no histrionics from him regarding being left out, he went back to the reserves, worked hard, and eventually won his first team place back again. He was first choice again when the 1955-56 season began and played in fifteen of the first sixteen fixtures, scoring just three more goals. On 12 November, United were defeated by 3-1 at Burnden Park, Bolton, and after that game Jackie was left out of the team in favour of John Doherty. Burnden Park was never a hospitable place for Manchester United, and the Trotters were a very physical team and always seemed to have United's measure there. Once again, as with the defeat by Manchester City in the previous seasons, Jackie seemed to be the one singled out. He was to play only one further game that season and that was at centre forward in place of Tommy Taylor late in the season when Taylor was away on international duty. United were blessed with three very, very good young inside-rights at the time; Blanchflower, Doherty, and Whelan. It is ironic that all three of them had played enough games in that championship winning season, to qualify for a winner's medal.

Jackie had gone back to the Reserves and it was in this environment that his versatility that began to show through. On the pre-season tour of Scandinavia in 1956, Jackie was actually selected in goal for one of the tour matches. Busby had also moved him back to the centre half position, and it was here that he really came into his own. However, Mark Jones was playing so well in the first team... two totally different kinds of player. Mark the big tall stopper type, but Jackie, much smaller, but very good ball playing type. What he lacked in physicality, Jackie made up for with brain and guile.

Jimmy Murphy, the Manchester United Assistant Manager summed Jackie up in his autobiography *Matt, United and Me* published by Souvenir Press in 1968:

Jackie began his professional career as an inside forward, and in a lot of ways he looked a more gifted player than his more famous brother Danny, being stronger on the ball, and certainly much better in the air. If he lacked Danny's ambition, and flair, both as a player and orator, few could deny that Jackie had immense talent and potential. As an inside forward he was not quite sharp enough for the First Division. As a wing half he was exceptionally good, but not good enough to displace Duncan Edwards. So in the course of time, Jackie became a centre half for both Northern Ireland, and Manchester United. He was a creative player, and like those other two famous English centre halves, Stan Cullis and Neil Franklin, was never content with a purely stopper role and was always trying to use the ball to initiate attacks for his own side. Thus, some of his best games were in European Cup games, where in those days, there was not quite so much physical contact as one gets in normal English League games.

The 1956-57 began and Jackie still languished in the Reserves although he was still a regular first choice for Northern Ireland. He made one appearance in the first team between August 1956, and 2 March, 1957, and it was in the very first European Cup game that Manchester United ever played, and that was in Belgium against Anderlecht on 12 September 1956. Trying to dislodge big Mark Jones was as hard as trying to win back his inside forward spot. However, on 2 March, 1957, in an FA Cup 6th Round tie, played at Dean Court in Bournemouth, Mark

Jackie Blanchflower, second from the left, looks down at the injured Manchester United goalkeeper, Ray Wood after he had been felled by a charge from Aston Villa's Peter McParland in the 1957 FA Cup Final at Wembley. The other Manchester United players in the picture are from the left, Roger Byrne, Duncan Edwards, and Bill Foulkes. Blanchflower took over the goalkeeper's jersey when Wood was unable to continue.

Jones injured his knee. It was an injury that would keep him out for at least a month. Jackie stepped in at centre-half and seized his opportunity with both hands. His displays were outstanding and even though Mark Jones was fit by the middle of April, Jackie had cemented his place as first choice. He played exceptionally well in both legs of the European Cup semi-final against Real Madrid, and walked out at Wembley in the FA Cup final against Aston Villa. That Final saw him give such a heroic display, as after just six minutes, Ray Wood was incapacitated due to a horrific piece of skullduggery by Villa's Peter McParland, and had to leave the field. Jackie went into goal and played there until the last nine minutes of the game, and although he conceded two goals, Jackie gave a tremendous performance and it was as though he had played in goal all his life.

The 1957-58 season started and Jackie was still first choice. He did miss a game through injury early on and Mark Jones deputized, but as soon as Jackie was fit again, he went straight back into the first team. He was ever present until 30 November, when he played against Tottenham Hotspur, at White Hart Lane, and in a game which turned out to be a seven goal thriller. Manchester United lost 4-3. Jackie picked up a hamstring injury in the game and little were we to know, that would be his last first team appearance for Manchester United's first-team . Mark Jones returned, and by his rock-solid performances, made it hard for Busby to leave him out.

Jackie returned to the reserves and prepared to battle to win his place back. On 3 February, 1958, he flew out to Belgrade with the first-team party for the European Cup second leg Quarter Final tie against Red Star. He went as cover should anything untoward happen and sat in the stands as United got the result that they needed to take them through to the semi-final. The next day was the blackest day in Manchester United's history and Jackie's life. The injuries that he sustained in the accident were so severe that he was in hospital for over two months before he was able to travel back to Manchester. He had suffered severe injuries to his arms, and also to his kidneys, and those injuries were ultimately responsible for the ending of his football career.

He tried to regain fitness but eventually a London specialist had to be firm with him, and tell him, that if he continued to play football, then there could be more damage done to his kidneys which could prove fatal. He was heartbroken. Football was all he had ever known. He was just twenty five years old, had only been married to his lovely wife Jean for a few years. He had lost his mates, (particularly Tommy Taylor who he was very close to) his trade, and his livelihood. It was such a devastating situation for which to find himself in. There was no counseling back then, nobody for him to lean on, and over the next few years he tried his hand at several different things... he bought a newspaper shop, worked for a bookmaker, became a publican, went back to school and became a finance officer... but nothing lasted more than 4-5 years. He had been cocooned in football and the bitterness swallowed him up... it was natural, and something that had counseling been available back then, would have helped him overcome it.

Life made him very cynical and especially about Manchester United. He stayed away from the club for years. Just a few years after the disaster, he and his family were asked to vacate their club house to accommodate Manchester United's new signing, Maurice Setters and his family. It was a heartless thing for the club to do. It was the same for a lot of the survivors and they harboured similar feelings. They felt that the club had let them down and could have done more.

Jackie mellowed in later life and he found his niche as an after dinner speaker. He was always in great demand, and he was such a treat to sit and listen to. He didn't concentrate on football all the time, although his stories would always keep you enthralled. Jackie was a naturally funny man, and his delivery and timing of his jokes etc. was perfect. He seemed so happy doing what he was doing, and he had started attending the Association of Former Player's dinners.

The evening which I spent in his company at that dinner in 1994, was a pleasure, and a privilege. He told me some wonderful stories and I'll always remember the love in his eyes when he talked about big Tommy Taylor. Tommy was his best buddy and was also his best man at his wedding. He was devastated by Taylor's passing and told people that after he got home from Munich, he couldn't even watch United on television. It was not the Manchester United which he had known, and he never again made another friendship like the one he shared with big Tom.

Jackie had me laughing as he impersonated Tommy's broad Yorkshire dialect, and he spoke of some of the scrapes that big Tommy got himself into. He talked of looking after Harry Gregg when he first arrived at Old Trafford and how he lit the place up. He waxed lyrical about Duncan, and little Eddie. There was such a wonderful look upon his face as he talked about his young friends and you could tell that he was remembering the happiness that he shared with them. Once the formalities of the dinner were over, Jackie had time for everybody..... He signed hundreds of menus and pictures, and had a continual smile upon his face. For me it was wonderful to see just how he was remembered and loved by the Manchester United fans.

Sadly, Jackie was diagnosed with cancer and it was to be his last battle. I last saw him speak at a Sportsman's Dinner evening at the Wythenshawe Labour Club, just over a year before he passed away. It was obvious then that he wasn't well, but it did not affect his performance. He did some Q & A after wards and I'll always remember something he said during that session: "*Life has been full of ups and downs, but without pathos there can be no comedy. The bitterness goes eventually and you start remembering the good times. I loved it at United. From this distance, even going through the accident was worth it for those years at Old Trafford.*" He added softly: "*I feel happy and at ease now.*"

Jackie slipped away on 2 September, 1998, and the world was a sadder place for the loss.

Sleep on in peace dear Jackie, not only were you a world class footballer, but you were also one of life's true gentlemen.

Jackie Blanchflower played 126 times for Manchester United and scored 26 goals.

He was capped 12 times by Northern Ireland and scored 1 goal

Duncan Edwards –
The Greatest of Them All

"The best player that I've ever seen, the best footballer that I've ever played with for United or England, the only other player who ever made me feel inferior."

Those are the words of one of the greatest players ever to grace the world football stage, one of the greatest ambassadors of the game, and most of all, one of life's gentlemen - Sir Bobby Charlton. The player whom he was talking about? Well, he was a young man - just. He played the game until he was only 21 years and 143 days old. But in that so short career, he left such an indelible mark, both on the game, and for the people that were fortunate enough to have watched him, on their memories. It says so much about him, that even now, 54 years after his passing, he is still talked about and remembered, not only by the fans of the club for which he played for and loved so much, and who cherish that memory so guardedly, but also, by football fans throughout the British Isles, Europe, and indeed the world.

He was a household name by the time that he had reached his eighteenth birthday. He was indeed world class, a colossus, a giant in the truest sense of the word, a great, and he has certainly become a legend. In the modern day, when these words are bandied about and bestowed upon players so freely and so easily, when they are used in connection with his career, no other words could describe him more aptly - he is of course, Duncan Edwards.

The town of Dudley is part of the West Midlands conurbation, and is situated just to the south of Wolverhampton. It is the largest town in the Black Country region of England. In this quiet corner of the country, which also borders the southern boundaries of Birmingham, and through which the River Severn winds its twisting path down to the Bristol Channel, two permanent tributes to this remarkable young player are now apportioned. In the middle of Dudley Town Centre stands a large bronze statue by sculptor James Butler. It depicts Edwards, resplendent in his England strip, kicking a ball with his right foot, and epitomizes the power, the strength, and the skill of this great player. For both residents, and visitors to Dudley, it acts as a point of remembrance to arguably the greatest young English player ever to play the game of football.

Just a short distance away in the Church of St. Francis, on Laurel Road, there are two small stained glass windows dedicated to the memory of Duncan Edwards. They are close to the font

Shown here are the two stained glass lead windows in St. Francis' Church, which is on Laurel Road, in Dudley, West Midlands. They are a tribute to the life and achievements of Duncan Edwards.

beside a picture of the gentle Jesus. Immediately above the two windows sit larger windows bearing images of St. George, and St. Francis. Below them and to the left, Edwards is depicted kneeling, in his Manchester United strip, carrying an unfurled banner with the inscription; *God is with us for our Captain.* The window to the right depicts Edwards, again kneeling, but this time in full England international strip, holding an unfurled banner with the inscription; *Though there may be many members, yet is there one body.*

Duncan Edwards was born on 1 October, 1936, to Gladstone, and Sara-Ann Edwards, in a little terraced house at number 23, Malvern Crescent, in the Black Country town of Dudley, Worcestershire. They were a typical hard working, working class family, just like so many of their contemporaries of that time. His late Mum used to tell the story about Duncan being able to kick a ball before he could even walk! His parents had a set of reins which they would tie around his waist, and whilst Gladstone would hold him upright, Duncan would kick the ball up and down their living room, much to their amusement.

He grew into a young giant for his age, having a huge frame - much bigger than children of his own age. He loved to play football. His waking hours were spent playing the game whenever the opportunity would arise, and if he wasn't actually playing football, then he would dream about it. It was obvious to anybody watching this young man, that he was so gifted and skillful where football was concerned. At the tender age of eight, he was playing in his School team against boys two, and three years, older than himself. By the time he was eleven years old, he was playing for his Town team, and also representing Worcestershire Schoolboys, his County team - he was three years younger than his team mates.

On 1 April, 1950, at aged just thirteen years old, Duncan strode out from the tunnel and onto the hallowed Wembley Stadium turf, in front of 100,000 spectators, wearing the shirt of England Schoolboys, representing his country, playing at left half, against the Wales Schoolboys team. He played in every England schoolboy international fixture for the next three seasons, and was even made England captain at just fourteen years old. That record of playing for three successive seasons for England schoolboys still stands today, as does his being the youngest ever captain, and I doubt very much if those two records will ever be broken.

Obviously, a talent such as this attracted a lot of attention. From the moment he became a schoolboy international, lots of the top professional clubs courted his parents in the hope that they would eventually land the signature of this remarkable young boy. All the big Midlands clubs were prominent, Wolves, Albion, Villa, Birmingham, as well as the big London clubs, Arsenal, Tottenham Hotspur, and Chelsea. A chance conversation between two old adversaries, as well as old army friends, was the beginning of the road to Old Trafford for Duncan. In 1950, Joe Mercer, then still playing for Arsenal, was doing some coaching with the England schoolboy team. After a game between United and Arsenal, Joe happened to remark to his friend Matt Busby, what a remarkable talent he had seen in the England schoolboys team, and that in his opinion; *"young Edwards is going to be some player".* This alerted Busby, and he sent his trusted chief scout, Joe Armstrong, down to Dudley to watch the young Edwards play. After just ten minutes, Armstrong had seen enough, and recommended that Busby should go and watch this young man for his self.

The following week, both Matt and Jimmy Murphy slipped unobtrusively into Dudley and watched Duncan play. They too, did not have to stay for too long watching Duncan play, and on the way back to Manchester; Busby told Jimmy that this was one young player that Manchester United must not miss out on. For the next two years they kept an eye on things. The fact that Duncan Edwards eventually signed for Manchester United, was due in no small measure to their Coach, Bert Whalley. Reg Priest, the United scout in the West Midlands, had informed United that there was pressure being brought to bear upon Edwards by several local Midlands clubs, and also Bolton Wanderers, to sign for them. Bert Whalley set off by car immediately to go down to the Edwards's home in Dudley and clinch the deal for Manchester United. Unfortunately, the vehicle which he was driving broke down, and he had to hitch a ride back to Manchester. Upon his arrival at Old Trafford, the club hired a rental car, and Whalley, accompanied by Jimmy Murphy, drove straight back down to Dudley.

At 2 am on the morning of 1 October, 1952, a bleary eyed Gladstone Edwards came downstairs to answer the knocking on the front door of his home. Stood there, outside in the darkness, were Bert Whalley and Jimmy Murphy. He invited both men into the living room, and called for Sara-Ann. For the next hour the four of them talked about the possibility of Duncan joining Manchester United. Gladstone told both of them that the decision would be left to Duncan as to which club he would like to join - unbeknown to him, Sara-Ann already knew the answer! Duncan had confided to her the previous morning.

Gladstone called Duncan, and this big giant of a boy arrived in the living room wearing his pajamas, rubbing the sleep out of his eyes and immediately upon recognizing the two men said; *"What's all the fuss about? I've already said there's only one club that I want to play football for, and that's Manchester United. I'd give anything to sign for them".*

It was as simple as that - he'd followed the exploits of the Manchester United team which had won the FA Cup in 1948, the First Division Championship in 1952, and who had also finished runners-up in the league on four other occasions. Their brand of football had captivated him. He was a United fan! A few minutes after meeting Bert Whalley, and Jimmy Murphy, Duncan was a Manchester United player, and a few days later he left the family home for digs in Stretford, and a career in professional football.

In no time at all Duncan had been promoted into the reserve team and his performances belied his young years. Even at this youthful age, he had a superb physique. Players of his own age looked under nourished compared to him! But for a big lad, he was exceptionally quick over the ground, could turn either way, and had a devastating body-swerve, had two great feet, a tremendous shot in either foot, was exceptionally powerful in the air, had the strength of an ox in the tackle, but most importantly, for one so young, his positional play was flawless because he read the game so well. It also soon became apparent that he could play anywhere in any position, and still be the most outstanding player on the park!

Proof of his exceptional talent came from manager Matt Busby. Busby himself looked for weaknesses in this young giant's make-up, but eventually he gave up and said; *"He is the greatest player of his age that I have ever seen."*

Just six months after the young giant had arrived at Old Trafford, the senior career of Duncan Edwards began. On Saturday, 2 April, 1953, at the age of sixteen years and one hundred and eighty five days, he appeared out of the tunnel wearing the number six shirt for Manchester United's first team. United's opponents that day were the Welsh club, Cardiff City, and it was a Football League, Division One match.

My earliest recollections of Duncan are of seeing him play in a reserve team game at Old Trafford early in 1953. It was astonishing to see this young giant playing amongst men. In hindsight, it was his age that first attracted me to him being a favourite of mine. United's reserve team wing halves in the second half of that season were two really young players - Jeff Whitefoot, who was younger than Duncan when he had made his first team debut, and Duncan himself. After he had made his debut, Duncan hardly appeared in a reserve game again, although he did play in the Youth team, and won a winners medal in the inaugural season of the FA Youth Cup.

In 1953-54, his reputation started to gain momentum, and even though he was just seventeen, he appeared for the England Under23 team against Italy, in Bologna - the first time that an England team had ever taken part in an Under23 match. He had already started to earn rave notices with his outstanding displays in the first team. In those days, there were some really outstanding players around who had huge reputations. They meant nothing at all to Duncan - even at such a young age, he just eclipsed them with the power and polish of his own performance.

Duncan could make players feel so inferior. He showed astonishing awesome power as he ran through the churning mud on pitches that the modern professional, so used to manicured fields which provide true playing surfaces at almost every time of the year, would find so hard to believe. His tackling was a series of tank traps, as ferocious as they were perfectly timed. His passing was penetrative and deadly accurate. Whatever the conditions, and however heavy the ball had become, his heading was always immaculate in its strength and direction. He simply had not a single flaw in his game.

The late Jackie Milburn used to tell the story of the day that he first came up against Duncan. He recalls early on in the game standing beside him and listening as Duncan told him;

"I know that you are a great player Mr. Milburn, and that you have a big reputation, but it means nothing at all to me. Today I am not going to allow you a kick at the ball."

This was from a young seventeen-years-old boy - it wasn't arrogance, or egotism, it was Duncan's inherent self-belief in his own ability. As Jackie was to say;

"The thing was, Duncan was absolutely true to his word, I hardly did get a kick throughout that game and United won 5-2. I just could not believe how mature this young kid was, and what ability and self-belief he had."

His reputation had already started to grow, but it never went to his head. He had his feet firmly planted on the ground. Duncan knew he was special, I don't think that he ever doubted that. He just loved to play, be it in the first team, or even the Youth team, he gave each game the same commitment. His appetite for playing was voracious. Jimmy Murphy who became so close to Duncan had many memories of him. He recalled another game, this time a Youth team match early in the stages of the competition against a well-known London team. From the very start of the game, there was a loud mouthed person sat behind Jimmy who kept on baiting him by shouting;

"Where's your famous Edwards then Murphy, where's this so-called superstar?"

Jimmy just gritted his teeth and said nothing until about ten minutes into the game, a tackle was won in the centre circle, and the tackler was away with the ball and moving towards goal. Several of the opposition players tried to get within touching distance of him, but he was just too strong for them, brushing them aside contemptuously. From a full thirty yards out from goal, he unleashed a tremendous shot that hardly got off the ground. Before the home goalkeeper could move, it was past him and nestling into the back of the net. Jimmy just smiled, turned around, looked the loud mouth straight in the eye, and said;

"That's Edwards!"

The youth team was formidable in those first years of the Youth Cup competition, and nigh on unbeatable - they won it for the first five years of its inception. In one of the very early rounds of the competition United had been drawn against Rotherham United, and the game was played at United's training ground at The Cliff, in Salford. Very early on, Duncan picked up a loose ball, beat three men and smashed it home from thirty yards. Andy Smailes, the Rotherham United Manager was at the game, and he remarked to Jimmy Murphy;

"How old did you say that this big fellow was?"

Jimmy responded that he was eligible to play in the FA Youth Cup for another two years. To which Andy responded;

"When I see boys like this, I think that this youth competition should be handicap like the Grand National!"

I personally can recall a semi-final against the Chelsea Youth team. Ted Drake had also put together a really good team of youngsters in 1954-55. The first leg had been drawn at Stamford Bridge 2-2. In the return leg played at Old Trafford on a Saturday morning in front of 30,000 spectators. Jimmy Murphy had given the following instructions before the start.

"Remember, this is a team game. Don't be too conscious of Duncan. Play your normal game."

Chelsea held the upper hand at half-time and led 1-0. Murphy went into the dressing room at the break and revised his pre-match instruction telling the players;

"Remember I told you not to automatically pass the ball to Duncan? Well forget what I said. Just look for Duncan. Give him the fucking ball whenever you can."

In the second half, Edwards moved up to centre forward. Within minutes of the re-start, Terry Beckett floated over a cross from the right, and there was Duncan powering into the area, soaring above everybody, to really thump the ball with his head past the goalkeeper, and level the tie. Sometime later, there was a corner to United on the left hand side at the Scoreboard End. Bobby Charlton floated it towards the penalty spot, and once again, Duncan's timing and power got him there before anybody could react, and another bullet header was planted into the back of the net. He then moved back to left half, and his influence on the young kids around him, made sure that they were never going to lose that tie.

He was such a wonderful young boy. He was a schoolboy in the forties and a teenager in the fifties. He was part of the generation which linked the hard, somber days of World War Two and rationing, with the more dashing, mobile times which followed. In those days, United players used to make their own way to the ground for home games. Duncan used to have an old Raleigh bicycle, and this was his mode of transport for getting to and from the ground. I would stand on the railway bridge and wait for him as he would come wheeling down what was then Warwick Road (now Sir Matt Busby Way). Once across the bridge he would turn left and free-wheel down to the old Ticket Office, with a stream of kids (me included) chasing after him. He would alight from his bicycle, prop it up against his leg, get all the kids to line up in front of him, and he would stand there signing all the books and bits of paper before finally, taking a piece of string out of his pocket, he would secure the bike to a drain pipe, and disappear inside the door to the old ticket office and then on into the dressing room. It was the same ritual in reverse after the game - out he would come, line up the kids once more, sign every book and bit of paper before untying the bike, climb aboard it, and then he was off, back up Warwick Road, and on to his digs in Stretford.

In April of 1955, he was selected to play for the full England team against Scotland at Wembley - he became the youngest player ever to play for his country at senior level at the age of just eighteen years and one hundred and eighty three days. Unheard of in those distant days

- teenagers just weren't good enough, nor experienced enough to play for England - or so the thought process went! *An Old International's* match report in the *Manchester Guardian* on the Monday after Duncan's international debut described his performance:

As for Edwards at left-half, not since Washbrook scored 160 in his first innings for Lancashire has any young colt stepped up into higher company with greater ease. All he was asked to do apparently, was to keep guard over a small area in front of Byrne, and whenever he got the ball to thump it vigorously in the direction of Mathews. This he did with obvious relish amid the "Oos" and "Ahs" of thousands of onlookers who were feasting their eyes on his mighty limbs for the first time. Naturally, boy-like, he could not suppress an air that this was easy meat compared with the thrust and parry of a Manchester needle match. Money for old rope so to say. Every now and then he seemed sorely tempted to run amok on his own, but a higher discipline pulled him back. W.Winterbottom's remote control, no doubt. "Play to orders, chaps. Big Brother is watching you."

Duncan had in fact represented England at schoolboy, Youth, Under-23, and B-team level before then. He took to international football like a duck to water, and was never left out of England's team again, unless he was injured. In the autumn of 1955, England went to Berlin to play the then World Champions, West Germany, at the Olympiastadion, in front of 100,000 spectators. For the first 20 minutes of the game, the Germans had given England a torrid time, but then Duncan made a tackle midway inside the German half and won the ball. His acceleration was so quick, it just took him past two startled German defenders, and from twenty five yards out, he just bombed the ball into the back of the net before the 'keeper could move. Even today, the Germans remember him by the nickname that they bestowed upon him that day - *"Boom-Boom!"*

The following winter, the Brazilians arrived at Wembley, testing the water for their assault on the World Cup Finals to be held in Sweden in the summer of 1958. Most of the players the Brazilians used in Sweden actually played in that game at Wembley. They were outclassed by an England team that won 4-2, and who also missed two penalties in the process! Tommy Taylor led their defence a merry dance, but Duncan eclipsed the man who was to be their big star in Sweden - Didi. Didi was made to look more than ordinary that day, and believe me; this fellow was up there with the best of them - Pele, Best, Di Stefano, and Puskas.

Edwards won eighteen caps in total and scored six international goals. There is no doubt in my mind that he would have played for England for a very long time but for fate. I also believe that England, and not Brazil, would have lifted the 1958 World Cup but for Munich, and also the cruel loss of Jeff Hall, the Birmingham City full back, to polio. The very heart was ripped out of a very, very, good England team.

In 1955-56, Matt Busby's famous *Babes* team became of age and lifted the Championship with an average age of just twenty two years, and by a margin of eleven points. They suffered a shock defeat in the FA Cup third round against Second Division Bristol Rovers at Eastville by the astonishing score line of 4-0. Last year, I had occasion to talk to a man who lives in Bristol, and who attended that game. I asked him to recall the game for me. He went quiet and a little misty eyed before saying to me;

"Aye, we won 4-0 that day, but you have to remember that Edwards did not play in that game."

That was the esteem that Duncan was held in by the British football fan.

On and off the field, Duncan Edwards was an amazing young man. He never smoked, nor touched alcohol, and even as a young boy, he was so professional in his approach to the game, and he was a shining example to all the youngsters of his time. Even when he was an established England international player, Jimmy Murphy only had to ask him if he would go down to The Cliff and help him out at a session with some young players he had to coach, and Duncan would never refuse. The youngsters idolized him, and the reason that he did things like that was because football to him was not just a living – although he knew where he was going in the game – it was more a way of life.

From late 1955 to late 1957, Duncan also had to serve his National Service, and did so in the Royal Army Ordnance Corps. He became 23145376 Lance Corporal Edwards D. He hated having to do this time in the Services, but like most of the young men of that time, he took it on the chin and just got on with it. He spent most of those two years stationed at an ammunition depot at Nescliffe, near Shrewsbury.

In 1956-57 he picked up another Championship winner's medal and also appeared in United's losing Cup Final team against Aston Villa. In that Final was the only time that he came close to losing self-control on the football pitch. He was horrified to watch the vicious assault by Villa winger Peter McParland upon Ray Wood in the United goal, during the opening minutes of that game. It effectively put Wood out of the game with a fractured cheek-bone and reduced United to 10 men. As McParland lay on the ground Duncan strode purposefully over to him, stood directly above him, but then held back before the red mist descended. He was scrupulously fair, and expected nothing less from opposing players.

He played in European competition that year also, My abiding memory of him during that European campaign was not of him in any of United's victories, but in the semi-final, second leg defeat by that great Real Madrid team of that era. Although that game had been drawn 2-2 at Old Trafford, United had been eliminated by 5-3 on aggregate. Over the two legs, the Spanish

The clock in the background shows five minutes to three o'clock on Saturday, 1 February 1958. The venue is Highbury, London, and Duncan Edwards signs an autograph for a young fan just prior to the kick-off in the Arsenal v Manchester United match. This was to be Duncan's last game played upon English soil.

Champions had employed some really dubious tactics, and also United were on the end of some very suspicious decisions from the referee in the away leg in Spain. Twice they had what seemed legitimate goals ruled out for offside. As he came off the field that evening at Old Trafford, I could see the hurt, and dejection etched in his face. He'd run his socks off that night, but even his superhuman efforts were not enough to pull off an almost impossible victory. It hurt him, you could see that.

The last time that I saw him play was on Saturday, January 25th 1958 in a 4th round FA Cup tie at Old Trafford, against Ipswich Town, which United won by 2-0. His last appearance in England was on February 1st 1958, against Arsenal at Highbury. It was fitting that it was a game that was an absolute classic, which United won by 5-4 and Duncan was outstanding, scoring very early in the game with one of his blockbuster specials. The result was of little importance in retrospect - football won that day. It left a lot of fans with the memory of a truly outstanding young footballer who performed in a truly outstanding young team.

His last appearance for Manchester United was on 5 February, 1958 in the Army Stadium in Belgrade in the 3-3 draw with Red Star, and again, it was fitting that he gave another outstanding performance. On a treacherous bone hard pitch which was full of ice, he floated and glided over it with grace and power. In the second half, when United's defence was on the rack, he tackled like a demon and marshalled everybody superbly, and again he was the outstanding player on the pitch.

Duncan was very reserved off the field, almost to the point where he was shy, and retiring. He just lived for football, and would have played every day if he had been allowed. Oh! Yes he knew that he was gifted, and he knew that he was special - but it never put an edge upon him. He didn't feel any different from any of his team mates. For his age he was so mature, and he allowed nobody to take liberties with him. Bill Foulkes recalled a tale from a game against West Brom in 1957. Maurice Setters (who was later to join United) was a really tough, abrasive, intimidating in your face, type of wing-half. Early on in the game, he made the mistake of trying to intimidate Duncan by standing nose to nose with him as Duncan tried to take a throw-in. Duncan just looked down at this craggy crew-cutted man - there was a slight movement of Duncan's chest, and Setters went flying backwards for almost ten yards on his backside. It was as though Duncan had just swatted a fly. Setters was nowhere to be seen after that. Bill was to say:

"It is easy to get carried away, but Duncan really did have everything. He was powerful, technically as good as anyone, and he could read the game as if he had been in the game thirty years, even when he was just seventeen. He was a freak to be honest, mature beyond his years. He always behaved in the correct way — everything that he did was correct. He had obviously been well tutored by his parents when he was young. He was one of the boys, but he was also a gentleman, the true model professional."

How many players have played for England at senior level one week, and their club's youth team the next? Duncan did. He was never in the media for the wrong reasons, and in fact the only time that he ever got into trouble was one Saturday evening after a derby game at Old Trafford in 1955. City had trounced United 5-0, and as usual, Duncan was on his way home on his bike feeling more than a little down. An overzealous policeman stopped him in on Chester Road, and booked him for riding a bicycle without lights. On the Monday morning he was fined 10 shillings in the Magistrate's Court, and upon arriving at Old Trafford, Sir Matt fined him two weeks wages for bringing the club's name into disrepute! He lived his life as the professional should. He conducted himself impeccably, looked after his body, and just loved the club that he played for. He was an icon to young boys like me, and without doubt was the perfect role model.

He survived for almost fifteen days after the tragedy. He fought my how he fought to live. His injuries were so severe though, especially to his kidneys. Dr. Georg Maurer the eminent doctor and surgeon at the Rechts der Isar Hospital in Munich, where all the injured were taken and treated, said that any less mortal than Duncan could never have survived those injuries for as long as Duncan did. His fitness, stamina and courage, were a testament to the way that this young man lived his life. His death was one which gave the deepest, most lasting pain to the Manchester community. Not because he was liked any more than the other players who perished, but because there was such a special appeal to people's ideals about him. He was the spirit of English football at that time, football that existed in children's daydreams; honest, brilliant, and irresistibly strong.

In the first few days after the tragedy, when Jimmy Murphy visited him as he lay there fighting for his life, Duncan asked him what had happened to the presentation gold watch that the Real Madrid club had given to him back in March 1957. Jimmy got people to go back to the aircraft wreckage and do a search. It was found, and brought back in a bad state. It just made Duncan happy to have it strapped back on his wrist. He didn't shout for it any more, he just kept asking:

"What time is the kick off against Wolves on Saturday Jimmy? I can't miss that one."

It must have broken Jimmy's heart to see his big champion lying broken, battered, and helpless, as he was. There was a very, very close bond between those two men. Jimmy used to tell a few stories about Duncan, but against himself. In an England v Wales game at Ninian Park in Cardiff, Jimmy as the Wales team manager was in the dressing room just prior to the game. One by one he was giving players their instructions on how to combat the England players. When he had finished, Reg Davies, the Newcastle United centre forward piped up:

"But Boss, you haven't mentioned this here fellow Edwards - what do we do about him? How do you want us to play him?"

Jimmy looked Reg straight in the eye and said:

"Stay out of his way son, stay out of his way. If you don't, you'll get hurt."

During the second half of that game, with England leading 4-0, Duncan had to collect the ball from close by the dugout so that he could take a throw in. Seeing Jimmy in that dugout, he looked up and said:

"Hey Jimmy, what time's the next train back to Manchester? You're wasting your time here!"

Jimmy exploded:

"Wait till I get you back in Manchester on Monday young man - I might even make you into a half decent player!"

Not long before the tragedy, Duncan became engaged to a young lady named Molly Leach. He had also bought a car, even though he couldn't drive! Sunday mornings would see both he and Molly outside his digs, busily polishing that car! It was his pride and joy. Again, it must have been heartbreaking for his parents, and also young Molly, to listen to him as he lay in that hospital bed. He told his Mum:

"I've got better things to do than lie here Mum. We've got an important game on Saturday."

She reminded him that he also had a car waiting at home for him, and he just whispered to her:

"Keep it on the road Mum, keep it on the road."

At 1:18a.m. On the morning of 21 February, 1958, this giant of a young man succumbed to those terrible injuries which he had received in the tragedy of two weeks before and that great heart of his stopped beating. When the news broke in the City of Manchester later that morning, once again another great pall of mourning enveloped the whole city to add to the heartache of the disaster of just over two weeks previous. Maybe it was better that he did pass away. The doctors had said that had he lived, he might have had to spend the rest of his life in a wheelchair. Duncan could never have stood that kind of imprisonment. Now, we who saw him play, and were so captivated by this human dynamo who was built along gargantuan lines, and oozed such class and personality, can remember him just as he was – the greatest thing that had happened to British football for years.

My memories of him never dim. I can still see him today as he comes bounding out from that old player's tunnel, taking those huge giant leaps into the air, and heading an imaginary ball. I can still see him standing there in the middle of the pitch expanding his chest and shouting to his team mates in that thick Black Country accent:

"Come on lads, we 'aven't come here for nuffink!"

He was special alright - in some ways he was a freak, and I say that in the nicest possible way. He was the perfect human being, the perfect footballer with the perfect technique, temperament, and the one player that I have seen that really did have everything and could play anywhere and still be the most outstanding player on the field. People often ask me today as to who would compare with him. Well, the honest answer is, I haven't seen anybody come near to him. To try and explain I tell them, take a little bit of Bobby Moore, a little bit of Bryan Robson, a little bit of Roy Keane, and a little bit of Patrick Viera - mix them together, and maybe, just maybe, you may just get a little bit of Duncan Edwards.

Today he lies resting in Dudley Cemetery. Even now, all these years after his passing, there are many, many visitors to his graveside every day of every week. Tributes in the form of scarves, flags, pictures, and flowers, are placed there in memory and respect of this gentle giant. The memorials in Dudley Town Centre, and St. Francis' Church, commemorate not only Duncan's outstanding football ability, but also the simple decency of a wonderful human being. He was idolized by the youth of his day, and he represented them in their thousands in their wish for courage, acclaim, and simple rare talent. That he had all three in abundance is without question. The hero is the creature other people strive to be – Duncan was such a man.

As Jimmy Murphy always liked to point out, there was once a famous athlete who years ago who used to proclaim:

"I am the greatest! I am the greatest!"

Murphy was to say:

"Well, unfortunately I have news for him. Even he got it wrong. You see, the greatest was a young 21 years

old wing half, who played for Manchester United and England and wore the number 6 shirt. In my opinion, he was the most complete player the game of football has ever witnessed. Talent and genius we will continually see again ...... but there will only ever be one Duncan Edwards"

Dear Dunc, I say it so often, the years roll by, but your memory never dims and your legend will live on forever. Sleep on in your peace.

Duncan Edwards made 177 appearances for Manchester United scoring 21 goals.

He made 19 senior appearances for England scoring 6 goals.

He was the youngest ever professional to play in the First Division when he made his debut against Cardiff City in April 1953.

He was the youngest ever footballer to play for England in a full international match when he made his international debut against Scotland in April 1955.

He played at every level for his country from schoolboy international through to full international.

Johnny Berry - The Wizard of the Wing

He was the smallest, the oldest, and the vice - captain of that great *Busby Babes* team of the 1950's. Johnny Berry was born on 1 June, 1926, in the Hampshire town of Aldershot, the son of a former professional soldier, and an Irish mother. Aldershot is probably Britain's most famous military town, being the home to many of the army's regiments, and corps. It is no surprise therefore that he lived in a small terraced house on the aptly named Crimea Road, not only with his own family, but also his mother's five brothers and one sister. Amazingly, there were another five more boys, and four, born to the Berry family. To say that the living conditions in the small three bedroom terraced house were intimate, is an understatement.

Conditions in the 1930s were never conducive to raising large families, and the financial implications of trying to support such a large family, were tough. Like most children of their time, the Berry's liked to concentrate, and burn off their energy, playing outdoor games. Crimea Road backed on to Sebastopol Road, and in the road between them, the boys played football. Like a lot of young players from all over Britain who went on to have careers in professional football, it was on those cobbled streets where Johnny honed his early football skills.

Johnny became two footed, and although small, he was more than a match for the bigger boys who possessed neither the skill nor speed to cope with him. Johnny attended St. Joseph's School in Aldershot, and he quickly progressed into the school team. As he developed, he gained his first football representative honour when he was selected to play for the Aldershot Town Boys' team. But for all his love of the game of football, Johnny also felt that he had a moral responsibility to try and help out with the family income, and so he took a job delivering newspapers both morning and night and handed over all of his earnings to his mother. He was also an altar boy at St. Joseph's church and he loved the days when there was weddings and funerals, and he had the job of pumping the bellows for the church organist, for which he would receive a few shillings.

Berry was well known around the Aldershot area as being a good player. His two footedness meant that he could play as a wingman on either flank. His local club Aldershot had a look at him and even gave him trials, but he was considered as being too small to make a career in professional football with the *'Shots*. Throughout his life, the small mindedness of the people at Aldershot Football club remained an irritant to him. How wrong could they have been! When he left school, with the help of a friend, Tony Brook, he took a job as a trainee cinema projectionist at the Ritz cinema. Aldershot was home to thousands of soldiers, and the town had five cinemas. John would work a shift at each of them, and it was whilst he was doing this that he met his future wife, Hilda.

In 1944 he was called up to serve his country in the armed forces and joined his father's old regiment, the Royal Artillery. His basic training was at Sunnyvale Camp, in Rhyl, North Wales, and it was here that he began to be noticed as a footballer. A man called R.E. Jones was in charge of the regimental football team, and many years later, in a letter to Johnny's son Neil, he recalled:

Very soon his ability as a footballer came to my notice in unit matches, but I was not the first to recognize his undoubted skills. There were two or three professional players in charge of Physical training, and almost immediately, he was playing for the Regiment, with some local clubs becoming very interested.

There followed some hectic bargaining and I was very pleased when he took the advice of an old professional, Fred Harris, the captain of Birmingham City who was one of my Physical Training Instructors. John signed for Birmingham City and I used to regularly take a group of my boys to see matches there.

Johnny Berry made his debut for the '*Brummies*" in a Wartime League game against arch rivals Aston Villa at the daunting Villa Park. Despite the game being rough physically, and Johnny taking some rough treatment from the Villa full back Cummings, he did much to impress. Unfortunately, just a few weeks after that match he was sent to India, where he was to remain for over two years. India at that time was not really the best place to find oneself. It was dangerous, tedious, and was above all, it was at a time of an inglorious British retreat from the jewel in their crown.

Because of his previous occupation as a cinema projectionist, Johnny was transferred to the Army Kinema Corps. It lightened his load somewhat and for the rest of his time in India, (he had been promoted to sergeant) he toured around the country in a lorry with two Indian Sikh soldiers showing films and newsreels to the troops to ward off boredom, and give them some relaxation from their duties of policing what was the end of the Empire. He was desperate to return to England and Birmingham City and finally, in 1947, he was able to return back home. He was demobbed, and immediately returned back home to Aldershot and married Hilda Reeves, the girl who he had left behind.

Johnny had a fairly productive time at St. Andrews and spent just four years there. In later life he often looked back on his time at St. Andrews with great fondness because he had many happy memories of his time there. In 1947-48, Birmingham City won the Second Division Championship, and the following season, despite being one of the favourites for relegation, kept their place in the First Division. Sadly, the season after that, they were again relegated back to the Second Division. Like most professionals of that era, every year Johnny took a summer job, and his was as a barber's assistant which helped supplement his income. It is something that one could never envisage happening today – going to the local barbers and having your haircut by one of your idols!

His journey to Old Trafford came out of the blue. With Jimmy Delaney having left a few months earlier for Aberdeen, United needed a fast, direct winger, who had experience to help with their push to achieve their first championship win since 1911. Matt Busby had never forgotten the problems that Berry had caused his defenders when Manchester United had last played Birmingham City. He'd given two of the most celebrated full backs in the game a real run around – Johnny Carey, and John Aston. The move was not without its problems though, because at first, he refused to move. It was not because he was not ambitious, but because he thought that the ten pounds signing on fee was a very small amount of personal financial gain, and it did not accurately reflect the contribution that he had made to Birmingham City both on and off the field. He was outraged that the huge profit which Birmingham City was going to make on his services was not going to be shared with him in any way. Eventually, the Birmingham directors reached a compromise with him seeing as they were just about to see a nice profit slip away, so they upped his compensation to five hundred pounds, and that was enough to make him change his mind and move to Manchester.

So in August 1951, United paid Birmingham £25,000 for the diminutive little winger. He had an immediate impact and United duly achieved their aim, being crowned First Division Champions at the end of the 1951-52 season for the first time in forty one years. Berry's debut game came on 1 September, 1951, at Burnden Park, in front of 52,239 fans, in a game played against Lancashire arch rivals, Bolton Wanderers, which United lost 0-1. United's team that day was; Allen; Carey, Redman; Gibson, Chilton, Cockburn; Berry, Pearson, Rowley, Downie, Bond. His first goal for the club came just two weeks later on 15 September at Maine Road in a 2-1 victory for United – a nice start to his derby career! He made a total of thirty six appearances that season scoring 6 goals, and collected his first Championship winner's medal.

Johnny was extremely quick and would run at defenders with pace and could move the ball with either foot and this enabled him to go either inside, or outside of his marker. He was an exquisite dribbler and was a nightmare for a full back to mark. His crossing was deadly accurate with either foot and United's strikers benefited a tremendous amount from the service that he provided. He was also dangerous in that he would also drift into the middle and suddenly arrive inside the penalty area unsuspected and would be there hammering the ball into the back of the net. For a little fellow, he packed quite a shot, again with both feet. He was a delight to watch especially when he was in full flight. That he only won four full caps for England is again one of football's travesties. You have to remember that occupying the outside right berth in the England team during those years was a certain ageing, Stanley Mathews. The national team was also picked by a Selection Committee at that time which was made up of several League Club Chairmen – a sad state of affairs, and the reason why the England team was hardly consistent from one game to the next!

I often wonder how today's fans would view Johnny Berry. To be honest, as they used to adore a certain young Portuguese young man who wore the number seven shirt, I am more than certain that they would also have taken Johnny to their hearts. For all of his short stature, Johnny had the heart of a lion. He faced some of the roughest and toughest full-backs in the game during his time at United, and was targeted for brutality on many occasions. This was a time when there was so much robust physical contact in the game and defenders could tackle from behind and get away with it. He had an unflappable temperament and was just so exciting to watch. Like Ronaldo, Berry could certainly get your backside on the edge of a seat – he completely baffled and bewitched full backs with his trickery, and this produced an awful lot of end-product for the other forwards!

As I said, his international career was so short. He went on the South American tour of 1953 and played in all three games. His next and last cap came some three years later in a game against Sweden in Rasunda which ended in a goalless draw. There was some tremendous wingers about during his time and no one could ever say that Tom Finney wasn't worth his place in the team – but he operated mainly in the left wing berth, and there were many players who got caps during Berry's time who were nowhere near as good as him. Stan Mathews, as Sir Matt once so aptly put it, loved to *"play the Palladium"*, meaning he loved London and particularly Wembley, but he never liked playing at the likes of Old Trafford, Burnden, Hampden Park, Ninian Park, or Windsor Park!

Johnny reveled in seeing the young *Babes* being introduced around him. He was vice-captain of the team and had the nickname of *'Digger'* which referred to his powerful shot. As the *Babes* came to the fore – in that Championship winning team of 1956, only he and Roger Byrne remained from the team that had won the Championship some four years earlier. As United entered the new European Cup competition, he was paranoid about flying and certainly didn't like it, which was the same for a few of the younger players as well. He was always suspicious of foreign food and used to take his own goodies with him on the foreign trips, together with a primus stove, which was often the source of merriment from the young lads.

Johnny Berry trains prior to the start of the 1957-58 season. Pictured left to right are; Duncan Edwards, Johnny Berry, Danish trialist Eric Dyroborg, Dennis Viollet, and Tommy Taylor.

He was an essential cog in that young team, and his form on the whole was so consistent. He also scored some very vital goals and amongst those that I can remember are the one against Bilbao at Maine Road that took United into the European Cup semi-final at their first attempt; the winner against Bournemouth at Dean Court in the FA Cup 6th round tie in 1957 that took them into semi-final; the winner in a crucial home League game against Blackpool at Old Trafford in April of 1956 which gave them a 2-1 victory that ensured the First Division title. He was also United's spot kick expert for a number of years, having taken over the role from Roger Byrne.

Unfortunately for Johnny, in the middle of the 1957-58 season, Busby decided he needed to freshen up his team, and in the December of 1957, after a run of bad results he took action. He bought Harry Gregg from Doncaster Rovers for a British record fee for a goalkeeper of 23,500 pounds. On Saturday, 21 December 1957, Gregg made his debut against Leicester City at Old Trafford, consigning Ray Wood to the Reserves. Also left out of the team were Johnny Berry, Billy Whelan, and David Pegg, and they made way for Kenny Morgans, Bobby Charlton and Albert Scanlon. Sadly for those left out, all but Johnny (and he was only to play once more) would ever play a competitive game in the first team again.

By this time, Johnny was 32 years old, and ever the pragmatist, he decided to ask for a move away from United. He figured that due to his age, Busby would be looking to bring in one of the younger players. He accepted this, but thought that after seven years at Old Trafford in which he had played 276 games, scored 45 goals, and had won three Championship winner's medals, had represented the Football league, England at both B and full international level, three Charity Shield winners plaques, and an appearance in an FA Cup Final; he believed that he could still play first team football, if not at United, then somewhere else.

Johnny knew that both Liverpool and Fulham had made enquiries to United about buying

him. Busby however, had no intentions of selling him. It angered Johnny Berry because he thought that he had

Johnny Berry on the extreme right, lines up with his Manchester united team-mates at Old Trafford in 1957. The other players, from left to right are; Eddie Colman, Dennis Viollet, Colin Webster, Jackie Blanchflower, Bill Foulkes, Geoff Bent, Liam Whelan, Tommy Taylor, Duncan Edwards, and Ray Wood.

given United seven years of loyal service, and considered that he had more than repaid the outlay that United had paid Birmingham City for him. Players back then were not paid the astronomical salaries that are seen in the game today, and Johnny thought that this might be the last chance for him to make some money from a nice signing on fee, or even from a *bung*. He did think that it was the right time for him to move on.

We all know that sad event of the tragedy and it is amazing that Johnny Berry ever survived at all. His injuries were so horrific; fractured skull, broken jaw; broken elbow, broken pelvis, broken leg. When his wife Hilda arrived at the Munich hospital her first sight was one of him surrounded by packs of ice which was there to try and keep the swellings and bruising to a minimum. He was also in a coma and remained so for almost two months. The ironical thing was that if Busby had granted his transfer request, then he would never have been on the aircraft at Munich, and both he and his family would have been spared the nightmare of the aftermath of this tragic event.

It was something that he remembered for the rest of his life and he felt that Matt Busby owed him the move. He had done his bit for United, and he deserved the chance to benefit from a move financially for the last time in his life. The move was denied to him and it was situation that he accepted (because he was contractually bound) but certainly did not enjoy. He felt that Busby had not looked after his interests, and it hurt him for the remainder of his years.

When Johnny Berry returned home to Manchester months after the accident, he still had no clear idea of what had happened, and initially thought that he had been in a car crash. On the flight home from Munich he was accompanied by two nurses who had a bag full of tranquilizers should he have had any sudden flashback to the accident. He was admitted into a Manchester hospital upon arrival and even then had to undergo the removal of all his teeth to help with the jaw injuries. His first knowledge of what had happened came when he picked up a newspaper which had a report of a United game on the back page, and when he saw the team line-up, he could not believe it. He badgered the nurse and she had to call a doctor who explained to him exactly what had happened. After Johnny asked about his team mates, the doctor went through the team name by name, and the doctor told him whether they had survived or not. Although he had been inside that ill-fated aircraft, he must have been the last person in the world to know it.

His injuries meant that he was never able to pursue his career in football again. He took a job with Massey Ferguson in Trafford Park but in 1960, United callously asked him to vacate their club house in Davyhulme to accommodate the signing of Maurice Setters. All I will say is that it was a sad state of affairs and one that made the Berry family understandably, very bitter.

The family moved back to Aldershot his home town, and Johnny and his brother Peter opened a sports shop in the little village of Cove, close by. In 1963 I can recall that I was playing in a match at Aldershot, and needed some studs for my boots. I called in to Berry's sports shop and it was John that actually served me. He spent great time advising me on what type of studs I needed and he actually fitted my boots with them for me. We spent time talking a little about Manchester but neither he nor I mentioned United. He looked a sick man even then. The sports shop business went on for 20 years, and Johnny spent the last few years of his working life as a store man in a television retail chain warehouse.

Sadly, Johnny did not enjoy a long retirement. He passed away on 16 September 1994 aged just 67 years.

Johnny Berry played 276 games in all competitions for United scoring 45 goals. Berry made 2 appearances for the senior England team.

Liam 'Billy' Whelan – The Quiet Man

He was probably the quietest in character of the *Busby Babes* but nonetheless, Liam Whelan, or Billy Whelan, as he was known to the fans on the terraces, made more than a significant contribution to the legacy left behind by that wonderful team known as the *Busby Babes*.

Saturday, 26 March 1955, was a red letter day in the short life of the young Irishman. When he woke up that morning, he must have felt nervous, but excited, and adrenalin would have coursed through his lithe young body. The day had arrived of which he had dreamed about ever since crossing the Irish Sea from his native Dublin, to sign for Manchester United in April 1953. Later that afternoon, at the Deepdale football ground in Preston, Lancashire, he would at last be making his first team debut for the affectionately named *Busby Babes* team against Preston North End.

Little did Liam know that Saturday morning that his first team career would last for just less than three years. He also didn't know what a prolific impact his short career would have upon Manchester United. However, in the following three years, he was to become an integral part of the best free scoring, inside trio, in the history of this famous club.

Cabra is a suburb on the north side of Dublin, in the Republic of Ireland. At the time of Liam Whelan's birth there on 1 April 1935, Cabra was very much on the edge of the city and comprised mostly of open fields, and open countryside. Five years later, the Dublin Corporation began a public housing programme, and started to build council houses in the district which enabled them to move people out of the tenements and rooms, which populated Dublin's city centre. The Whelans were a large family comprising of Mum Elizabeth, Dad John, three brothers, Christy, Michael, and Liam, and three sisters, Rita, Maura, and Alice. Sadly, in 1943, tragedy struck, and the father, John, died. Christy, the oldest brother, who was to have a big influence on the young Liam, took over as the family's father figure.

As the houses in Cabra started to be built, the population of the area began to expand with the arrival of the inner city families, and their

Liam 'Billy' Whelan pictured at Old Trafford in 1956.

children. Children playing football on the open patches of land around the area became a common sight. The Whelan family lived at number 28, St. Attracta Road, Cabra. Liam had an appetite for the game just as his two brothers had. But Liam was more gifted. By the time he was ten he was playing in local teams, and at twelve years of age, he joined the famous Irish club which has provided so many famous players to English football, and Manchester United in particular – Home Farm.

Christy, Liam's older brother recalled in an interview the Irish television station RTE:

He went up to Home Farm, and he was only 12 at the time, and they took him on. When he was playing under17, Home Farm Minors were playing in the FAI Minor Cup Final, and Liam was brought on to help them because he was such a good player and that day he helped to strengthen the team.

There was one day when he was playing at Home Farm, and he came in, and was then going out, and I said;

'Where are you going?' He said 'I'm playing tonight' and I replied 'who are you playing for?', and he replied 'I'm playing for the UL side and they're playing Merrion Rovers in an important match, and I'm playing. Vinny Ryan is playing in the match with us.'

Vinny Ryan was a young player like him and he was all the talk, he was always in the papers, it was – Vinny Ryan is going to Celtic, Vinny Ryan is going to United, all that was going on and there still wasn't a mention with Liam. I went up to watch the match as usual because I never missed a match that Liam played with Home Farm that I can remember, from the time he was 14. My brother Michael and me, on our bikes would spin out to where he was playing wherever it was. I went up to Home farm that night and they were playing Merrion Rovers and as usual he was great.

Bert Whalley, who died in the crash as well, he was there, and he was watching the boy Vinny Ryan. John Doherty, who was in the United first team, but was also eligible for the United youth team, and he had got injured. They needed somebody very much for the youth team in his place. You see they think an awful lot of the youths over there, and the youth matches, and they wanted somebody good to replace him. So Bert Whalley had come over to run the rule over Vinny Ryan, and at half time he was turned to Billy Behan and he says:

'Forget about Ryan for the time being; get that lad Whelan signed up.'

I was in bed later that evening and the next thing something shook me on the shoulder. It was Liam, and I said 'What's wrong?' 'Can you come downstairs for a moment' he said, and I again said 'What's wrong?' He said 'There's somebody downstairs from Manchester United' and I said, 'Well it's about bloody time.'

So I got up, I had no dressing gown at the time, so I put an overcoat on me, and down I went, and I sat down. It was Billy Behan, the United scout, a famous United scout, and Tom Smith, who was the main coach at Home Farm, and he was looking after Liam's team. I looked at Tom and I said, 'What's wrong Tom?' and he looked at me and said 'This is Billy Behan, from Manchester United' and I shook hands with him. 'They want Liam' Tom said. I looked at Billy Behan and I asked him, 'What way do you want him? If this is a trial I'm not interested in it.' 'No' said Billy Behan, 'We want to sign him full time immediately, and we want him to come over and take a place in the youth team.' So I turned to our mother and I said, 'Well, I have no objections' and I also said, 'If you want to let him go then I won't say anything.' So she looked up at Liam, and she said, 'Well I suppose we'll have to let you go.' That was on a Friday evening, a Friday night, and on the Sunday evening he was gone away.

I remember we went up to Manchester, it was after the Cup Final time, and United were playing Blackpool. Stanley Mathews was the player of the day at that time, and this is a well known fact, it's in print, and Mathews was a great dribbler. He went by Roger Byrne, but a figure came around the side and took the ball off him — it was Liam. I was down by the corner flag, and Liam just started pushing the ball from foot to foot, he did this for a few seconds, and then he 'nutmegged' Stanley Mathews who was the 'Prince of Dribblers' and he nutmegged him, and away he went! The crowd just went mad — 'Go on Billy, show them what dribbling's all about!'

Liam had not come to the attention of the many English Football League scouts in Ireland despite some blistering displays for the Home Farm junior teams. He had even slipped under Manchester United's radar in the country, and that was very unusual as few gifted young Irish players at that time escaped their notice. However, as his brother Christy said, due to an injury to United's John Doherty in a Youth team game, Liam's move to Old Trafford was surprising, but accelerated. United needed a talented replacement for inside forward John Doherty as they were to play in the Final of the 1953 FA Youth Cup against Stan Cullis's young lions from the famed Wolverhampton Wanderers club in the West Midlands. Initially, they were watching other young players, but Liam was the one that Bert Whalley wanted once he had watched him play, and he made sure that he came away from Dublin with his signature.

Liam answered the call and his impact was immediate, seeing him play the starring role in a 7-1 demolition of the young Wolves team in the first leg of that final. It is interesting to read the very first team that United ever fielded in that first FA Youth Cup Final;

Gordon Clayton; Bryce Fulton, Paddy Kennedy; Eddie Colman, Ronnie Cope, Duncan Edwards; Noel McFarlane, Liam Whelan, Eddie Lewis, David Pegg and Albert Scanlon.

From that team, the young full back Paddy Kennedy had played in the same team as Liam at Home Farm less than a year previously. That 7-1 win made the second leg a formality and it ended in a 2-2 draw. Manchester United were the first ever winners of the FA Youth Cup. Liam had immediately made a huge impression on Tom Curry, Bert Whalley, and most of all, upon Jimmy Murphy.

Immediately after the 1952-53 season ended, Manchester United's Youth team travelled over to Switzerland to play in what was fast becoming Europe's premier youth tournament – The Blue Star Tournament. Once again, Liam turned in some tremendous performances which helped United win the trophy. So well did he play during that tournament that United were to receive enquiries from the Santos Club from Brazil, as to whether they would release Liam, and allow him to play for them in South America.

For the next two years, the quiet unassuming young Irishman was left to develop in the Central League team. It was to be an examination of not only his skill, but also his temperament, and his courage. The Central League, or Reserve League, as it was known back then was a tough environment for young players to come in to. Most teams in that league had a number of older professionals who were either returning from injury, or were seeing out their careers with their clubs... it was certainly not a place for the faint hearted.

United's coaches kept a watching eye on Liam's development and he became a prolific goal scorer at that level. Jimmy Murphy would spend many an extra hour on the training ground with him. Murphy described him as thus:

"Billy Whelan was an absolute genius with the ball at his feet. If he would just believe in himself a bit more he would be sensational. They talk about these Continental and South American players and what great ball jugglers they are. Well, Billy Whelan could do what they did only better. He did it in competitive games and in all kinds of conditions. He could think faster than those cowboys in the Wild West in their shoot-outs."

He also filled out in physique somewhat during those two years. For an inside-forward he was tall and gangly, standing over six feet. But he was deceptive and although a lot of pundits were of the opinion that he lacked pace, that was not true. He covered the ground a lot quicker than a lot of people realized. He had tremendous dribbling skills and could go past players very easily. If there was a weakness in his game it was that he was not a great header of the ball. His passing was a joy to see and like Pat Crerand a few years later, Liam had a real eye for the opening and could pass a ball through the eye of needle – long or short.

Off the field Liam was quiet and shy. He was the typical young Irish boy, away from his home and his family. There were times when he was very homesick and longed to be back in Dublin and would travel back home whenever the opportunity arose. However, like most young men of his age, he was to settle down eventually and he mixed well with the other young boys at

United. Initially, at Mrs. Watson's Boarding House in Old Trafford, he shared digs with Bobby Charlton, Duncan Edwards, Jackie Blanchflower, David Pegg, Mark Jones, Tommy Taylor, and Bobby Charlton, and he was often seen out and about with them.

In the RTE interview his brother Christy told the story of Liam's homesickness:

He was always wanting to be home. I remember him saying to me one time; 'I wish with all my life that this was over and that I was going home again.' That stayed with him for many years, the homesickness. But one of the things that did happen then, and which did help him, was, my pal Sean Dolan, who lived next door to me in Fosser Road, his brother lived in Stockport. They had a lovely big house over there. He was the manager of a canning factory that was owned by the future United Chairman, Louis Edwards.

I was over one time with Sean my pal, and we went up to Brendan's place and we had a lovely big stew which Bid had made for us, and Liam had tucked into it. When we had finished, and when we were going, Bid, Brendan's wife, she called to me and said:

"Christy. Did you see Liam eating that stew?"

I said, " yes, he really tucked in to it." Then she said;

"Would he like to eat more of them?", and I asked her, "What do you mean Bid?" and she replied:

"Would he like to come and stay with us?" I said that I was sure that he would, so she asked me to ask him. We were going into town and Sean was with us, and I said to Liam:

"What did you think of the dinner today, it was like mammy's wasn't it?" And I asked him, "how would you like to live with Bid and Brendan and their two lovely children, Elizabeth and Michael?" Liam looked at me and he said:

"Ahhh that would be grand if I could live with them, it would be grand." I told him, "You can if you want to." He looked at me and said; "What do you mean?" I told him that Bid had told me that he could go and live with them if he wanted to. "Is that right- that's great" he replied.

So he went to live with them but unfortunately there wasn't much time before the accident, however it did help. He was great, and he settled in and used to enjoy being with the two children, taking them to the pictures — you know, that sort of thing. He was more back into the family life.

He would write or telephone the family two doors from us and sent Mammy £3 every week. He never forgot his mum. Until he went to the Dolans one of the problems he had was how he spent the days. He would train all morning and then finish about 1 pm and go to the pictures in town, but he got fed up with that. He would go to Mass, of course, and he was very friendly with Father Mulholland, but the afternoons were a terrible drag. But at the Dolan's he was really happy.

On 26 March 1955, just five days before his 20th birthday, Matt Busby pitched him into the hurly burly of First Division football by giving him his debut at Deepdale, against Preston North

End. A paltry total of just 13,327 fans witnessed the likeable young Irishman's first game at senior level as United won 2-0 with goals by Roger Byrne, and another youngster, Albert Scanlon. The following week he scored his first goal as he helped United go nap against Sheffield United winning by 5-0. Liam was to play in the next five games, and although he did not score in any of them, he had made a good impression on both the United manager, and the coaches. There was still a lot more to come from this talented youngster.

The season 1955-56 was the season in which United's team of young *Babes* came of age by winning the First Division Championship. Liam was used sporadically through that season playing in just thirteen games and scoring four goals, but it was enough for him to qualify for a Championship winner's medal. There was some stiff opposition for the inside right berth at that time, and the appearances throughout that season were also shared by John Doherty, Jackie Blanchflower, and Welshman, Colin Webster.

At the start of the 1956-57 season, Busby made Liam his first choice inside-right, and Liam repaid him with some astonishing performances and a bag full of goals. Manchester United's prolific strikers at that time were centre-forward Tommy Taylor, and inside-left Dennis Viollet. It was a fearsome duo and a partnership that scored goals on a regular basis. This was also the season that United went into Europe for the first time, and Liam's contribution in the campaign that season can never be underestimated, particularly in the quarter final, first leg tie against the Basque club, Bilbao, in Spain.

Liam scored an incredible thirty three goals that season in fifty four games (twenty six in forty appearances in the League; four from six appearances in the FA Cup; and three from eight appearances in the European Cup) and this was from what would be termed a mid-field player today! When you consider that the strike duo of Taylor and Viollet also scored thirty four and twenty six goals respectively, in all competitions, it does not take a genius to see why they retained their league title that season, and also reached the FA Cup Final, and the European Cup semi-final. Ninety three goals shared between three players is an astonishing strike rate by any stretch of the imagination - especially in top class football.

The late Frank Taylor who was a journalist who covered Manchester United's matches remembered the game in Bilbao, Spain in January 1957:

"United were losing 5-2 as the game got to the closing stages. It looked as though nothing could save them. But hold on, in those dying minutes, there is 'Billy'Whelan, the quiet boy from Dublin, on the ball over on the far right hand side and in his own half. When Whelan had the ball under control like that, he was always liable to make it do anything but talk. That weird shuffle; the sudden quickening of speed; the rolling shoulders hunched over the ball protecting it lovingly; the pull back with the ball; the sudden feints and

stops; the crazy corkscrew turns that bore no resemblance to sleek athletic movement; but when Whelan did it on a football field, it could be quite devastating.

He took the ball in his stride, lazily, and then started to dribble, coaxing it along through the heavy waves of mud, beating first one man, and then another, gradually gathering pace all the time. A shrug of the shoulders, a jink and a turn, and then a change of direction, until he had wiggled his way diagonally across field from right to left. Then he started to come back again into the middle, leaving a trail of five Bilbaoans in his wake. For more than forty yards the wandering Whelan took the ball until one wondered how he had the strength, after such a hard slogging match; or whether in fact he would ever muster the strength to draw back his foot and try to shoot. Whelan ploughed on until Carmelo came out of his goal, and from a spot just inside the penalty area Whelan hit the ball hard and true into the top left-hand corner of the net. It was a goal to remember in any conditions. In the murderous quagmire of mud in Bilbao, it was a miracle goal that kept United's European Cup hopes alive."

Bill Foulkes also remembered that goal in an interview with local radio in Manchester;
"It was one of the most thrilling goals that I ever witnessed, and it restored our hope, and duly we won the tie. After that, he did the same sort of thing on plenty of occasions, pulling off the seemingly impossible, roaming free then rifling home from distance. Billy scored more than 50 goals for United in less than 100 senior appearances, a fantastic record, and although he had lost his place to Bobby Charlton at the time of Munich, I am sure that had he lived, he would have taken a major role in the club's future. I am not saying that he would have kept Bobby out in the long run — I don't think that anybody could have done that — but somehow, space would have been found for Billy more often than not.

As well as being a superb footballer, this softly-spoken Dubliner was one of the loveliest men that I ever met, so modest and decent. He was very religious too, with a certain tranquility about him, and sometimes he used to come out with sayings which made me think that he might have been a priest. I was sitting near him as our plane attempted to take off for the third time on that fateful afternoon at Munich and I heard Billy say something along the lines of; 'If anything happens then I am ready for it.' With all the tension, with people scurrying around the aircraft as they changed seats, he was utterly calm. In that moment, it didn't really occur to me what he was talking about, but when I discussed it later with Teresa, I realized. Billy was a devout Catholic, and he was preparing himself for the worst if it happened. What a character, and what a player he would have become had he been spared."

Liam was a joy to watch and if he had a flaw, it was that he did not realize just how good he was. At times he seemed to have an inferiority complex. There was so much talent around at Old Trafford at that time, and he used to wonder if he was really good enough. His performances belied those thoughts. He was such a quiet boy and you would never ever see him in the newspapers or the media. As soon as the game was over he would be bathed and then off home to his digs. For the kids who idolized him at that time, he was always happy to stand and sign their autograph books and he never refused. My good friend John White, who has followed Manchester United for as long as I have, recalled a lovely tale from that season:

"Why was he my favourite? Well, I've thought back some 56 years or so and I can only say that it HAD to have been because of the game against Aston Villa at home on 25 February 1956, not long after my tenth birthday and some five weeks away from his twenty first birthday. Ironically and meaningfully, which has just dawned on me as I was putting this together, it was also less than two years away from his death.

It was a typical cold Saturday in February, and strangely, I have learned that Old Trafford was not full as it seemed it was. There were only 36,277 in the ground for the visit of Villa and I honestly remember very little of the detail of the game but I do remember it was pissing down throughout, and I did remember that we won 1-0, and Liam scored the winner.

It wasn't that this goal was THE goal of the century that made him my favourite. It wasn't that he had played out of his skin to win the day that did it either. It was simply this. I stood around (as lads did back then) in a soaking Duffle coat at the player's entrance to get autographs as the lads came out after the game. As they started to come out, I'd seen big Dunc dart off followed by Eddie Colman without any hanging about at all. The rain was absolutely atrocious it's fair to say, but the only man who patiently stood and signed for us lads that evening was Liam. Even our captain Roger Byrne sneaked round the back of the posse of lads gathered around Liam and made off as Liam was encircled by us grateful lads.

I can see him now, with his belted grey gabardine mac, and his trilby hat jauntily dripping water all over our autograph books, as he signed until there was no-one left waiting. So it is that night more than anything that made Liam my favourite. It is also such memories of a hero who had that personal touch that remain with you all your life."

Twenty one years of age and he wore a trilby hat – hard to believe in this day and age. My own memories of him were very similar. He was always one of the gang that would congregate at the Galleon Swimming Baths in Manchester, during the summer. He would be there with his quiet unassuming smile, cigarette in hand, as he relaxed and enjoyed the company of his team mates and friends. Like so many of them he was so approachable and especially where kids were concerned.

His quiet unassuming personality touched everybody who came into contact with him. Christy, his brother tells some lovely stories about him:

"There was many a time when the local school children would find out that Liam was at home. They would come knocking on the door and ask, 'Is Liam coming out?' He would go to the door and they would ask him,

'are you coming out to play a match Liam?' and he would answer them saying, 'Yeah, have you got a ball?' and they would say, 'no'. Unhesitatingly he would put his hand in his pocket, take out some money and say, 'Here, go up the bridge and get a ball and I'll be out shortly.' That bridge is the one that's now named after him. It was the bridge where all the shops were and played a big part in his short life. He had to go over it every day to go to school, he had to go over it to go to the shops, and he would go over it when he was going off to matches. But he used to go out with the youngsters and he'd be playing ball in the road with them.

On one particular occasion, Belmore Football club had organized a big five-a-side competition which was played at Dalymount Park. The tournament was over two nights and each night the ground was packed. The tournament attracted a good few international teams as well, and Liam had asked the 'Boss' could he take a United team over to Dublin to play in it. Busby said yes, and along with Liam, Ray Wood, Eddie Colman, Duncan Edwards, Albert Scanlon, Dennis Viollet, and a few others, they all came over. The boys were staying at The Gresham Hotel, but Liam was at home.

The first night they won all their matches, and on the second day, Liam was at home in Cabra, and was outside playing ball with kids. My mother said to me, 'Christy' as she looked at her watch, 'it's getting late and he has still to get down to the ground to play.' So I went out and said to him, 'Liam, it's getting a bit on now and Mammy's getting a bit concerned.' He just smiled and said to the youngsters, 'okay – next goal is the winner.' When it was over he came running in, had a quick wash and changed his shoes, and he RAN down to Dalymount! He came home that night and he said to our Ma', 'what do you think of that then Ma?' She said, 'what do I think of what?' and Liam replied, 'Two hat-tricks in the one day.' 'What are you talking about two hat-tricks in one day?' 'Well I scored a hat-trick out in the road with the youngsters, and I went down to Dalymount and scored a hat-trick against Shamrock Rovers, with Eamonn D'Arcy in goal!' That was the type of boy that he was. He was always so well liked in Cabra."

The 1957-58 season started for him at Leicester City's Filbert Street ground in the opening day's game. He started off where he had left off just a few months before — he

Liam 'Billy' Whelan takes a corner kick at the Racecourse Ground, Wrexham, during an FA Cup 4th Round tie on Saturday 26 January 1957.

scored all three goals in the 3-0 win! He was to score a further eleven goals before on 21 December 1957, he was left out of the team along with Ray Wood, Johnny Berry and David Pegg. Ray Wood's omission came as no surprise as Busby had paid a world record fee for a goalkeeper earlier in the week when he had signed Harry Gregg, the Northern Irish international 'keeper who came from Doncaster Rovers. When the team changes were announced just half an hour before the return game against Leicester City at Old Trafford, I can recall that there was much head shaking and gasps of astonishment.

Manchester United had hit something of a stutter but it seemed to be defensively that they were suffering because the forwards were still scoring goals. Unfortunately the defence had conceded some silly goals in high scoring games that had cost the team points. Liam's last appearance in a first team shirt came at home to Chelsea in a 1-0 defeat on 14 December 1957. He was replaced by Bobby Charlton for the Leicester game.

There was no banging on the Manager's door and asking for a transfer. He went back into the reserve team and got on with his game. In my opinion, Liam was just too good a player not to have won his place back again and at some time in the future would have returned. He travelled to Belgrade for the second leg European Cup quarter-final tie as one of United's reserves. The great sadness was that in the days beforehand, he had made a request to Matt Busby to see if he could be left behind in Manchester. He was suffering from a heavy cold and thought that a few days back home in Dublin would do him much better than the long trip out to Belgrade, especially as he would not be playing. Busby turned down his request saying it would not be right if he didn't travel with the whole squad.

On Thursday afternoon, 6 February, 1958, as the ill-fated Elizabethan aircraft thundered down the slush filled runway at Munich's Reim Airport for the third and last time, he was to utter his final words among the quietness and apprehension inside that aircraft cabin: *"If this is death, then I am ready for it"* a reference to his strong religious beliefs. Liam was a staunch Roman Catholic who took great comfort from his faith. Sadly, moments after he uttered those words, he left this world so tragically. He left behind a broken hearted family, and also a broken hearted fiancée, Ruby McCullagh, who he was to have married in June, 1958. He had met Ruby through his sister Rita and they had worked together at a local biscuit factory.

When his body was returned home to Dublin, and to his beloved family, he was buried at Glasnevin Cemetery. It is estimated that more than 20,000 people lined the funeral cortege's route to the cemetery on the day of his funeral. He was so popular within his local community and country. Even today, the mere mention of his name to the older generation of Manchester United fans, and the older people of his home in Cabra, brings a smile that really does light up their faces, as the memories of the quiet, unassuming young inside-forward come flooding back.

Personally, I will always remember his quiet polite manner, his lovely smile, and the soft Irish brogue when he spoke, and also the fact that he was a wonderful player to watch. The most underestimated player in that great team, and the man who had a phenomenal strike rate.

Sleep on in peace Liam, you are still so loved by your family, friends, and the many fans that were so privileged to see you play.

Liam Whelan played 96 games for Manchester United and scored 52 goals.

He also won 4 caps for his native Eire.

Tommy Taylor - The Smiling Executioner

His smile would have brightened even the darkest room. With his black curly hair, mischievous eyes, that smile, and the good looks, Tommy Taylor, standing at 6'1" tall, and weighing in at 13 stones, was the epitome of the professional athlete. Like the *Bestie* of a few years later, it is true to say that Tommy Taylor would not have looked out of place on a Hollywood film set. It is also true to say that the female contingent of Manchester United's following back in the 1950s, looked upon him as a replica of Adonis!

Tommy Taylor was born on 29 January 1932, at number 4, Quarry Street, in the Smithies district of Barnsley, Yorkshire, and into a working class mining family. He first attended Burton Road Junior School before moving on to Raley Secondary Modern School. Raley was a unique school for its time, for in addition to its academic buildings, it also comprised a gymnasium and swimming pool, and had its own soccer and rugby pitches. It was a school that produced Olympic shot putter, Arthur Rowe, and also the former Yorkshire cricketer and Test Match umpire, Harold *'Dicky'* Bird MBE.

Surprisingly, although his family had a football background (his Grandfather played for Barnsley St Peter, the forerunner of Barnsley Football Club, and his Father played for Wakefield City in the Yorkshire League) in his early years, Tommy was not drawn to the game. In fact you could say that there was a distinct lack of enthusiasm on his part. It was not until he was twelve years old that he actually started playing, and then it was as a full back. Eventually he moved to the centre forward position, and it was there that he began to shine.

The amazing thing was that Tommy never actually owned a pair of football boots whilst he was at school! Whenever he was playing for the school, or even for the Barnsley Boys town team, he would borrow a pair from his various school friends. Eventually it was to cause him a problem and one which he carried with him into later life. On two separate occasions he turned up for school matches with no boots. A certain schoolteacher took umbrage at Tommy not owning a pair, and he ordered him to play in his clogs. Tommy refused, and he was never to play another game for his school again. What upset Tommy was the fact that the schoolteacher also discriminated against Tommy's younger brother, Bill, and he too was also never selected to play for the school again.

Years later, when Tommy had become a famous name, he was at home in Barnsley when the same schoolteacher spotted him on the High Street, and made a bee-line for him. Obviously the teacher was delighted to let people know that one of his former pupils had made the grade in First Division football, but Tom was having none of it – he completely ignored him. It was completely out of character for him because he had such a bubbly, effervescent type of character. But deep down, Tommy had never forgotten the teacher, not so much for leaving him out of the school football team, but for discriminating against his younger brother.

Once he left school, Tommy's disinterest in making football a career continued. He was just a happy go lucky young boy who just wanted to be knocking around with his young mates. Football never entered his young head. It was not surprising that as soon as he left school, he followed a lot of the young men in Barnsley, by choosing to pursue a career as a surface worker with the National Coal Board. He was employed at the local Wharncliff Woodmoor Colliery. It was hard work, but nonetheless, he enjoyed it, and especially when the weekend would arrive and he could go for a pint with his mates. Apart from a kick-about on a pitch that they knew as the *Bog;* in the immediate two years after he left school, Tommy Taylor played no part in organized, competitive football.

In his early formative years, Taylor was on the small side, but as he moved towards his middle teens, he grew, and filled out physically. It was a pure fluke that he started playing football again. There was a local pub team named *Smithies United* and they were a man short for a forthcoming fixture, so they sent a person round to the Taylor home to ask him if he would help them out and play. He did – at centre forward, and the game seemed to rekindle his enthusiasm for football. He played well and scored a goal. After just three more games for the pub team, he began to draw the attention of Football League clubs. Scouts from Hull City, and his home town team Barnsley, began to push for his signature.

Despite Hull's interest, Tommy was only ever going to sign for his home town team, and this he did, joining the Barnsley Groundstaff. *Smithies United* profited by the enormous sum of ten pounds when Tommy signed for Barnsley as a professional on 25 July 1949. Not a bad return for a future England international and one of the greatest centre forwards to have ever played the game.

When he first joined Barnsley, Johnny Steele was the youth team coach, and in an interview with a local newspaper many years later, he recalled:

Tommy carried a little too much puppy fat and we had to tutor him about his eating habits. He listened and acted accordingly. At that time he was just beginning to fill out and grow.

But he possessed a terrific shot in both feet and he also had the uncanny knack of being able to virtually hang in the air and get tremendous power and direction behind his headed efforts. He could head the ball much harder and further than many players could by kicking it. He was a natural, but he still had to be taught the right and wrong ways of doing things on the field. However, we brought him along slowly, through the junior and A teams and so on.

When the young Taylor arrived at Barnsley, the senior team was blessed with an abundance of talent. Players like Danny Blanchflower, the Chilean brothers George, and Ted Robledo, (who were later to star at Newcastle United) Jimmy Baxter, Beaumont Asquith, Jimmy Kelly, 'Skinner' Normanton, and Gordon Pallister. They were good players for youngsters to learn from, and they all took an interest in the progress of young Tommy Taylor. However, a little thing called National Service was to rear its head and this meant Tommy having to go off and serve two years in the armed forces.

Joe Richards, the Barnsley Chairman (later to become Sir Joe Richards – President of the Football League) hatched a plan that would keep Taylor at Oakwell, and for him to further progress his career as a professional footballer. Richards sat on the National Coal Board Committee, and he suggested that Tommy should be given a token job at one of the local coal pits. To all intents and purposes, this would make him a miner, and be exempt from National Service duty. However, Tommy put a stop to the plan when he heard about it, and off he went to serve his country, becoming 22366853 Gunner Taylor T. of the Royal Artillery.

The Army brought out the best in him. Their rigorous training methods helped to develop him not only physically, but mentally as well. He starred for his regimental team and was selected to play for the Army in a team which included some very well-known players; John Charles, Mel Charles, Geoff Twentyman, Dennis Viollet, Jack Parry, Johnny Anderson, to name but a few. With players of this quality around him, Tommy could only improve – and he did! He was stationed in Tonfirnan, in North Wales, when Barnsley called him up to play his first game in league football. In October 1950, he played at inside-right in a game at Oakwell, against Grimsby Town. He did not score in the game, but his all action play was a huge contributory factor to centre forward Cec McCormack scoring a hat-trick. The Barnsley fans immediately took to Tommy, and he became a firm favourite. Two weeks after his debut game, he was to score his own first ever hat-trick in the Football League in a 7-0 victory over Queens Park Rangers.

After he had made his debut in the Barnsley first team, the goals began to flow. Being a local boy, Taylor was blissfully happy playing for his home town team. Everybody knew him, he could live at home, and he was able to stay around his close circle of friends. But as the goals flowed, so his reputation was enhanced, and scouts from the top First Division clubs began to be seen at Oakwell, Barnsley's home ground, in large numbers. It did not faze him, and he had no intentions of moving on — he was happy. Talking about this part of his career a few years on, he was to say in an interview with the *Manchester Evening Chronicle*:

I loved the club, the staff, everything about the place. My girlfriend was a Barnsley lass, and all my family lived in Smithies. Although the club could have been said to have been struggling, I certainly had no intention of leaving a sinking ship. I knew that the club needed money, but I was hoping that getting it would not be at my expense.

Manchester United at this time was in a period of rebuilding after their First Division Championship win in season 1951-52. A lot of that team was on the wrong side of thirty years of age, and United were having trouble finding a goal scoring centre forward. Jack Rowley had moved out to outside left, and Roger Byrne had moved to left full-back. Busby had experimented with playing John Aston Senior in the pivotal forward position, but this could only ever be considered to be a short term project. Eddie Lewis filled the spot for a dozen or so games and wasn't unsuccessful in that he found the net six times. However, the lad lacked that little bit of pace, and he was still young and raw. In the reserves, United were also experimenting with playing Bill Foulkes at centre forward and he was having quite a time. Bill hit the net regularly, and in one reserve game up at St. James's Park in Newcastle, he scored four times! Busby was about to give Foulkes his head in the first team but an untimely ankle injury put paid to that plan. So in March 1953, he decided to take the plunge in the transfer market.

For the previous seven months, both Busby and Jimmy Murphy went to watch Taylor closely at Barnsley's matches. Both knew that there was a bevy of First Division clubs watching this exciting, athletic, young centre forward. On Murphy's last visit to the Oakwell, he informed Busby that there had been more Managers, Chairmen, and Scouts from other clubs in attendance, that he thought that there had been a general meeting of the Football League. Busby decided to strike. Both he and Murphy made contact with the Barnsley chairman Joe Richards and were allowed to speak to Taylor. Richards warned them that they would have a hard job persuading Taylor to move. Barnsley could never have been said to have been a rich club and Richards and his Board desperately needed a big fee to ease the financial situation at Oakwell.

Once Jimmy and Matt were able to talk with Taylor, they found that one of their biggest problems was trying to convince the boy that he was good enough to play in the First Division. He was such a modest young man. It was the charm and the charisma of Matt Busby which eventually turned the tide as he outlined the future plan that he had for Manchester United. Busby sold him on the prospect of being part of a very young team, and a club full of home grown young players – one of them, Mark Jones, also hailing from the Wombwell area of Barnsley. Jimmy Murphy convinced him that should he join United, the sky was the limit as to what he could achieve on the football field:

"They will be world beaters and so will you when you join us. Look, you can't be responsible for the plight that Barnsley is in. It's not your fault. Besides, you are much too good a player to be playing in the Third Division."

Busby sold Manchester United to Tommy with not only his charm, but his persona as well. It is well documented that he pulled off a coup in beating some twenty other chasing clubs for Taylor's signature. Taylor realized:

"I quickly realized after talking to Mr. Busby and Mr. Murphy that it was in everybody's benefit if I moved, and so I chose Manchester United. Firstly, Manchester was just a short distance from Barnsley, and secondly, they had an unenviable record in post-war football. I knew that I would get absolutely first class coaching there under the guidance of both of these great men."

But the mark of Busby's managerial qualities also came out in the finalizing of Taylor's move. Barnsley would not settle for less than £30,000, which in 1953 was an astronomical figure. The British transfer record at that time was for inside-forward Jackie Sewell who had moved in 1951 from Notts County to Sheffield Wednesday for a fee of £35,000. Busby did not want to burden young Taylor as being a *'£30,000 player'*, so taking out his wallet, he pulled from it a one pound note and handed it to Lil Wilby, the lady who had been serving up the teas in the boardroom. The transfer went ahead for the agreed sum of £29,999 and finally, Taylor's signature was secured and he became a Manchester United player on 4 March, 1953.

He moved over to Manchester and was placed into digs at Mrs. Watson's at 5, Birch Avenue, in Old Trafford. It was just a five minute walk from the Old Trafford ground. Sharing those digs with him, along with other players, was Mark Jones and David Pegg, both staunch Yorkshiremen. It was the beginning of a strong friendship that would only end for all three at the end of a snow filled Munich runway just less than five years ahead. Young David had made his debut for United in the December of 1952 away at Middlesborough, and he had begun to make the outside left position in the team his own. Mark had made his debut some three years earlier in 1950, but was struggling to displace the consistent Allenby Chilton in the first team, so his appearances were few and far between.

On Saturday, 7 March, 1953, in front of 52,590 fans at Old Trafford, Tommy Taylor made his debut in the red shirt of Manchester United, against their Lancashire rivals from Deepdale, Preston North End. It is interesting to look at the team that lined up that afternoon;

Crompton; Aston (Snr), Byrne; Carey, Chilton, Cockburn; Berry, Rowley, Taylor, Pearson, Pegg.

Seven members of that team were over thirty years of age! However, it was a great introduction for the young Yorkshireman as he scored twice. His new friend Pegg scored twice, and the 'Gunner' Jack Rowley, completed a 5-2 rout for United. The *Manchester Evening News* reported his debut as follows:

Tommy Taylor's story book debut..... He deserves a huge slice of credit for the way he overcame the psychological handicap of having to look, think, and reacts like a player worthy of that £30,000 transfer label. After his bullet-speed header brought him his first goal —he deserves great praise.

George Follows (who was to die alongside Taylor at Munich) was chief football writer for the *Daily Herald* and covered Manchester United's matches. His headline the following Monday morning read:

Tommy Taylor has the Lawton Look. He then went on to write;

Enter the shy and smiling executioner, Tommy Taylor. The home-sweet-home boy from Barnsley, kisses all around from his family afterwards, is deadly in the penalty box. And Manchester United have bought a full £30,000 worth of goal filled footballer, perhaps more. He looks a little like Trevor Ford, a little like Jack Rowley, and in his ruthless execution near goal, he is a lot like Tommy Lawton.

For the United fans of this era, it was the beginning of the club's ascendancy to the summit of the football ladder. They were exciting times. The addition of Taylor was very instrumental to the team that was beginning to evolve. One by one Busby introduced his youngsters. Wood in goal; Bill Foulkes at right back; first Jeff Whitefoot and then Eddie Colman at right half; Mark Jones at centre half; Duncan Edwards at left half; Jackie Blanchflower and then Billy Whelan at inside right; Dennis Viollett at inside left. It took two years from Taylor's signing before the team really gelled, but once it did, they took British football by storm.

Taylor was a big strong, hard running forward who did not exactly fill the common perception of the normal barnstorming centre forward of those days. He had great movement, and real pace. For a big man he also had tremendous grace, and he moved wide to both the left and right flanks, instead of ploughing the proverbial furrow down the middle of the pitch. He had two great feet and could really hit a ball with venom with either. In the air, in my opinion he was the greatest header of a ball that I have seen. He had a prodigious leap and he seemed to hang in the air, but he still got tremendous force behind the ball when he connected with it. I heard him tell that as a young boy, he used to practice standing jumps. There was a small brick

Tommy Taylor trains alone at a deserted Old Trafford in 1956. In the background is the original Stretford End – a far cry to what it is today. Also notice that despite the heavy waterlogged pitch, Tommy's training footwear is nothing more than plimsols!

wall alongside a church, close to where he lived in Barnsley, and he was eventually able to leap over it from a standing position. His timing was impeccable, and to see him hurtling across the goal area to meet either a cross, free kick, or corner kick, was one of football's joys. He had the ideal temperament – never let foul play get to him, and I saw him take a lot of stick from some of the better known defenders of his time. But he never retaliated, he just got up, got on with the game, and did what he did best – stuck the ball in the back of the opponent's net. And boy, when he did – did that smile light up the stadiums.

George Follows was a journalist who wrote for the *Daily Herald*, a national morning newspaper of that time. It was George who christened Tommy *The Smiling Executioner* – so apt for the big man. He really was a centre-half's nightmare because he would drag them all over the place and create so much space through the middle for the other forwards to capitalize on. He had the perfect foil in Dennis Viollet, and Dennis profited from so many balls knocked down to his feet by big Tom.

Just two months after joining United, Tommy became an international player. England embarked upon a South American tour in May 1953, and on 17th of that month, in Buenos Aries, Tommy debuted against Argentina in front of 91, 397 fans in a match that lasted just twenty three minutes, and had to be abandoned because of torrential rain. Seven days later, and on that same tour, he appeared against Chile, in the capital Santiago, and scored the opening goal in a 2-1 England win. A week later in Montevideo, Uruguay, he scored once again when the Uruguayans defeated England 2-1. It's interesting to note that the Referee in all three of those tour games was none other than Arthur Ellis, the Yorkshire man – yes, the same guy who compered the BBC Television programme, *It's a Knockout*.

Tommy embraced the Manchester United family, just as that family embraced him. He was a fun boy with a perpetual smile. He never let the success that he found ever go to his head. Certainly, I don't think that there was ever a bigger catch for the ladies than Tommy, but he had

The Manchester United players pictured at Manchester Town Hall after clinching the Division One Championship in 1956. The players are; back row left to right; Dennis Viollet, Tommy Taylor, Roger Byrne and Johnny Berry, holding the trophy; Mark Jones, Ian Greaves. Front Row left to right; Duncan Edwards, John Doherty, Ray Wood, David Pegg, Eddie Colman.

a local girl friend back home in Barnsley, and she traveled over the Pennines to be with him of a weekend. Both he and David Pegg embraced Bobby Charlton into their friendship and they were seen around together a lot. They used to love going into the local parks during the afternoon and watched the kids playing football. They liked nothing better of an evening than to walk into Manchester city centre (yes, I did say walk because they said that going on the bus was boring!) to go to the cinema. They were just every day, down to earth, boy-next-door type of lads. No pretensions, no heads in the clouds. Tommy and David Pegg both had broad Yorkshire accents, and stood a lot of mickey taking from the other lads. But they both took it in good nature, and certainly gave back as good as they got.

Two games from Tommy's career stand out in my memory. The first was an international game at Wembley on 9 May 1956, against Brazil. Tommy led the Brazilian defence a merry dance that afternoon and they couldn't cope with him. He was in the thick of the game from the very first minute. He scored twice; one a rasping left foot drive in the opening minutes, and the second, a thumping header that left Gylmar, the Brazilian 'keeper flat footed. England won the game by 4-2 and it was also a game in which they missed two penalties – Tommy's Manchester United team mate and captain, Roger Byrne, being one of the culprits. His strong running and aerial prowess caused the Brazilians all sorts of problems and they just had no answer to him. Two years later, with the nucleus of the team that turned out on that May afternoon, Brazil was World Champions.

The second game, and for me, probably his finest game in a Manchester United shirt, came on 6 February1957, at Maine Road, against the Spanish Champions, Bilbao, in the return leg of United's first ever European Cup quarter-final. Down 3-5 from the first leg, United were really up against it. Directly opposing Taylor that evening was probably one of the finest centre halves in world football at that time – Jesus Garay. Tommy ran his socks off that night, and inspired by the roars of the crowd, put in a superlative performance. He drifted, right, he drifted left, he was always there to receive the ball from defenders under pressure – no ball out of defence was a lost cause. He dragged Garay into positions he should never have been.

Tommy scored the second goal that night, but during the last fifteen minutes, as the United player's exertions began to take their toll, tiredness started to become a factor. They were defending the eighteen yards area when a cross from the left was aimed in and Mark Jones towered above all and thundered a headed clearance away, and out to the right hand side. For the umpteenth time that night, big Tommy was after it, followed by his shadow, Garay. He collected the ball on the half way line, turned, and there was Garay showing him the touchline. Tommy held the ball inviting the tackle, but Garay was having none of it. They jockeyed each other down that touchline, and Garay looked quite comfortable. Big Tom started to take the ball towards the big Spanish centre half, just about in line with the eighteen yards line. He showed Garay the ball and then a quick dip of his left shoulder and movement towards the left and Garay pounced flying towards the ball. Alas, it wasn't there! Tommy pulled the ball back onto his right foot and was away a yard. Looking up he released a cross of stunning quality aiming and landing the ball just on or around the penalty spot - normally the area where he himself would be. But of all the big lads United had, not one of them was there - instead, the smallest man in United's team, little Johnny Berry was haring in at full speed. He met the ball full on the volley with his right foot and crashed the ball into the back of the net - it sped in like the speed of a bullet.

Maine Road really did erupt as did the United players. I had never seen the big Duncan Edwards jump and cavort about like he did at that moment, nor had I ever seen Roger Byrne so emotional – but none of them forgot the lad who had set it up. That was Tommy Taylor, prolific goal scorer that he was, he had unselfishness about him that few players had. He covered acres that night, and after the game, Gray was magnificent in defeat, claiming that Taylor was the best centre forward he had ever played against.

He may have been a star, an established international player, but he never forgot where he came from. He had time for the fans but most of all, time for the kids. You would always see him walking up Warwick Road and off to his digs in Greatstone Road, in Stretford, after home games. Tommy had a great relationship with the press and in particular Henry Rose of the *Daily Express*. Henry was Tommy's biggest critic, and had once stated that in a match against Billy Wright and his Wolves team, that if Taylor scored, he'd walk back to the *Express* offices in Ancoats, barefoot. Tommy scored twice that afternoon and dear old Henry kept his promise –

followed by a huge posse of kids — it was like watching the Pied Piper! He loved the banter with the fans, loved the camaraderie, loved his club and loved football. Never in the news for the wrong reasons, he was just simply a lovely, lovely, person.

I will leave the last word to his dear friend Harold 'Dicky' Bird, the former cricket Test Match umpire, when unveiling a Blue Heritage Plaque on the wall of his former digs at number 22, Greatstone Road, Old Trafford in June, 2011:

"Tommy was my friend. We were brought up together in Barnsley in a little place called Smithies. We went to the same school, Burton Road primary, and then Raley Secondary Modern School. We both played for the school team, he played centre forward and I played inside right to him. At school, Tommy's nickname was "Tucker" Taylor. I think that he got that label because he tucked the goals away.

Both of our fathers were close friends, having worked at the same coal face down the pit. At weekends they would enjoy a pint together, and they would argue with each other as to who was the best player, Tommy or me! Both of our fathers agreed that neither of us would ever go down the mines to work, and it gave them both a tremendous satisfaction when Tommy signed for Barnsley FC, and I signed for Yorkshire Cricket Club. That's how it all started for us both.

We used to practice for hours together just the two of us. Tommy, from a standing start could jump over a garden gate. He could also jump on top of a snooker table as well from a standing position. When we were playing matches together, he always wanted me to cross the ball at head height for him so that he could rise and head the ball. He had this remarkable gift of being able to rise and hang in the air. I am convinced to this day, that this gift made him the best header of a ball that the game of football has seen.

I've seen four defenders marking him in the box, waiting for the ball coming in high, and though being pulled and tugged he has left his markers flat-footed as he suddenly took off in the air. It was if he was on a cushion of air or something. Majestic. On top of that he had pace, he had two very good feet, and he was tremendous in getting himself into the right positions. And his bravery knew no bounds. Really, he had everything! Which is why, if the newspaper reports were accurate, Real Madrid were prepared to pay United £70,000 for his transfer whilst at the same time, the Italian clubs were bidding between £55,000 and £65,000, for his services.

Tommy was in these digs next to the Lancashire Cricket Ground after he signed for Manchester United. He loved cricket and spent a lot of time at Old Trafford cricket ground. He loved it also when Yorkshire played there against Lancashire and he would always come up to the dressing room to visit me. Though he was idolized in Manchester, there was not the slightest sign of any big headedness about my old school friend. If anything, he was rather shy. He was very proud of his roots, a typical, warm hearted Yorkshire lad.

Tommy, I know that you will be in heaven mate, because you were a good and honest man. You gave millions of people a lot of pleasure. You were the greatest centre forward that I ever saw and I have seen *them all from Tommy Lawton to Alan Shearer. Your achievements are all there in the record books for everybody to see. What would you have achieved if you had not lost your life so tragically in the Munich Air Disaster of 1958?*

I always talk about you whenever football is mentioned, no matter what company I am with. It only seems like yesterday that we were both young kids practicing both football and cricket on broken glass, in fields, and on any old rough ground. I think that it gave us both the will and determination to succeed in both our chosen professions. They were poor, but oh! So happy days all those years ago.

I am so proud and honoured that Tommy was my friend."

Rest on in Peace Tom – you gave us so much to remember.

Tommy Taylor played a total of 191 games in all competitions for Manchester United scoring 131 goals.

He was capped 18 times for England and scored 16 goals.

Dennis Viollet – The Man for All Seasons

Dennis Sydney Viollet was born in Fallowfield, Manchester on 20 September, 1932. He lived, and went to school, in close proximity to Manchester City's famous old stadium, Maine Road. As he grew up through the war years, and then the immediate post war years, he became a prolific schoolboy footballer. His progression from school team to Area team, and on to the Manchester Boys team, brought him to the attention of first the Lancashire County Schoolboy selectors, and after playing in the North versus South schoolboy's game, to the England Schoolboy selectors. He was a young player that had enormous potential to progress to the professional game, and during the six times that he played for England Schoolboys, there was no shortage of football scouts from England's top teams sat there watching him perform with a hope that they could persuade him to sign for their club.

The opinion of that time was that despite the bevy of League clubs who were chasing his signature, he would sign for Manchester City. However, not for the first time the Maine Road club took things for granted and a unique player would slip from their grasp and join their arch rivals. Frank Swift, the legendary England and Manchester City goalkeeper had recommended to his club that they should go all-out and sign this talented youngster. He thought that his advice was being heeded, but one afternoon he bumped into Dennis' father and asked him if the club had been in touch. He was staggered when Mr. Viollet told him that they had not.

Swift was angry and went straight over to Maine Road and made arrangements for the City officials to meet with Dennis and his father. On the appointed day and time, Dennis and his father turned up at Maine Road, and were told to sit down and wait until the club officials were ready to see them. Two hours passed and they were still waiting. Mr. Viollet became annoyed and asked the receptionist what the delay was. He was told that the officials were still not ready to see him and his boy. Another hour passed and when he enquired again, he was told that the officials had gone out on other appointments and would not be back until later on. Mr. Viollet lost his temper after being kept waiting without an apology, or an explanation. He marched Dennis out of Maine Road immediately.

When Frank Swift got to know what had happened, he was extremely angry, and let his bosses at Maine Road know about it. The day after the scheduled meeting at Maine Road, Matt Busby turned up on the Viollet's front doorstep in Fallowfield. He charmed Dennis' parents and left them to think over the offer he had made to them about Dennis joining Manchester United. In the next few days the family received visits from Jimmy Murphy, Bert Whalley, and

Joe Armstrong. Eventually, Dennis parents turned to big Frank Swift and asked about the offer from Manchester United. Unhesitatingly Swift told them:

"I played with Matt Busby and he is a wonderful fellow. You won't find a better manager or a better club."

Swift's advice closed the deal, and just a few days later, on 1 September, 1949, Dennis was to become one of the very first *Busby Babes*. He was signed on by Joe Armstrong, at the GPO offices in Central Manchester, where Armstrong worked as a telephone engineer.

For the next few years he played for the junior and A and B teams where his progress was monitored under the watchful eyes of Jimmy Murphy, and Bert Whalley. Dennis watched as more and more talented youngsters joined the Manchester United playing staff. In an interview with my very good friend Brian Hughes MBE, Dennis was to say:

"Jimmy Murphy and Bert Whalley were like father figures to us young players. We had some great young players at the club in the early fifties and every close season they would sign more schoolboy internationals. The competition for places in the team was tough, extremely tough. Matt Busby would be seen now and again training with the youngsters or the first team, but he was very tied up with the running of the club so the main coaching was done by Jimmy and Bert. They would spend hours with bags of patience and understanding with us kids. Bert was a kindly uncle whereas Jimmy could be gruff, strict, and had a no-nonsense approach. He would play hell with us when he thought that we needed it, then, he would give us a little bit of sugar. By that I mean that he would put his arm around your shoulder and quietly explain what he wanted you to do.

In 1952, the FA Youth Cup began but I was slightly too old to play in this competition. I was gutted because it was a great platform from which to get noticed and a great many of United's first team players came through from that competition. Jimmy Murphy made me the footballer I later became. He was the one who would tell Matt Busby when a young player was ready for a run out in the first team. He talked sense, and everything that he told you was aimed to make you professional. He taught me that football had always been, and should always be, a game to be enjoyed. He also believed that young players would improve by simply listening to older, more experienced players."

Dennis' performances were good and by 1951-52 he had become something of regular in the United reserve team. It was difficult for him to break into the first team as Stan Pearson, and Johnny Downie, United's inside forwards, were on top form in a season which saw Manchester United lift the First Division Championship for the first time since 1911. However, that championship winning team was getting old, and the following season Busby experimented with different players – and especially after Tommy Taylor was signed and he tried to find the perfect foil for him. Frank Clempson, Eddie Lewis, and particularly Jack Rowley, were all tried as inside forwards.

On 11 April 1953, at St. James' Park, Newcastle, Dennis Viollet made his first team debut. It was also a significant day for another young man who was to play a major part in Manchester United's history some years later.... Les Olive. Les, who went on to become the Manchester United Club Secretary immediately after Munich, made the first of his only two appearances ever, in the first team. It was a Manchester United team that had a real unfamiliar look about it and read; Olive; McNulty, Byrne; Carey, Chilton, Whitefoot; Viollet, Pearson, Aston, Taylor and Rowley.

United won the game by 2-1 with Tommy Taylor scoring both goals.

In that same interview with Brian Hughes MBE, Dennis recalled:

"When I made my debut at Newcastle United, Jimmy was as pleased as punch for me, and his enthusiasm at my promotion was genuine."

The following week the very same team earned a 2-2 draw against West Bromwich Albion and Dennis was able to celebrate after scoring one of United's goals – the first of many in his career. He was left out of the next game, a home league fixture against Liverpool which was won 3-1 at Old Trafford, but he returned for the last game of the 1952-53 season which was away at Middlesborough, and United crashed to a 5-0 defeat. He had played in three of the last four games of that season, and he had proved to himself that he could play at that level.

The following season, 1953-54 was to be Dennis Viollet's breakthrough season. He played in a couple of games earlier on, but then on October 31st 1953, in the famous game at Leeds Road, Huddersfield, when Alf Clarke christened the team *Busby's Bouncing Babes,* he was selected along with several other youngsters notably, Edwards, and Blanchflower. From that moment on, he became first choice inside-left, and he forged a tremendous partnership with Tommy Taylor, one that was to produce a phenomenal number of goals between them. Their understanding became telepathic, and they complimented each other so well. They could read each other's play and Dennis would profit from the many times big Taylor would hang in the air, and nonchalantly nod the ball down into the space into which Viollet would ghost into. On the reverse side, Dennis was adept at slipping quick through balls between the opposing defenders which would set Taylor free, and it was not very often that he missed.

Dennis played a huge part in helping the *Babes* secure their first, First Division title in 1955-56, and the following year, 1956-57, he was absolutely outstanding and it was certainly a travesty that he was not capped for England at that time. United had gone into Europe and

Dennis Viollet, on the right, and skipper Roger Byrne return back up the player's tunnel at Old Trafford on 15 January 1958, after defeating Red Star Belgrade 2-1 in their European Cup Quarter Final first leg.

again his performances and goal scoring feats were tremendous. Unfortunately for him, he picked up a groin injury towards the end of that 1956-57 season, and that was to cost him dearly. He played in a number of games when he wasn't fully fit and he missed a number of games towards the end of that season. He was back for the last two league games but he was still struggling and Busby decided to leave him out of the FA Cup Final line up against Aston Villa at Wembley, preferring to play the young Bobby Charlton. It was devastating for him.

The following season between late October and early December, he missed nine games because the injury flared up again. He came back against Birmingham City on 7 December, and between that date and the game in Belgrade against Red Star on February 5th 1958, he scored fourteen goals in thirteen games. Of course then came Munich and Dennis received some bad head injuries. He did return to first team duty in late April of 1958 in the hope of helping United lift the FA Cup. He played in two games prior to the Final and it was obvious that he still needed time. However Jimmy Murphy did select him to play in the Final against Bolton Wanderers, but Dennis did not function so well and the same could be said for the rest of the team. The emotion, and time, had caught up with them.

After the season of 1957-58 finished, Dennis went away and recharged his batteries. Although he was capped for England, and broke the club scoring record, he still was not the player he was before the accident. My good friend John White recalls:

"There have been so many players in my 55 years of watching Manchester United, some great, some not so great. Memories can fade quite quickly, some linger for a time and then fade away, but always with players of quality, the memory seemingly is as fresh today as it was those many years ago. Dennis Viollet fell into the quality category, for he was a player with presence and you NEVER forget the players that have that!

Make no mistake about it - for those of you who unlucky enough never to see him play, Dennis Viollet was a player. His movement was not unlike that of our other Denis, Denis Law. Like Law, he too was only 5'9" and 10 stone wringing wet. He was quick was Dennis, not just physically, but also in his thinking and over that vital first couple of yards. He was a natural goal scorer of course and natural goal scorers 'see' situations that others can't spot. He could read the game - the ebb and flow and pattern of it - and then decide where he HAD to be at the crucial moment. That just can't be taught - you've either got it or you haven't. If you haven't got it, then you can never acquire it – it's a born-with thing. Dennis had it in abundance. He was mercurial.

Over the years since the crash I have often thought what would have become of Manchester United had the crash never been. We would I'm certain have succeeded to the throne of European football held by that great but ageing Real Madrid side who dominated the European Cup in the 50's. Not a doubt in my mind about that. Furthermore, the English players coming through Matt's sides would have solidly served England's World Cup bids in '58 and again in '62. Maybe England might have won the World Cup before '66. But if's, butt's, and maybe's can't disguise the fact that it was we United fans that suffered the greatest loss.

I have also spent a lot of time thinking about how good a player Dennis Violet might have become had Munich never happened. He would have become something very special. I'm convinced of that. He was only just turned 24 by the time of the Munich crash and the whole side were beginning to hum like a well-oiled machine. There maybe would never have been any need for the signing of our other great Denis.

Some of the boys of 58 lost their careers as a result of the crash. It wasn't so with Dennis but I have always felt he lost something special too. He lost the potential or the desire for true greatness that would and should have been his. He like other survivors played on through the dark days that followed Munich. The burden wasn't only that United's make-shift side was struggling to find anything like a rhythm. Dennis and Bobby along with Albert Scanlon, Harry Gregg, Billy Foulkes and Kenny Morgans had to bear the burden - and the guilt - of having survived!! Jackie Blanchflower and Johnny Berry had their careers finished by the crash-induced injuries. Ray Wood hardly ever stood between the sticks again for United.

To have seen United pre-Munich, and then to see them during 59, 60, and 61, was a very sad experience. For me, to see these lads trying to re-launch our club's hopes and dreams and to re-ignite that fire of greatness - at the same time as each of them had to have been living and battling through the most horrible personal nightmare - was a shockingly destructive experience. It was for me the hidden tragedy resulting from Munich, and so many promising young careers were certainly destroyed by them being forced to grow much before their time.

Like a great number of United fans, I was both shocked and saddened to hear that Dennis was to leave Old Trafford in January 1962. Perhaps the arrival of David Herd and the imminent arrival of Denis Law were factors in Matt Busby's decision to sell Dennis to Stoke City – who knows?

It was never made clear but on he went on to a very successful second career with Stoke City – a club who to their eternal credit, gave Dennis a testimonial after his 5 years , 200 + appearances, 66 goals from midfield for the Potters , a 2nd division winner's medal and a League cup runner's –up medal in '64. – Which Dennis delivered - playing like a good old pro - from midfield!!

Like all great goal-scorers, he would get in amongst the flailing feet without regard to his own safety in pursuit of netting THE critical goal. Although never a big man as I've said, he was like many other dedicated *goal-scorers, brave beyond the call of duty. He was called upon to demonstrate that bravery in his final challenge - the one against brain cancer in the States where he made his home in Jacksonville Florida."*

How good was he? Well, if I was asked to compare any modern day player with Dennis Viollet, then there is only one – and that one would be Paul Scholes. Paul reminded me so much of Dennis – unselfish, wily, cunning, being difficult for defenders to pick up, always seeing the bigger picture, having the ability to pick out the killer pass, and being lethal in front of goal. However, unlike Scholes, Viollet never ever gave the referee an excuse to pull out his notebook and pencil. Both had similar temperaments – nothing fazed them at all. Like Paul, Dennis shunned the press and the limelight - he just went to work, did his job, and slipped away afterwards.

If I had to pick a couple of games out of the 293 which he played for United to remember him by, then I would select the game against Anderlecht on 26 September, 1957, when he scored four goals in a 10-0 blitz of the Belgian champions, Anderlecht RSC. That total could have been larger, because he spent much of the last fifteen minutes of the game trying to tee a goal up for David Pegg, the only forward not to score on that memorable night.

The other game would again be in that same season and that first European campaign, when United played the Spanish champions, Bilbao at Maine Road on 6 February, 1957. United were down 5-3 from the first leg, and Dennis worked his socks off that night, fetching and carrying, and trying to get that all important first goal. He had one goal dubiously disallowed for offside, but just before half-time he suddenly appeared ghosting into the box and fired home. That was the lift that

the team needed, and in the second half he was so conspicuous with his supply of the ball to the United wingmen, and Tommy Taylor. It built pressure on the Spaniards, and eventually they cracked as United scored two more goals and went through 6-5 on aggregate.

Dennis Viollet on the left, talks to a young Bobby Charlton in the Manchester United dressing room after a training session in 1960.

149

Dennis Viollet poses for the camera in the England World Cup winning team dressing room prior to his testimonial game at the Victoria Ground in Stoke in 1966. The England players from left to right are; Geoff Hurst, Gordon Banks, Johnny Byrne, Tony Allen, John Fantham, Bobby Moore, George Eastham, Bobby Charlton, Jimmy Armfield, Nobby Stiles and Martin Peters.

It was a shock for the United fans when he was allowed to leave the club in 1962 – he had been at Old Trafford since leaving school in 1948. But Denis being Denis, he hid his disappointment and went off to Stoke City, and he enjoyed five memorable years at the Victoria Grounds. Stoke City were then in the Second Division, but in his second season with the *Potters*, he helped them gain promotion back to the top flight. Over the next few years, the Stoke City manager, Tony Waddington assembled an array of ageing stars for his team – Stanley Mathews, Jimmy McIlroy, Roy Vernon, Jackie Mudie, Peter Dobing, Eddie Clamp, Ron Stuart, Maurice Setters to name but a few. The Stoke City dressing room was a fun place to be. For Waddington, those old stars had so much experience and they gave him the time to bring his younger players through.

There was a human side to Dennis and there are so many tales to tell about him. He touched the lives of everybody he met and they were far better for the experience. Once, when he found himself at Manchester Airport late on a Saturday evening, as he was about to leave he spotted a young boy bedding down for the night on the seating there. There was nobody about, and all flights had departed for that day. Dennis went across and spoke to the young man and found out that he was a United fan making his way back to Ireland, but had missed his flight and had to wait until the Sunday morning until he could continue his journey. Dennis did no more, took the lad home, billeted and fed him, and got him back to the airport the following morning. You could not imagine anything like that happening today.

In 1967, when his time was up at Stoke City they gave him a testimonial game which was played against England's World Cup team. Dennis had an old school friend named Alan Wallace.

They had played together in the same school team back in the late '40's, and Dennis told him: *"You were there at the start of my soccer career, and I would like you to be there at the end of it."*

Alan recalled:

"I was delighted to be invited to Dennis' testimonial. He wrote me a letter telling me that he was delighted I had accepted the invitation to be at the game. He took me into the England dressing room and introduced me to every one of the players. He also took me into the Stoke City dressing room and did the same thing. He treated me like a king."

Dennis gave Alan his fullest attention, introducing him to people and showing him the same warm friendship that was shown to the other more famous personalities present.

Dennis befriended Stoke player Bill Asprey. Asprey grew up in Dudley, the same home town as Duncan Edwards. Through Duncan, he got to know a lot of the United players of that time, and he remembered:

"The first time that I actually met Dennis was one Saturday night in the Continental Club, in Manchester. Dennis and Bobby Charlton were on stage singing a duet. It was great! Tommy Taylor also liked a sing along as well. All those lads from the 'Babes' were characters and wonderful company. Those nights were unforgettable occasions.

Dennis was a lovely fellow — down-to-earth, always ready for a bit of fun. As a player his technique was first class and his reading of situations was uncanny. I never ever saw him in trouble with a referee. He relied on his skill and brilliant football brain. I never once in my career ever heard anybody speak derogatory of Dennis — a great footballer, a tremendous friend, and a wonderful human being."

Dennis Smith the old Stoke centre half had just started his managerial career and was managing Oxford United. At an away fixture, after the game was over, he was seen and heard to be ushering his players out of the dressing room and onto the team coach as he was in a hurry to get away. Smith was stopped by a person who went on to say how much he had admired Smith as a player. The man then mentioned Dennis Viollet. The young Oxford manager stopped and told him, *"I was in awe of Dennis Viollet"*, and he then proceeded to talk to the man for over half an hour about him.

The late Sir Stanley Mathews was to say:

"There were moments in games when the ball came to Dennis and it was if a spotlight had fallen on him and every other player was in his shadow. Your eyes were drawn to him as he engineered, first space to work in, then proceeded to conjure up his own special brand of magic. Only when the ball had left Dennis' feet

151

did you see the opening as the ball glided across the turf just in front of one of our galloping forwards for the course of the game to be altered. Short pass, long pass, low pass, high pass, it mattered not one jot. Whatever it was, it was always the right pass when it came from Dennis."

In an interview with Roger Day from BBC Radio Kent, the late Albert Scanlon, Dennis' left wing partner in so many games, had this to say when talking about the *Busby Babes:*

"The best footballer that was at the club, and who had everything, was a young man named Dennis Viollet. Dennis Viollet was magnificent. He was about five feet nine inches tall and weighed ten stones, and was all muscle and bone. He would go where others feared to tread and that was in the penalty box — he was lethal. When he came back after the accident, he was absolutely phenomenal and scored more than thirty League goals. His record still stands today He really was such an outstanding player."

After leaving Stoke City, Dennis moved to the USA and the North American Soccer League. He joined the Baltimore Bays and he stayed for just a year. When he returned to UK he turned his hand to coaching and had stints at both Witton Albion, and Preston North End. In 1972 Dennis moved back to the USA and Baltimore Bays again, moving with them to Washington DC when they became the Washington Diplomats. In 1978, Noel Cantwell, the former Manchester United captain, took over as head coach at the New England Tea Men.

Noel was to recall:

"I hadn't seen Dennis for a few years. The next time I met up with him was when I had been offered the job with the New England Tea Men in Boston. Phil Woosnam whom I had known at West Ham and was one of the first British coaches to go to America, advised me to take it. I knew nothing about American soccer, so I thought to myself; "who can I get to help me?" I thought of Dennis, got in touch with him, and he accepted the position of assistant coach. We got things moving in Boston and won our Eastern Division, and I was named Coach of the Year. The reality was that Dennis did as much coaching as I did, so really we were both Coaches of the Year. He was brilliant in every respect. Our families became very close and spent a number of years together in the States. It was the most enjoyable relationship of my life, a lovely man with a beautiful loving family."

The Tea Men were moved to Jacksonville, in Florida, and in 1983, Dennis was appointed Head Coach when the team joined the American Soccer League. The team won Jacksonville's first, and only, professional sports championship. He was then appointed as Staff Coach to the Florida Youth Soccer Association. He progressed the game at all levels. He moved the game into the local colleges and University, and took control of both the men's and women's programmes at

Jacksonville University. His contribution to the development of the game in the United States cannot be questioned and it is a story that needs telling.

Dennis Viollet was a player who once seen, could never be forgotten. He was one of those players who were blessed with style. He did not run, he glided. He did not strike the ball, he stroked it. He was an engaging companion who bore the trauma of Munich with fortitude and no little humour. In the history of Manchester United he tends to be overlooked, engulfed by the shadows of Byrne, Edwards, Taylor, Charlton, Law, Best, Robson, Keane, and Cantona. His partnership with Tommy Taylor was as subtle as it was effective. Taylor was the spearhead, powerful in the air, quick over the ground; Dennis lurking in space, prospered from the confusion his team-mate created. Without doubt the two of them formed the most potent striking partnership that I have ever seen in a lifetime of watching football. Add to those two, the scoring exploits of the young Irishman, Liam Whelan, and there is no doubt in my mind that those three were Manchester United's original *Trinity*. Sadly, there are no statues or other recognizable memorabilia around Old Trafford today that would reinforce this opinion.

No bigger accolade can be given to Dennis Viollet than in a story recalled by his former team mate and great friend, Noel Cantwell:

"I remember sitting with Denis Law and Matt Busby in a restaurant. Dennis had moved on to Stoke and we were discussing the merits of certain great players to have graced Old Trafford, and Matt turned to us and said: 'I would have Dennis Viollet in my best team that has ever played for Manchester United!' That was some tribute wasn't it? Matt loved Dennis, he thought the world of him. I agreed with him because he was so easy to play with. He wasn't an individualist like Bobby. Although Bobby was a brilliant, world-class player, he would drop his shoulder and go off on one of those surging, electrifying runs, beating man after man. You never knew what he was likely to do — but you knew what Dennis would do, which is a great advantage when you're playing."

The last words are Dennis' after he retired from playing:

"No player has gained more pleasure from the great game of football than I have. But as I bow out, there is a little sadness for me. I see that the game is changing. The pattern is less colourful, and the individuals grow fewer and fewer. Football is now regimentation. Yet I have been privileged to spend the major part of my career with a club I have always considered the finest in the world — Manchester United. During those years, and after, I played with the greats like Duncan Edwards, Roger Byrne, Tommy Taylor, and the rest. I have also been thrilled to play with the illustrious Stanley Mathews, and against mighty footballers like Puskas, and di Stefano. To me these were the football kinds, ruling the game with their brilliance and overwhelming authority."

Poignantly, at just after 3.00 pm on Saturday 6 March 1999, (Kick–off time) Dennis slipped away at the age of 65.

He was inducted into the first class of the United States Soccer Hall of Fame in 2002. The annual University of North Florid-Jacksonville University football match has been contested for the *Viollet Cup* since 2001.

God bless you Dennis – sleep in Peace. Thank you for your tremendous contribution – both to my personal memories and to the cause of Manchester United over those momentous years of the 50s and early 60s.

Dennis Viollet played 293 games for Manchester United in all competitions and scored 179 goals.

He won 2 England caps scoring 1 goal.

David Pegg – The Flying Yorkshireman

David Pegg was born in the Yorkshire village of Highfields, which is situated just to the north of Doncaster, on 20 September 1935 – he shared the same birth-date as Dennis Viollet, although Viollet was three years older. Like most young boys of his age, David took to playing football and became so good at the game that by the time he was fourteen years of age, all the top English professional clubs were after his signature. He became an established English Schoolboy international during the 1950-51 season, playing in the same team as Duncan Edwards.

With his obvious talent, the Pegg family had a lot of Football League club scouts knocking on their front door, hoping to persuade them to allow David to sign for them. His Mother, Jessie, was not so sure that he should leave home to become a professional footballer. Thankfully for Manchester United, their chief scout Mr. Joe Armstrong, did a wonderful job in selling the club to David and his family, but what tipped the scales in United securing his signing, was Matt Busby's charm and charisma. Jessie was so impressed with his manner and honesty when he called at their home to speak to the family, that from that moment on, there was only ever one club that young David was going to join.

Pegg joined the ground staff at Old Trafford at the same time as Albert, and initially, with David playing at inside left, and Albert at outside left, they formed a potent left sided scoring partnership in the junior and youth teams. When the FA Youth Cup first began in 1952-53, David had already made progress through to the Reserve team even though he had only just reached his seventeenth birthday. Jimmy Murphy had also switched him from an inside forward position, to that of an out and out left-wing forward. He was probably the first of Busby's young *"Babes"* to breakthrough at first team level. On 6 December 1952, he made his first team debut in a game at Old Trafford against Middlesborough, and he was to enjoy a run of some twenty

one games during that season. He scored his first goal for the club at Roker Park, Sunderland, in a 2-2 draw in February of 1953.

Speaking to the *Manchester Evening Chronicle* shortly after his debut game, he said:

I have had some wonderful moments in my short career. To play for England boys was a rare thing, but to face Wales at the most famous

David Pegg pictured at Old Trafford prior to the start of the Manchester derby fixture with Manchester City on 31 August 1957.

stadium in the country was absolutely incredible. I can recall that time as if it was only a week ago. Given the day off school, I travelled down to London to meet the rest of the boys and officials. After booking into the hotel, and this was a treat in itself to a youngster like me, we were whisked off to another glamorous location - Highbury. I had read in the football magazines about Arsenal and the traditions of this club were something I knew about long before that first visit to train for the following day's match. We beat Wales 3-0 Jimmy Murphy always screws his face up when I remind him of this occasion, which is quite often. Behind me in the England team was a big, chunky lad, who already looked man-sized. His name was Duncan Edwards! Little did we know then that only a few years later we would be together in a championship team with Manchester United.

Edwards would appear with David in every representative game he was selected for, both as a junior, and as a senior.

What a great help it has been to get the service from this outstanding half-back, David continued. I couldn't be happier playing for the Red Devils. My biggest problem was leaving home for the first time at fifteen; still, the time passed quickly. I was an apprentice joiner for my first two years and only trained on Tuesday and Thursday evenings. After a spell in the third team and some great coaching from Jimmy Murphy, I was selected to play for the reserves in 1951. This was a wonderful opportunity and a huge step up the ladder.

About a year later, I signed as a professional, and another milestone. December 5th 1952 was the date. It was a Friday and the team sheet seemed longer than usual coming down from Matt Busby's office. When it was pinned the notice board in the dressing room, I hurried over to look. I felt disappointed - my name wasn't on the reserve team sheet - but in a split second as I noticed this, I saw I was selected for the first team. Also making his debut was another 17-year-old, inside-right Johnny Doherty, and we must have brought the team good luck.

Playing inside to David that day was the legendary Stan Pearson.

Stan was a lovely, quiet person, and he taught me a tremendous amount. So too did Johnny Aston, the former England full-back. Jimmy Murphy was also pleased as punch for me and he influenced me a great deal.

In March of 1953, Manchester United signed centre forward Tommy Taylor from Barnsley. He was placed into digs with David in Stretford, and it was the start of a friendship that would only be ended in the most tragic of circumstances. David and big Tom became inseparable! Together with Mark Jones, who was also from Barnsley, they formed a strong Yorkshire trio, and each of them was blessed with that strong Yorkshire wit and charm. David and Tom were two very good looking boys and were always so popular with the female fans. They were mischievous, and fun to be around, and both of them had a smile that could melt even the strongest of hearts! They were both single and enjoyed life to the full.

But football was their game, and with the arrival of Taylor, Jack Rowley was moved from centre forward to outside left and this cost David his place in the first team. The following season 1953-54 he started in the first three games of the season, but was only to make six more appearances at the top level after that. Early in the season Busby was still trying to find the right blend for the team and though he introduced several youngsters into the team for the game at Huddersfield on the last day of October, David was disappointed not to be one of them. The following season 1954-55 Jack Rowley was still hanging on to the left wing berth even though he was 35 years of age. By this time Albert Scanlon had also progressed and he too was knocking on the first team door. David played in four games in early 1955 but sadly, three of them ended in defeat including a 5-0 home drubbing by Manchester City. Jack Rowley's career at Old Trafford came to an end the week after that "derby" defeat when Manchester City knocked United out of the FA Cup by 2-0 in a fourth round tie at Maine Road. David was in for the next two games which ended in defeat by 4-2 at home against Wolves, and then by 3-0 at Ninian Park, to Cardiff City. After the Cardiff City game he was left out, and Albert Scanlon became the first choice.

It was in the following season that he made his breakthrough and made the left wing position his own. He had developed a strong running type of game and could run at defenders with pace, and his delivery of the ball into the penalty box set up so many goals for the other forwards. He played in thirty five league games and one FA Cup game that season, but helped the team win their first Championship. This enabled the club to enter the new European Cup competition the following season and meant that they were chasing three trophies; European Cup, First Division Championship, and FA Cup. Manchester United played fifty seven games that season, and David played in fifty three of them. Some of his performances were absolutely breathtaking, and two which I remember in particular came in the European Cup.

On 26th September 1956, in the first ever European Cup game played upon English soil, a second leg Preliminary Round tie against Anderlecht at Maine Road; David ran the Belgian side ragged. United won by the astonishing score of 10-0 that evening and David was instrumental in setting up most of the goals, even though he did not get on the score sheet himself. Later on that season, in March of 1957, in the semi-final first leg tie against Real Madrid at their magnificent Bernabeau Stadium, he played magnificently and gave the big Spanish full back Lesmes a real chasing. So much so, that for the return leg at Old Trafford, Real Madrid used a

David Pegg pictured wearing his 1957 FA Cup Final shirt.

very obscure competition rule, and signed the best right full back in Spain, Torres, for a period of fourteen days, just so that he could counter the threat of Pegg's strong running game. Although United went out of the competition at that stage, they did retain their First Division title and David picked up another winner's medal. He also appeared in the FA Cup Final at Wembley against Aston Villa, but with the injury to Ray Wood so early in the game, it disrupted United's formation and playing 10 men against 11 on the tiring Wembley surface, proved just a little too much for them.

Just two weeks after the FA Cup Final saw David's breakthrough at International level when he was capped in a World Cup Qualifying match against Eire at Dublin's Dalymont Park which finished in a 1-1 draw. Byrne, Edwards, and Taylor from United also played in that match. Sadly, it was to be David's solitary cap.

Season 1957-58 saw David play in the first twenty six matches of the season. He had scored eight goals in a forward line that on paper was doing its job. They had scored sixty five goals – 2.5 goals per game, no mean average. The defence had conceded thirty eight goals in those games, so although the team was not supposedly firing on all cylinders, their form was not that bad. They had dropped some silly points but mainly through careless individual defensive errors. On 21 December, for the game against Leicester City, everybody knew that there would be a change in goal... Harry Gregg had been brought in from Doncaster Rovers. However, at 2:30 p.m. that afternoon, when the stadium announcer spelled out the team changes, there were gasps of astonishment by the fans because three forwards who were virtually nailed on regular first team choices were left out – Berry, Whelan... and David Pegg. Sadly, we were not to see David play in the first team ever again, his final appearance being in a 1-0 defeat at Stamford Bridge on December 14th 1957.

Nobody saw those changes coming, but United were trailing Wolves by some six points in the chase for the title, and Busby explained himself by saying that he felt that the team needed freshening up... so in came eighteen years old Kenny Morgans, nineteen years old Bobby Charlton, and twenty two years old Albert Scanlon.

David went back into the reserves and began the quest to win his place back. Over the next seven weeks, the first team went undefeated in eleven games scoring thirty four goals in the process. Busby would not change a winning team. David went to Belgrade as a travelling reserve. Just before the third aborted take-off, both he and Tommy Taylor moved from their original seats to the back of the aircraft as they believed that they would be safer there. Sadly, both of these great friends were to perish in the accident.

I have lots of memories of David Pegg. Of seeing his happy smiling face emerge from the player's entrance after a game. Always ready to stand and sign autographs and pass time of day with the fans. The days spent at the Galleon swimming pool during the summer months in the close season. He got to know several of us kids and always acknowledged us. I will never forget him coming off the field in a game at Preston's Deepdale ground, at half time, on a day when torrential rain was pouring down. As he got towards the player's tunnel, he spotted me sat inside the trainer's dugout and he just burst out laughing. He was a wonderful boy, full of life and zest and inseparable from his mate Tommy Taylor. They could be seen at weekends in the local dance halls enjoying themselves... never too big to spend time chatting with supporters.

David was laid to rest in the Redhouse Cemetery close to his home village of Highfields. He was just 22 years of age – one of the youngest to perish in the tragedy. Sleep on in peace dear David, you gave this youngster so many, many happy moments to remember and cherish... you'll never be forgotten.

David Pegg played 127 times for Manchester United and scored 24 goals.

He was capped once at full international level and also won 3 caps at Under 23 level.

Albert Scanlon – Mr. Happy Go Lucky

Albert Scanlon was a thoroughbred Mancunian. He was also the nephew of former Manchester United and England left winger, Charlie Mitten. Scanlon was born in the inner city district of Hulme, just over one mile away from the Manchester city centre on October 10th 1935. Hulme was a tough district to survive in at that time and Albert attended a tough school, St. Wilfred's Catholic School. He was the typical inner city boy who spent most of his leisure time outdoors playing football with his young pals. Albert was brought up in a family that was ardent Manchester City supporters and as his abilities as a schoolboy footballer progressed, it was Manchester City who seemed to be favourites to sign him.

By the time he was 14 years old Albert was the star player in his school team. Although he had played for his Area Boys team, and had made it into the Manchester Boys team, he was not always first choice for Manchester. Unbeknown to him though, he had come to the notice of Manchester United's chief scout, Mr. Joe Armstrong. However, in 1949, fate decreed that this would soon be remedied. The first choice left winger in the Manchester Boys team was a youngster named Will Smith from the Xavarian College. In March of 1949, Manchester Boys played Barnsley Boys in the semi-final of the English schools shield at Manchester City's Maine Road. It was a game they won by 1-0, but unfortunately it was also the game in which young Smith also broke his leg.

The following Monday morning Albert was playing with friends on a croft in Hulme when they were approached by a Mr. Whetton. He enquired which one of them was Albert Scanlon and was met with a wall of silence. In those days kids and people were suspicious of anybody who was well dressed coming and enquiring about local people...for all they knew, the enquirer could be a policeman! However, Mr. Whetton did identify Albert and he then asked him had he got a Birth Certificate! Albert replied that he had but it was at home and his parents were at work. It turned out that Mr. Whetton was a member of the Manchester Schools Football Association and they had selected Albert to fill Will Smith's place in the City schoolboy's team. The English Schools Trophy Final was just six days away and they needed a copy of the Birth Certificate to make sure that Albert was eligible.

Without ado, Mr. Whetton took Albert to the Manchester Register Office which was then situated in All Saints, and a copy of his Birth certificate was obtained. Mr. Whetton then told him that he had to be at the Queen Victoria monument in Manchester's Piccadilly at 3p.m. the following Wednesday afternoon, where he would congregate with the other boys and that he

160

would be playing against Bolton Boys that evening. His family was ecstatic when they were told and they were all present at the game to watch young Albert score in a 3-0 win. He then went on to play in the English Schools Trophy Final against Swansea Boys.

Albert also found himself in the Lancashire Schoolboys team that played Yorkshire schoolboys in a game that was played at Rochdale's Spotland ground and he scored three goals in a 5-3 win. His family had travelled to watch him and when they caught the bus to return back to Manchester. Also on the bus was Joe Armstrong. The bus was crowded with passengers and many people were standing as it trundled its way back along the Rochdale Road. The Scanlon family was unaware of who this little grey haired old fellow was who was standing near the bus platform, but he stood up and called out:

"Ladies and gentlemen, I'd like you to give a round of applause to this young lad here who has just scored three goals in a football match against Yorkshire Boys."

The bus resonated to the sound of applause and Albert had tasted his first experience of fame! Although they lost that English Schools Final to Swansea, several of the boys went to League clubs immediately afterwards. The captain and right half was Colin Booth who went on to have a wonderful career with Wolverhampton Wanderers. Several were snapped up by Manchester United including Albert.

Albert initially wanted to be plumber and there was an apprenticeship lined up for him, but upon his arrival as a youngster at Old Trafford, Bert Whalley and Jimmy Murphy decided that plumbing was not for him and that he was joining the Ground Staff. On his first day as a Ground Staff Boy at Old Trafford in the summer of 1949, Albert, together with a few other young boys, was given a paint brush and a tin of red paint, and they were sent out into the Old Trafford Stadium, to paint all the stands and hoardings that were coloured red. Upon the completion of that task, they had to go and wash their paint brushes, collect another tin of paint, this time white, and paint over everything that was coloured white inside the stadium including the lines on the various passageways around the stadium and the picket fence that surrounded the running track! From there they progressed to mopping out the gymnasium daily! What an introduction to life as a Manchester United footballer!

Albert's first game for Manchester United was in the junior team which played in the Eccles and District League. It was an away fixture at a park in Burnage at the back of the old Hans Renold factory which I believe later became Mellands playing field. Back then though it was on land that was surrounded by a pig farm. In an interview with Roger Day from BBC Radio Kent in February 1968, Albert recalled:

"We'd all meet up and travel to our matches on the bus. We were under the watchful eye of Bert Fishbourne who looked after the junior team. We would all get on the bus and he would pay the bus fares, there, and back. You all carried your own boots and shin pads. And we got off at a place called Hans Renolds and that was in Burnage. There was a big engineering works and nobody knew where we were going. And we was all stood around and then Bert said 'follow me' and we walked down a path at the side of Hans Renolds and we just kept going, and going, and must have been about a mile down this path. On the left hand side we appeared at a football field and it was fenced off - your ground had to be fenced off - and there was a fellow in the field at the side and he was tending pigs. A few of the lads were now laughing. And one or two said to him 'what is this?' He said, 'it's a football pitch I rent it out' - he said 'it's mine - I'm a pig farmer'. Playing on that pitch, you can imagine the smell of pig shit that permeated the air! When the match was over and we'd again travelled back on the bus, Bert would give each player a Half Crown (12½ pence today!) for their expenses!"

Unfortunately after just a few games in his initial season, Albert injured his back and didn't play another game that season nor did he do any training. Instead he did ground staff duties around the stadium which also included cleaning out the dressing rooms after matches. Again, in the BBC interview he recalled:

"My first job was painting the ground. They gave us a five gallon drum of red oxide, a paint brush, and they said go out and paint everything red. Then, when we'd painted everything red, they'd come back with a drum of white and a different bucket and give you that and you'd go out and paint everything white that was white. You never sort of got involved in anything else but just Old Trafford as it was then. We did all the odd jobs. We'd sweep. You see there was such a lot of building work going on. They were building a stand - a firm called Woods was building the first stand you know after the war. That was at Old Trafford. And you'd clean up. And then there was an old gym outside the dressing rooms and the only thing in the gymnasium was mats, big square mats and two medicine balls and a few weights. And Ted Dalton, the physiotherapist, he had his treatment room in there and every day, Monday to Friday, we swept and locked it and that was the job I finished with. And you were covered in dirt, - the water was rotten. All it was - it kept you there and you could train and we trained Tuesday and Thursday."

The following year Albert began his progression through the United ranks. It was hard going because there were so many good youngsters arriving on the scene at Old Trafford, including the new painters, Eddie Colman and Duncan Edwards! The FA instituted the FA Youth Cup for the 1952-53 season, and for Manchester United, it was like manna from heaven. The very first youth team in the competition read; Gordon Clayton; Paddy Kennedy, Bryce Fulton; Eddie

Colman, Ronnie Cope (Capt), Duncan Edwards; Noel MacFarlane, John Doherty, Eddie Lewis, David Pegg, and Albert Scanlon. They took the competition by storm and won it very easily and over the next five years, it was to become their own personal property. David Pegg was converted into an outside left and it was he who made the break through into the first team first, making his first team debut at aged just seventeen years of age, in December of 1952. Over the next two years, he vied for the first team place with the ageing Jack Rowley. Albert was patient and became a regular in the Reserve team.

On 20 November 1954, the day that he had long awaited arrived – his first team debut and it was against Arsenal at Old Trafford in a 2-1 victory. In early 1955, Jack Rowley left United and the left wing berth was then a battle for the shirt between Albert Scanlon, and David. Immediately after two bad defeats by Manchester City in February of 1955, David Pegg was reintroduced to the first team in place of Rowley. However the next two games ended in a 4-2 defeat at home to Wolves and a 3-0 defeat away at Cardiff. For the game against Burnley on 5 March, Albert was recalled and was ever present until the season ended. He scored his first goal for the club against Everton on 19 March and was to score a further three before the season ended. Albert had at last arrived!

He began the 1955-56 season as first choice but unfortunately, after just six games he suffered an injury in a game at Everton, and David Peg replaced him for the following game. Such was Peg's form that Busby could not leave him out of the team and when Albert regained fitness, it was back to the Reserves. This was the season in which the *Babes* won their first Division One title, but sadly, those six games Albert played in that season were not enough to warrant a winner's medal. It was much the same the following season, 1956-57 and Albert only played five games towards the end of the season. Again, it was a Championship winning season and the team reached the FA Cup Final at Wembley...... but once again, Albert missed out on the medals.

The following season 1957-58 started off where the previous season had left off. In October of 1957, Albert passed his 22nd birthday and he was restless for first team football. There were stories about a move to Arsenal for him but nothing materialized. In November in the game against Dukla Prague at Old Trafford, right winger John Berry picked up a niggling knee injury and for the following three games, Albert returned to the first team, but at outside right, not outside left. When Berry regained fitness again, Albert returned to the Reserves. The first team was not firing on all cylinders and suffered some careless defeats. On 21 December 1957, Busby surprised everybody for the game against Leicester City at Old Trafford by leaving out Johnny Berry, Liam Whelan, and David Pegg. I say surprised everybody because it was thought that the attack were performing well and scoring goals, but that the defence was leaking silly goals which were proving costly. Into the team came eighteen years old Kenny Morgans; nineteen years old Bobby Charlton; and Albert. He seized the opportunity with both hands and his performances were electric, none more so than in that wonderful game at Highbury on 1 February 1958, when United beat the 'Gunners' by 5-4. He was instrumental in three of the goals that afternoon and Stan Charlton the Arsenal full back who faced Albert that afternoon reckons it was the biggest chasing that he ever got in a first class game. It was such an enthralling and exciting game that kept the fans rooted to the spot — nobody left the ground early! Both teams left the field when the final whistle went to thunderous applause. Albert recalled a conversation with Dennis Viollet as they got into the dressing room:

Viollet:
"Nobody's moved, Nobody's moved" (meaning the spectators). "You'd better go back out there and help him (meaning Stan Charlton the Arsenal full back) because he's not moved either! He's still trying to work out which way you went!"

Albert went to Belgrade with his young mates and played his part in the 3-3 draw that took this great young team into the semi-final of the European Cup for the second year running. He recalled the evening after the game with much fondness and just how happy the players were. *"After the Red Star game, we had a real good night out. Roger had a word, and the Boss let us go at the end of the speeches at the after-match reception. We all trooped off together. Going around different places you would lose people, and find them again in other places later. Tom Curry would not go to bed until the last player was back at the hotel. He would sit at the bottom of the stairs, and players would try to sneak past him. They would get so far and his voice would boom out; 'Good evening Gentlemen'."*

The following morning after breakfast they left for the airport and the first leg of the journey to Munich which proved to be uneventful. He remembers the ill fated third attempt to take off. Just prior to the attempted take off, Tommy Taylor and little Eddie Colman decided to move to the back of the aircraft. David Pegg who had been sat alongside Albert playing cards also decided that he was going to the back as well. Johnny Berry called out; *"We're all going to get fucking killed".* Billy Whelan who was across the aisle from him said; *"Albert, if this is death then I'm ready for it."* Albert recalled watching the wheels through the bulkhead window churning through the slush.... And then nothing... everything went black. He has no recollection of the actual accident at all. He woke up in the hospital wrestling with a lady who was on top of him (he was later to find out that it was a nun) trying to hold him down whilst they operated upon his head. He'd suffered head injuries, shoulder injuries, kidney injuries, and leg injuries. He was to stay in hospital in Munich for more than nine weeks encased in plaster.

Although he suspected the severity of the accident and that there had been fatalities, but it was an Australian Catholic priest, Father O'Hagan, who eventually gently broke the news to him of who had perished. Although BEA offered to fly Albert back to Manchester when he was fit enough, he opted to return by rail and ferry. He'd missed the outpouring of grief in the city by the time he got back home, and as soon as he was able, he began the battle for fitness and the quest to return to first team football. It is a tremendous credit to his resilience, determination, courage and bravery that he was ready to play again by the start of the 1958-59 season. Albert played in every game that season and his form was astonishing. He played forty two games and scored sixteen goals helping United to the runners-up spot in the First Division and just missing out to Wolves for the actual title. It was an astonishing feat coming as soon after the disaster as it did.

The 1959-60 season was nowhere near as successful and the team struggled. It was to be expected really and the effort at keeping the club at the forefront of English football took its toll on a lot of the players and their form was erratic. Albert played in thirty five first team games that season but was nowhere near as prolific as he had been the previous season and

Albert Scanlon lifts the ball over Manchester City's German goalkeeper Bert Trautmann in the Manchester "derby" match at Maine Road in 1960.

The last time I saw him. Albert Scanlon poses with a female admirer at Old Trafford in May 2009. He is seen carrying a copy of my book Forever a Babe.

sometimes, like the others, couldn't find the consistency he needed. The following season 1960-61 was his last at Old Trafford, and his final appearance in a Manchester United shirt was on 2 November 1960, away at Bradford City in an inglorious 2-1 defeat in the newly formed League Cup competition. Busby had started to play Bobby Charlton at outside left in a number of games, and you could say that Albert's days were numbered. There was no inkling of his departure though although there were some stories about off the field discretions, but he left for Newcastle United in November 1960.

Shortly after his arrival at St. James' Park he broke a leg in a league game and was never the same again. Although he was at Newcastle some twenty months, he only made twenty two appearances for the Magpies before he moved down the league to Lincoln City where he stayed just over a season making forty seven appearances. He then moved to Mansfield Town and stayed for three years making one hundred and eight appearances. In 1966 shortly after moving to Newport County, Albert retired from football.

From then on life was somewhat of struggle. He finally took a job as a docker on Manchester Docks under the shadow of the ground which he had graced for so long as a young man. Unfortunately, containerization was about to begin its march into industry and Manchester Docks was hard hit, eventually becoming a redundant port. Albert always retained his sense of humour. The bitterness did disappear, and his love for Manchester United was always as deep rooted as it ever was. In his later years, he attended some games at Old Trafford, and was always able to return his thoughts back to those halcyon years of the 1950s when he could still see those young friends with whom he grew up with at Old Trafford, so clearly.

Albert passed away peacefully in Salford Royal Hospital on 22 December 2009. He left us with so many, many, happy memories. Sleep on in your peace Albert.

Albert Scanlon played 115 games for Manchester United and scored 34 goals.

He was capped 5 times at England Under23 level, and played 1 game for the Football League.

Geoff Bent – Mr. Loyalty

On February 1st 1958, Geoff Bent and Ronnie Cope, two young Manchester United Reserve players, played together in a Central League fixture at Old Trafford. Events that afternoon down at Highbury, in London, where the first team were playing away to Arsenal, were to impact both their young lives significantly. For one of them, Geoff Bent, it would end in tragedy.

Geoff Bent was born in Pendleton, Salford, on September 27th 1932. In his early years he attended St. John's Junior School and after passing the 11-plus examination, he went off to Tootal Road Grammar School. In August of 1948, just before his 16th birthday he joined the Manchester United ground staff. For a young boy who was Manchester United crazy, coming almost immediately after the ravages of the Second World War, it must have been a dream come true. My good friend John White recalls;

"In many respects, Geoff was probably like any number of understudies anywhere - good enough in his own right to get a place at almost any football club in the land."

Little could he have known then that secure and valuable to his club as he certainly was, his United career was to be a brief and not so glorious one, being kept well in the background at Old Trafford as cover for the man who would ascend to the captaincy of Manchester United - and also automatic left back for England - Manchester-born Roger Byrne.

All this was in the future back then and Geoff must have been on cloud nine as he signed his name on that first contract for Matt Busby in August 1948. I'll bet he was even more ecstatic in May of the following year when he signed his professional contract!

I genuinely hope that Geoff gleaned every moment of personal joy from those two highlight events - because the lad wouldn't be getting much joy in the way of appearances for the Reds! It was actually well over 5 long years later before he made his first team debut in the away game at Turf Moor in the 4-2 win over Burnley in late 1954 which speak volumes for the health, form and consistency of performance from Roger Byrne who kept the lad out for all those years.

Probably THE highlight of his career (in his own view anyway) was taking the ball off the legendary Tom Finney in a game against Preston (one of his total of only 12 first-team games). He treasured the newspaper cutting of the event he valued so much. I think that it is simultaneously wonderfully poignant and yet carries in it the joy of a footballer who was also a huge fan of the games finest."

Geoff Bent pictured before the start of the 1954/55 season.

Although Geoff's appearances in the first team were sporadic and spread out to say the least, there was no histrionics from the likeable, quiet Salfordian. No banging on the Manager's door demanding a transfer. On February 1st 1958, Geoff was already 25 years old and I think that it would be a fair assumption that given the amount of talent that was coming through from the junior teams at Old Trafford, if he wanted to progress his career as a First Division footballer, then a move to another club was almost inevitable.

Towards the end of the 1956/57 season, Geoff broke his leg playing in a Reserve team fixture. It was the second time in his career that he had suffered such an injury. He worked hard on his rehabilitation through the summer months and by September 1957, he was fit enough to continue playing once again.

The party to travel to Belgrade on February 3rd had already been named, and big Ronnie Cope was one of the 16 players scheduled to be in the party. However, after the game at Highbury on February 1st, Roger Byrne reported a slight thigh strain. On the way back to Manchester that evening, Busby mulled over the matter and then the following morning made the decision that Cope would not travel, but that Geoff Bent would as cover in case Byrne was not fit to play in Belgrade. He was reasonable in his thinking – the original party contained two centre-halfs – Cope and Blanchflower. Notwithstanding Blanchflower's versatility – Bent was an out and out full back and left sided at that. So it was logical that Cope would be the one to be left behind.

Big Ronnie wasn't happy about the situation and spoke to Jimmy Murphy about it on the Sunday morning before Jimmy left for Wales to become involved in their World Cup Qualifying match against Israel, which was scheduled for the same day as United were playing in Belgrade. Cope said that he would be handing in a transfer request, and Jimmy told him to sleep on it.

Geoff Bent was a very quiet individual. He was married to Marion, a local Salford girl and just four months previously, they were overjoyed with the arrival of their baby daughter, Karen. Geoff was probably the lowest profile player with the "Busby Babes" and was quite happy to keep it that way. Like the rest of the married lads in the club, once training or a match had finished, he just wanted to get home to his family.

The day before the game in Belgrade, skipper Roger Byrne declared himself fit to play, and Geoff had to be content with a seat in the stands. Sadly, the following afternoon in Munich, he was one of the seven players to lose their lives. It was so tragic and broke Marion's heart. I also often think about how this affected Ronnie Cope in the years that followed. Geoff's daughter Karen grew up not knowing her father. She went on to have a fairly successful career in the music and entertainment industry.

Geoff was laid to rest in St. John's CE Church, Irlam o'th' Heights. God grant you eternal rest Geoff and on behalf of all those many fans who never got the chance to say it, a huge retrospective thank you to you for your absolute loyalty to United's cause.

Geoff Bent played 12 first team games for Manchester United.

Kenny Morgans – The Flying Welshman

At the time of the Munich tragedy, Kenny Morgans was the youngest of the "Busby Babes". He was born in Swansea on March 16th 1939 and joined Manchester united shortly after his 15th birthday in 1954. Like many of the young boys who joined Manchester United at that time, he was initially taken on as a Ground Staff boy, and like many of his predecessors, worked around the stadium painting the stands, helping in the boot room, tending the laundry, and cleaning out the dressing rooms and baths. Far removed from what was perceived to be the life of a budding professional footballer.

Kenny was the quiet, self effacing Welsh boy. But he had an abundance of skill. This did not go unnoticed by the Manchester united Coaching staff. He was a right winger who possessed all the trickery needed to take on some of the tough uncompromising defenders that played in the game at all levels at that time. He had great feet, similar to a certain young Irishman who was to come to the fore a good few years later. Kenny had a great feel for the ball and was able to keep it close to either foot as he ran at full backs. Aligned to that, he had terrific pace and once he had turned them, there was no catching him and he would then deliver quality balls into the penalty box to the delight of the other forwards.

He progressed from the junior team through the A and B teams and was also the star in two FA youth cup winning teams in 1955-56, and 1956-57. He was also playing in the Youth team that began its defence of the trophy in 1957-58. My own memories of him were seeing him initially in the Youth team during the 1955-56 season, particularly against Chesterfield in the Final first leg at Old Trafford. This young Welsh boy, with the frail physique, tormented the bigger Chesterfield defenders throughout the game and he was responsible for laying on two of the three goals that United's young team scored that evening. I can recall that when the final whistle was blown, and United had won by 3-2, as the players left the pitch hordes of young kids ran on to the pitch and surrounded two players. One was Chesterfield's young seventeen years old goalkeeper who had put in an astonishing performance which kept the score line respectable (it was none other than Gordon Banks) and the other was young Morgans.

Kenny began to develop a reputation and fast became a favourite of those fans who went to watch the Reserve team on a regular basis. Towards the end of that 1955-56 season, he had started to appear as a regular name on the Reserve team sheet. At this time, United were blessed with some top class wingers; David Pegg, Johnny Berry, Albert Scanlon, Johnny Scott, Noel MacFarlane, and even fellow Welshman and international, Colin Webster. So progressing to the first team was going to be a challenge but it was one that he quietly got on with.

The following season, 1956-57, he was again appearing regularly at reserve team level and again starred in the Youth team which retained the FA Youth Cup beating West Ham united 8-2 on aggregate in the Final. His performances at both levels were beginning to make people to take notice. Johnny Berry though had been Mr. Consistency for the previous five seasons, and he was a delight to watch. In today's modern game, Berry would have had people sitting on the edge of their seats! I think that it would also be truthful to say that Morgans, once he had broken into the first team, would have had the same effect.

I recall a Wednesday evening in November of 1957 when I went to watch the Manchester United Youth team play in a Youth Cup tie at Maine Road against arch rivals Manchester City. Over 25,000 fans turned up that evening to watch Morgans put on a dazzling display of wing play which if my memory is correct, was the biggest factor in United winning comfortably by 4-1. He was mesmeric that evening and the young City defence just could not cope with his dribbling skills and his pace… he simply tore them apart. He was certainly ready for first team football even though he was just 18 years of age.

His big day came on December 21st 1957 when Busby freshened up his team and left Berry out to introduce young Morgans. The match was against Leicester City at Old Trafford and was won by 4-1. He only missed 1 game, and that was against Luton Town on Boxing Day 1957, out

Kenny Morgans pictured playing in his first senior Manchester derby match at Maine Road against Manchester City on 28 December 1957.

of the next 11 which took them to the ill fated journey to Belgrade. He had become a fixture and first choice, and Berry would have a battle on his hands to regain his place. Big Tommy Taylor particularly, took a liking to the service that Morgans wing play provided for him and he told him;

"Dai, you hit those crosses as hard as you like, but remember this...make sure that they're nine feet high!"

Once around his full back, Kenny would look up and put it exactly where the big Yorkshireman wanted it... on his head.

The horror of Munich could have been even greater because if it hadn't been for the vigilance of two German journalists. Initially, as the horror of the accident unfolded, amongst all the chaos, Morgans was not on the survivors list, nor was he on the roll of people who had died. The reason for this was that he wasn't found until five hours after the accident had happened, and it was the two German journalists who had returned to the broken tail section of the aircraft to look for two cans of film that they had put on the aircraft earlier. As they searched around they saw something move and found Morgans underneath one of the aircraft wheels and surrounded by a lot of the luggage. They had found that he was breathing, called for help, and got him to the hospital. In getting him out of the wreckage, they had to cut him out of his new Italian suit. The trip had been his first into Europe with the first team and he'd been fitted out for a suit just like the rest of the other players. It's a miracle that he hadn't frozen to death in the five hours that had elapsed since the time of impact until the time that the reporters found him. He was in a coma and did not wake up in the hospital until Sunday, February 9th, 1958.

Kenny suffered head injuries and he woke up in a room that was also occupied by Bobby Charlton, Albert Scanlon, and Ray Wood. Initially, he thought that a lot of players were upstairs on another floor in that hospital, but sadly, after a few days, the full stark reality of what had happened, was there before him. Upon leaving hospital in late march, the physicians advised him not to try and play competitive football again that season, but in his own words;

"I was desperate to get playing again because I wanted to play for Duncan, for Tommy, and all those boys who never came back. They'd played in the Cup Final the year before and lost and I was prepared to play my heart out in the Final against Bolton."

Sadly, that was not to be. He'd returned to first team action On Easter Saturday 1958, in a home game against Preston North End which ended 0-0. He was then virtually ever present until the end of the season. It was sad that Jimmy Murphy left him out of the Cup Final team in 1958.

My own theory on this is that he was left out to accommodate the inclusion of Dennis Viollet. Alex Dawson who was a centre forward was moved to outside right. According to Kenny, Jimmy's reasoning for leaving him out was that he had lost weight and thought that the occasion would be too much for him emotionally. United lost that Final by 2-0 but on the following Thursday evening, he was selected for the team that defeated AC Milan 2-1 in the first leg of the European Cup Semi-Final at Old Trafford, and he was man of the match. Jimmy regretted leaving him out of the Final line up at Wembley the previous Saturday and admitted to Kenny the morning after the AC Milan game.

For the next two years he fought to re-establish himself as a top First Division performer but there were so many obstacles. As he recalls;

"I stayed for two more years but I wasn't really interested. I missed the boys so much. Because of what had happened to them, I just didn't seem to care. I tried, but the players were not the same and that upset me. We used to have two dressing rooms, one for the first team, and the other for the reserves.

"When I came back after the crash, all the reserves were in the first-team dressing room. Some of them were never good enough to be there. The Babes were the best team there'd ever been.

"The sadness is there - every time I look at that painting of the last line up. Had they all lived, they would have been the best team in the world. People laugh at me when I say it, but the Babes were so good, they never made mistakes. You know, I never lost a game with the old team."

Kenny left Manchester United for his home town club of Swansea in 1961 and he stayed there for three years making 54 appearances. He then moved on to Newport County where between 1964 and 1967 making 125 appearances before he retired from first class football. Today he lives quietly with his wife Stefanie in Swansea."

Kenny Morgans made 24 first class appearances for Manchester United.

Bobby Charlton –
The Face of Manchester United

Saturday, October 6th 1956, was a rather special day for a certain young man who was just approaching his 19th birthday, which would be celebrated on the following, Thursday, October 11th. He was at that time, serving his country doing two years National Service with the Royal Army Ordnance Corps in Shropshire. Manchester was his adopted city and home, and he had first arrived there in 1953, from his home town of Ashington, in Northumberland. He was a very shy, fresh faced, good humoured type of person with a mischievous smile. But most importantly, when not tied down by the rigours of his mandatory military life, he was employed by a very special establishment, which just a few months earlier had won the hearts of the English nation, when they lifted the First Division Championship title of the Football League, with a football team that had an average age of just 22 years each. That establishment was of course, Manchester United.

Bobby Charlton had been a schoolboy prodigy, and his signature had been courted by a large number of First Division clubs, including the team which he supported, and who were his local team - Newcastle United. The village of Ashington, where he lived, was a mining village deep in the heart of the Northumberland coal field, and not unexpected, his father was a miner. His mother, 'Cissie came from the famous north-eastern footballing family, the Milburns. The Milburn it would be true to say, are probably the most famous family in the history of the game of football and are synonymous with the North East of England.

The very first Milburn was named Jack. He played for Shankhouse, and also Northumberland, during the early pioneering days of the game in the Nineteenth Century. After him came a real feisty character who went under the name of 'Warhorse' Milburn and was famous in local football throughout the Northumberland area. This fellow had thirteen children and several of them went on to play football at a decent level. *'Tanner'* Milburn was one of these children and he appeared for Ashington during their Football League days, and the Milburn family tree grew further branches when this particular Milburn had four sons, as well as three daughters. Inevitably, the boys played football.

One of *'Tanner's'* brothers was named Alec and he also played for Ashington, after turning down the chance to travel south and play for 'Spurs. It was Alec who produced the son who later, was to become so famous, and idolized on Tyneside, and known as *'Wor Jackie.'* *'Tanner's'* four male offspring also all turned out in League football. Sons George, Jim, and Jack all turned out for Leeds United, whilst Stan made his name as a tough tackling full-back with Chesterfield and Leicester City, and he also appeared for the Football League. 'Cissie Milburn was one of 'Tanner's' daughters and she married a miner named Bob, and they too had four sons. Of these sons, two were to become famous in the football world in their own right, Bobby and older brother Jackie.

The story of how Bobby Charlton first started his journey on the road to a career in football with Manchester United is fascinating. In 1952, Mr. Ellis Smith was the Member of Parliament for Stoke-on-Trent South. He was an avid Manchester United fan and was on very good terms with manager Matt Busby. Mr. Smith was attending a party conference in the Lancashire seaside town of Morecambe when one evening, he got talking about football with another delegate. The man was a schoolteacher, and he went on to tell Mr. Smith that he also did some scouting in the North-East for three different league clubs. He told Ellis Smith;

"There's a schoolboy by the name of Charlton I rate as a future England player. But I just can't get any of my clubs to take an interest in him. They think that he's a bit frail, but I'm convinced that he'll make a good 'un."

That schoolteacher was a headmaster from a different school to the one which Bobby attended. The headmaster was in fact the principal at his Brother Jack's school and was named, Mr. Hemmingway. Little did he know at the time of his conversation with Ellis Smith, that he was helping write as big a sporting history page as any masterpiece produced by the famous American author of the same name! Smith contacted Matt Busby and let him know about this outstanding schoolboy. Busby then began the process which would eventually bring Bobby Charlton to Old Trafford. He informed Chief Scout Joe Armstrong that he wanted the boy watched.

Talking to the former Blackpool, and England full-back, Jimmy Armfield in an interview on BBC Radio in 1999, Bobby recalled his childhood days;

"When I was nine years old, I was playing for my school in eleven years old league football. On a Sunday morning at Hirst Park, in Ashington, we used to start playing football at about 9am, and we would play non-stop until it was dark, right through the day. People used to join in this match and leave it, either to go for their lunch, or to go to the pub, but the game continued every time there was a break. You played football, everybody played football. If there was no spare ground available, or you didn't have ball, then you would find an old tin can to kick around, and you would have a game in the street.

There were a lot of miner's terraced houses in Ashington. The local pit was the centre of the community, and that's where most local people went to work. My dad was a miner for fifty years. The only way people got out of going down the pit was if they joined the Navy, or went away playing professional football. That's why football was so important. Football was everything"

In local Northumberland circles it was widely believed that Bobby Charlton would join either of the big North-Eastern clubs, Sunderland, or Newcastle United. The ties with the Milburn family strongly supported that theory. In 1953, on a cold February morning in the North-Eastern town of Jarrow, the town boys team was playing Hebburn Boys in a youth game. As was normal, it was 'Cissie Charlton who had gone along to watch her son play. When he was leaving the field of play, Bobby noticed a dapper little fellow talking to his mother. It was said in the dressing room that the person his mother was seen talking to was a Manchester United scout. It proved to be that the scout was Joe Armstrong who had traveled up to the North-East to watch Bobby. Manchester United was in fact the first Football League club to show any real interest in Bobby. The list of interested parties grew longer after Bobby scored a couple of goals for England Schoolboys at Wembley Stadium just a few months later. He played for England against Wales Schoolboys and 93,000 spectators watched the game which ended in a 3-3 draw. Afterwards, eighteen different football clubs eventually joined the chase for young Charlton's signature.

That Joe Armstrong had taken the trouble to travel up from Manchester to watch him play, and that it was United who first showed interest in signing him, made a big impression upon the young Charlton. He was desperate to become a professional footballer. Charlton had no affinity with Manchester United at that time, and he was of the opinion that whichever club came in first for him, he would join. That it was Manchester United who was the first with an approach was their good fortune. Newcastle, Wolves, Middlesborough, Arsenal, Chelsea, Chesterfield, and even Manchester City, were just a few of the clubs chasing him. After a schoolboy representative match which was played at Manchester city's Maine Road ground, Bobby was approached in the tunnel after he came off the pitch, by the then Manchester city centre-forward, Don Revie, who asked him would he like to join the club. By this time however, bobby had made his mind up that it was to be Manchester United for him.

His mother 'Cissie, also turned to her famous cousin, *'Wor Jackie'* for advice as to which of the clubs pursuing Bobby's signature, would be best suited for her boy. Jackie Milburn didn't even hesitate, and recommended that she send Bobby to Manchester United! His reasoning was that with the youth policy put into place by Matt Busby, Bobby would have a better chance of progressing to League football with United, and that they were a club who had a big reputation for looking after their young players and giving them every chance to succeed.

Bobby's own words on joining United, sum it up;

"I must have been smitten by whatever bug bites you here at Old Trafford. At that time, the cream of youth was here and I wanted to match myself against them. Wonderful young people like Duncan Edwards, Jeff Whitefoot, Wilf McGuinness, Albert Scanlon, Eddie Colman and many others. Duncan in fact became a great pal and he looked after me like a father! He was a lovely person, naïve in many ways; not crafty. He just loved life, and lived for United and his football, at which he was more gifted than any other player that I have ever seen. Yes, that's why I joined United. I just wanted to. It was as simple as that."

Bobby's father, Bob senior, naturally wanted to make sure that his son was not being blinded by the glamour of the name of a big club, and also whether Bobby might be going too far away from home. Being a miner and from the same kind of background as Jimmy Murphy, the two of them spoke the same language. Jimmy was to tell him;

"Mr. Charlton. My father worked down the pit like you. When I became an £8 a week first teamer with West Brom, I was eventually able to save up enough to make it possible for my father to leave the coal face for good. If I never had another thing out of football that precious moment when I was able to get my father out of the pit, was worth it.

Bobby himself was to say;

"The distance really did not enter into it. If I didn't go to Sunderland or Newcastle, then Manchester seemed to be the next big place on the railway line."

So in the summer of 1953, he joined United. For the next three years he worked exceptionally hard and listened intently to what the coaches drilled in to all the young players. Manchester United Football Club was awash with young talent and Matt Busby was at last starting the conveyer belt that took players to the first team. But first, Jimmy Murphy had to work hard with young Bobby. As a 15 year-old, he had a thunderbolt shot in his left foot. When the ball was at his feet, Charlton was such a graceful mover, able to drift to the right or to the left of an opponent with consummate ease. He looked a different class. However, he had one big fault. He would hit long balls to the left or right wing and then stand admiring what he had done. Jimmy Murphy and Coach Bert Whalley had to spend hour upon hour, day after day, teaching him the short game. The message was always the same;

"Play it short son........ Play it short. Get the slow steady build up......... And leave the long balls alone until they are on."

Bobby played in the junior, A and B teams, and these teams played in open age football leagues, often against players much older than they were. They were subjected to a lot of rough physical treatment as well as verbal abuse when they played, but it was all part of the toughening process. The surfaces that they played on back in those days would make people gasp in amazement in this modern day. But all those junior teams were successful – especially the Manchester United Youth team who from the inaugural FA Youth Cup competition started in 1952-53, made that trophy their own. The youngsters were also encouraged to join in some of the ad-hoc kick-abouts with the senior players that used to take place on the gravel, outside the ground, at the back of the Stretford End. These games certainly weren't for the faint hearted! Jimmy Murphy would often cast an eye over these games and would watch the youngsters with a view to judging their temperament and heart and 'bottle.' Many a youngster failed the acid test on that area of gravel and the back of the Stretford End saw the demise of many a young career before it even got started!

Bobby relished the challenge. He had a wonderful temperament and a huge big heart. In 1955 he had made it through to the Reserve team and it was here that he started to make people outside of the club begin to take notice. He had a thunderbolt shot in either foot and his name began to appear regularly on the score sheet. His reputation at Reserve team level began to grow, and to the United fans of that era who went to watch the Reserves play (and back then it wasn't uncommon for there to be 10,000 or more fans to be present) it was obvious that young Charlton was knocking on the door for selection to the first team. Already from his youth team days, Colman, Edwards, Whelan, and Pegg, were established in the first team.

Although he was doing his National Service, he was getting plenty of football, not only turning out for United's teams at weekends, but also playing in mid-week for his Regimental team, and when necessary, also for his Command and full Army teams. International football was played on sporadic weekends throughout the season back in those days, and clubs were not allowed to postpone League games because they had players who would be away with their respective international teams. If you had four or five players away on international duty, so be it – players from the reserve team were promoted to the first team to fill their places.

So it was for the 6th October, 1956. Fixtures for the Home International Tournament were scheduled for that day, and England was away in Belfast, to play Northern Ireland at Windsor Park. Selected for England (there were no substitutes allowed in those days) for that fixture

Bobby Charlton scores the first goal of his senior career against Charlton Athletic at Old Trafford on Saturday October 6th, 1956. The other Manchester United player in the picture is Liam 'Billy' Whelan.

were three players from Manchester United; Roger Byrne, Duncan Edwards, and Tommy Taylor. Manchester United also had a Division One Football League fixture to negotiate that day against Charlton Athletic at Old Trafford. Busby pondered his selection for this fixture knowing that he was without three crucial first team regulars. At full back, he drafted in young Geoff Bent in place of Roger Byrne. At left half-back, he drafted in Edwards' regular replacement whenever he was injured, away on international duty, or playing at inside-left; Wilf McGuinness. The final selection was the one that most of the fans had been waiting to see! In place of the great Tommy Taylor at centre-forward, he selected Bobby Charlton!

I attended the game against Charlton Athletic that afternoon and have fond memories of it. The United team lined up; Wood; Foulkes and Bent; Colman, Jones, and McGuinness; Berry, Whelan, Charlton, Viollet and Pegg.

41,439 fans turned up to watch that afternoon, and little did we all know back then that we were watching the start of a real piece of soccer history. Johnny Berry was Captain of the team in Roger Byrne's absence. Charlton were no match for United that day, and they had already made a dreadful start to the season, which was to end in relegation for them. I cannot clearly recall the sequence in which the goals were scored but do remember the moment that every young player dreams about. United were attacking the Scoreboard End, and Charlton received the ball pretty central to the goal and just outside of the area. Without any hesitation, the ball was dispatched as though fired from a canon and high into the Charlton net past a stationary Willie Duffy (I think that was his name) the Charlton goalkeeper. Old Trafford erupted in appreciation, and it wasn't too long after that that young Charlton got his second goal in a similar way. Billy Whelan and Johnny Berry also scored that afternoon and United were winners by 4-2. To say that the fans were delighted was an understatement. Another tremendous young player had emerged off the conveyer belt of youth. United were reigning Champions, and were on course to retaining their title. I can clearly recall the newspaper reports the day after the match, and in one of them, the headline ran; *W'or Bobby Will Do!* It was a quote from his father's reaction the previous afternoon after the game had finished.

Bobby Charlton takes on West Germany's Franz Beckenbauer in a World Cup tie played in Leon, Mexico, in 1970.

From the day of his debut onwards, that *W'or Bobby* would do was never in doubt. Jimmy Armfield in the BBC interview asked bobby how did he feel trying to break into a forward line which contained Berry, Whelan, Taylor, Viollet, and Pegg? Bobby's response was;

"There was no age to them so it was always going to be difficult. Matt Busby always did say though that if you were good enough, you would get a chance. With Busby, there was times when, if things were not going too well, he would leave two or three out, so that chance was always there. He kept me waiting for ages before he did throw me in because Tommy Taylor was away on international duty. After that, I only got in when Whelan, Viollet, or Taylor were away or injured. In December 1957 Busby decided to freshen things up a little and I got in on merit, replacing Billy Whelan and I was in on a regular basis. Just two months later however, Munich happened, and that changed everything."

What could never have been foreseen at the time of Bobby's debut game against Charlton Athletic was the tragedy that was lying in wait less than eighteen months hence. Less than five years after he joined United, he was to suffer the agonies of the Munich tragedy. He lost those that were closest to him, namely; Duncan Edwards, Eddie Colman, Tommy Taylor, and David Pegg. He was a veteran before his time and in the immediate aftermath of that tragedy his nerves were shattered. When he did come back, he played like a man possessed; it was as though he was carrying the full weight of the club on his own young shoulders. Some of the goals that he scored had they been captured on video tape would make today's fan salivate at the sight of them.

His first international goal was at Hampden Park, Glasgow against the *'auld enemy'*. 134,000 partisan Scottish fans packed the old stadium that April afternoon, and saw probably the greatest goal ever scored there, and certainly the hardest shot. Standing centrally and just inside the penalty area, he watched as Tom Finney jinked around the full back. Finney's cross was inch perfect and above waist height. A slight movement to his left and Charlton took off in mid-air, swinging that lethal left foot of his at the ball. It connected full on the volley and the ball thundered past Tommy Younger in the Scottish goal with such force, that it almost ripped the net pegs out of the ground. The Hampden Stadium thundered its applause and Younger, who had been left motionless and rooted to the spot, proceeded to run half the length of the field to shake Charlton's hand.

His playing career at Manchester United was to last for another sixteen years after his debut, and during that time, he was only ever "booked" once – for a confrontation with of all people, Jimmy Scoular, the craggy, hard, Scot who captained Newcastle United. In a long career he carved a name as a chivalrous, scrupulous opponent. Yet for me, it will be the explosive facets of his play that will always stay fresh in my memory. To see him in full flight was akin to watching a China Clipper cut its way through a tempestuous sea. That jinking run, the sudden swerve and change of foot and direction as he would turn so elegantly on the ball as he accelerated through a gap surrendered by a confused defender – he could be gone like a ship in full sail. It was no surprise that in his playing career, Bobby Charlton was to win every major honour available to him in the game, including European Cup, and World Cup winning medals.

He suffered internally after Munich and his character did change. It also happened to Bill Foulkes, and to Harry Gregg. He has often given out an impression of aloofness, but to those that really do get to know him, it couldn't be further from the truth. His face can wear that elusive look of anxiety or fun, and as much as he wants to endure relaxation, he finds it hard to find. He is also difficult to get to know and to get inside of, but that is not to say that he doesn't care. He does, and passionately. His heart is genuinely betrothed to Manchester United, irrespective of what is said about him today. I will finish this chapter with a quote which he made in the Manchester United Centenary Souvenir Programme back in 1978, when he named Old Trafford, 'The Theatre of Dreams';

"I'll always have a great affection for this place. I suppose that I have put a lot of blood and tears into it. And to see the place as it is now, as opposed to when I first arrived here, makes me fully realize that I did have a little part in all that change. I find that so rewarding. Look at it now – it must be the envy of every club in the country.

As for the man on the street, the guys on the terraces, they're everything. They're not a part of the backroom politics and all the in-fighting that goes on. They don't really understand that side of it. What they do understand is that they have their team and their whole lives revolve around coming down here to Old Trafford.

They are a part of a never ending story. They are a Theatre of Dreams!"

Bobby Charlton made 758 appearances for Manchester United scoring 249 goals.

He was capped at every level for his country from Schoolboy through to full International.

For the England senior team he made 106 appearances, scoring 49 goals.

Wilf McGuinness –
'Compared to Duncan Edwards.........'

On 20 May 2011, together with my wife Cheryl, we made a visit to the Stretford High School which is situated in Greatstone Road, Old Trafford, almost in the shadow of Manchester United's magnificent stadium at Old Trafford. Our purpose was to visit with the staff and pupils of Form Seven, who I had worked closely with for almost a year, on a project which would eventually see two *'Blue Heritage'* plaques erected on the walls of the two small council houses, situated very close the school. The houses were homes in which both Tommy Taylor, and Duncan Edwards, had lodged at during their careers at Manchester United.

Upon arrival we had been met by the school's Director of Learning, Chris Hirst, who was the instigator of the *'Blue Plaque Project'*, and we were taken to the Headmaster's study where we met the School Principal, Jim Hasledine. From the moment that we had arrived at the school, we had sensed that there was a great feeling of excitement and expectancy in the air. Something *'special'* was obviously happening in the school that morning.

As we sat taking coffee and indulging in small-talk in the Principal's small lounge, there was a knock on the Principal's door. Seconds later, one of the school's receptionists led a small, bald headed, stocky man, who had a craggy, toothy smile, through the door and into the lounge. Immediately the smiles upon the faces of all present told the story that this was indeed, a special person. For myself, I had met him many times before, and I knew that he was etched into the fabric and folklore of his beloved Manchester United Football Club. The others present looked on in awe as he shook hands with everybody, and put all at their ease.

This man was now 74 years of age, and the stylish dark hair had been lost in years long ago. The gait in his walk betrayed the passing of all those years. However, he still retained that same bubbling, effervescent personality, that I had first witnessed some 58 years previously, when I had watched him play for the very first time in the Manchester Boys Schools team at Belle Vue, Manchester, in the *'Coronation Cup'* against the London Schools team. The person was Wilf McGuinness, one of only two men who have both played for, and managed, Manchester United Football Club. Just a few weeks earlier I had spoken to Wilf and had asked if would go to the school and speak to the Year Seven students and talk to them about his career in football, and particularly about his time as a *Busby Babe.* I passed on the details to Christ Hirst, and he liaised with Wilf to set the date and time for his talk.

The schoolchildren were packed into the school's auditorium, and as Wilf entered, he was met by a crescendo of cheers. The event began at noon on that day, and many of the schoolteachers gave up their lunchtime and lunches just to join the children in the auditorium and sit and listen to him. For the next hour, McGuinness kept everybody enthralled as with great passion, vigour, and much humour, he recounted the tales of his past.

The suburb of Collyhurst lies less than a mile to the north of Manchester's city centre. Over the years it has become synonymous as an area which has provided professional footballers for both of the Manchester clubs. The most notable would be Nobby Stiles MBE, who was both a World Cup, and European Cup winner with Manchester United. Wilf McGuinness was born on 25th October 1937, in a small terraced house in Twyford Street, Collyhurst, to parents Lawrence, and May. His stay there was a short one as while he was still an infant, his family moved out to the north of Manchester, and the more green and airy suburb of Blackley.

The McGuinness family went to live at number 51, Westleigh Street, Blackley. It was a street which was vastly different from where he had begun his life. Instead of small grimy, terraced houses, this street was given to larger terraced type houses, built in the 1930s with big, front bay windows. The house was just a stone's throw away from the lovely vast open spaces of a large park named Boggart Hole Clough and during his early years, this was where he spent a lot of his time.

Wilf attended the Mount Carmel Catholic School in Blackley, and it was while he there that he came under the influence of his very first mentor, schoolmaster James Mulligan. Mulligan was a full-back with Manchester City in the 1920s and had been good enough to win a full international cap for Northern Ireland. Like most young boys in Manchester at that time, McGuinness developed a love of football and would spend all his free time playing, and practicing. Mulligan saw something special in the football talent of this enthusiastic young boy and carefully nurtured it.

Wilf's father, Lawrence, also loved to watch football. Lawrence had served in the Army during World War Two, as a driver in one of the logistic corps. When Wilf was just four years old, he had been called upon to join the British Eighth Army in North Africa, and Italy. On the cessation of hostilities in June 1945, he returned back to Manchester, and once again was able to rejoin his family. He took a great interest in Wilf's football progression and tried to attend all his competitive schoolboy matches. Lawrence also began taking him to watch Manchester United at Maine Road, and it was he who nurtured the love of the club which would play such a huge part in Wilf's later life.

He began playing organized, competitive football, as a young Baden-Powell, Wolf Cub when he was just ten years of age. Initially he was a centre-forward and was a prolific goal scorer in schools football. As a young boy, he was very sure of himself, and he had a dominating personality, so it was not surprising that most of the teams of which he was a member, he was also captain. Even at such a young age, Wilf was dedicated to the game of football. He would spend hour, after hour, kicking a ball against the gable end wall of their house; controlling the ball as it came off at different angles; passing, shooting, heading, chipping, and even saving. Just a few years later, he was to experience a similar exercise at Old Trafford under Jimmy Murphy's watchful eye. He also spent long hours practicing taking throw-ins, hurling the ball against that gable end, and then throwing it high against the chimney stack of the house from across the road. By the time that he was 14 years old, Wilf could hurl the ball from the touchline of a football pitch, and into the six yards box of a penalty area.

All those hours of practice and single minded determination were to pay off for the young McGuinness. He made it into his schools teams, and then the Northern area of Manchester team. Then at just 13 he was selected for the Manchester Boys team and also the Manchester Catholic Boys team and he also forced his way into the Lancashire County Schoolboys team. At that time, James Mulligan was also Chairman of the Manchester Schools Football Association, and it was he who recommended Wilf McGuinness for an England Schoolboys trial. Wilf traveled to Bournville, in Birmingham, for the trial and caught the eye of the England selectors. So much so, that for the first schoolboy international of the 1951-52 season against Northern Ireland at York City's, Bootham Crescent, he was selected and also made captain. It was a game which England won easily by 5-1.

The following season he was again captain for the first game against the Republic of Ireland Schools, played at Portsmouth's, Fratton Park Stadium. It was another easy win for England by 8-0. Starring in that same schoolboys' international team in that 1952-53 season was a certain Robert Charlton from East Northumberland Schools. The biggest thrill for Wilf that season was that he was selected to lead his young England team out of the famous old tunnel at Wembley Stadium, in a match against Wales schoolboys, which ended in a 3-3 draw. Incredibly, 90,000 spectators watched that game.

It was no surprise that as Wilf neared school leaving age, his signature was being courted by a number of the First Division's leading clubs; Bolton, Wolves, Chelsea, Manchester City, to name but a few, as well as his beloved Manchester United. As we sat in the school auditorium on that Friday lunchtime, it was compelling to listen to him as he explained to all, the reasons why he actually joined Manchester United:

"There were two main reasons why I joined Manchester United, and none of them involved under-the-counter payments to my parents, or anything of that nature. Those two main reasons were two terrific young

players named Eddie Colman, and Duncan Edwards. When I captained Manchester, Lancashire and England schoolboys, a lot of clubs were chasing me. With me in the England team were Jimmy Melia, who went to Liverpool, and Bobby Charlton. A lot of offers came in. I saw these two boys playing in the Manchester United Youth Team in the inaugural season of the FA Cup Youth Cup. In the first leg of the final at Old Trafford, against Stan Cullis's young lions from Wolves, they won by 7-1 with people like Eddie, Duncan, and David Pegg in the team. Eddie and Duncan were the architects of that victory.

Little Eddie had only played for Salford Boys but he had not played for England Boys like I had, and the way that he was playing I thought, 'If they can improve him and make him play like that, what can they do for me, a schoolboy international?'

Watching that team more than anything, made me want to join Matt Busby and Manchester United. My first impression of Sir Matt was the lovely way he spoke, how gentle his voice was. I met him first with my parents, and the way that we were looked after was great; he seemed to know my family background, and whenever we were chatting, he always mentioned my parents and my brother Laurence."

Wilf McGuinness signed as an amateur for Manchester United in June 1953, on the very same day that Bobby Charlton joined the club as well. Initially like most amateurs on the club's books, Wilf had to train on Tuesday and Thursday evenings down at The Cliff training ground in Salford. For his services, he was paid the princely sum of just £2 per week, although his parents did receive a subsistence and lodging allowance (which wasn't quite strictly legal) of £6 per week. The latter was money which Wilf's Mum never spent, and saved it for him for a 'rainy day.'

In November 1954, shortly after his 17th birthday, he signed his very first professional contract with Manchester United. Over the next few years, Wilf came under the tutorship of Jimmy Murphy, and also Coach Bert Whalley. Jimmy particularly, was a hard taskmaster and his criticisms were at times, hard for the young players to take. Many of them ended up in tears, but that was Jimmy's way – he knew what it took to mould them into professional footballers.

Manchester United at this time was seeing something of a transformation. Slowly but surely, the players that had made up the fabulous teams which had won the FA Cup in 1948, and the First Division Championship in 1952, began to disappear from the first team. There was an abundance of young players, most still in their teens, and there was an exuberance all around Old Trafford. Busby and Murphy had created a family atmosphere at the club, and all the young players were growing up together and learning their trade. They also bonded on and off the field as they were all great friends and used to socialize together. Wilf became very close with Eddie Colman, and Bobby Charlton. They would go on holiday together in the close-season to places like Butlins at Pwhelli in North Wales, and over to the Isle of Man. They spent time visiting Bobby's home in Ashington. Bobby's parents would stay at Wilf's home in Blackley, whenever they were down in Manchester. Many a Saturday evening would find all three of them at Colman's home in Archie Street, in Ordsall, listening to Eddie's Grandfather Dick, regaling them with tales of his past, and his Uncle Bill belting out songs for them, fuelled by jugs of beer brought in from the local off-licence!

Wilf's progression was fairly quick, and he moved through the Junior, A and B teams fairly quickly, and also played in three consecutive FA Youth Cup winning teams, 1953-54, 1954-55, and 1955-56, the latter team which he captained. The FA Youth Cup was virtually Manchester United's own property between 1953-58 they won the competition for the first five years of its existence. It is interesting to note that during those first five seasons, the club used a total of thirty five young players in those five finals. Of those, twenty five would go on to play in the first team at one time or another — a terrific example of how the club's youth policy was producing dividends and of Busby and Murphy's faith in what they were doing. If they were good enough, they were young enough, and this is why Joe Armstrong was able to cajole parents into allowing their offspring to join Manchester United. They knew that their boys would be given every chance of making a career as a professional football player.

Wilf was an all action wing-half who had a high-stepping running action. He was a tremendous tackler and knew how to distribute the ball once he had won it. His anticipation and reading of the game was superb, and if he was playing in today's modern era, he would probably fill the central midfield holding position. He had an abundance of stamina and when he was out on the pitch, he certainly caught the eye. Once he forced his way into the Reserve team at left-half, he was understudy to Duncan Edwards. Even Wilf realized that he had no real chance of displacing the young colossus from the team on a permanent basis, but as he told the spellbound young schoolchildren;

"When Bobby Charlton said that he couldn't lick Duncan Edwards's boots, you can imagine just how good Duncan was. Duncan played for United at 16, England at 18 and was only 21 when he died. He was left-half but could play anywhere. You would have been talking about him the way people talk about Pele, Maradona, and Di Stefano.

Off the field he was a shy, modest guy, a gentle giant with a strong Midlands accent. But on the field he was anything but shy and retiring. He could do anything, and he excelled at everything. He was a powerhouse and wanted the ball all the time. He stood out like a beacon. He would definitely have been England's captain at the 1966 World Cup, and I was proud to be his understudy. I didn't mind that. I have to admit that trying to get a game in his position was like trying to climb Mount Everest twice in a day

But I was always a confident person, and never shy about my own ability, and my own way of thinking was, that if I played well enough, he was such a great, great player who could play anywhere; I would get in, and they would move Duncan to another position."

McGuinness' first-team debut came on Saturday, 8 October 1955. Duncan Edwards went down with 'flu on the Friday morning, and Wilf was rushed to join the first team at the Norbreck Hydro Hotel in Blackpool where they stayed on a regular basis before important first team matches. The following lunchtime the team left by coach for Old Trafford where they would be playing against a very strong Wolverhampton Wanderers team. Playing against Stan Cullis's Wolves teams was always difficult. They were a team packed full of international players and they were always very physical. For a young 17 years old, facing that team could have been a very daunting prospect. However, Jimmy Murphy worked his motivational magic. Seeing Wilf sat in the corner of the dressing room shortly before the game, and obviously nervous, Jimmy talked to him for a few minutes. He put Wilf at his ease, so much so that he had a very good game in a hard fought game in which United won by 4-3.

Over the next two years, he was to play in a further twenty three games as a *'Babe'* before the Munich tragedy occurred. In the 1956-57 season when he was just eighteen years old, he played in thirteen league games which enabled him to collect a First Division Championship winner's medal. During that run of twenty four games, he also took part in some very good matches of note. One was in the European Cup against the German team Borrussia Dortmund, which was played at the Rote Erde Stadion, in Dortmund in November 1956. On a frozen ground, and with all the team's rubber studs having mysteriously gone missing from the kit skip, United had to fight a rearguard action all through the game, while defending a slender 3-2 advantage gained in the first-leg at Maine Road. With Tommy Taylor out injured, Edwards was moved up to centre-forward and Wilf came in at left-half. For the whole of the ninety minutes, United fought like tigers to defend that lead, and Wilf was tenacious throughout the game – tackling, harassing, and covering his other defenders. United escaped with a 0-0 draw and he had more than played his part in securing the result which took United through to the next round.

In October 1956, he had played in the home game against Charlton Athletic which saw Bobby Charlton make his Manchester United debut, and in March 1957, he played in the very first game ever to be played under floodlights at Old Trafford, against local neighbours, Bolton Wanderers. He also played in the famous win over Burnley at Old Trafford, on Easter Monday 1957 when Busby made nine changes from the team which had retained their First Division title

A young Wilf McGuinness pictured playing for Manchester United against Everton at Goodison Park on 6 March 1957. The famous St Luke's Church can be seen to the left of the Gwladys Street Stand. It was a landmark that was famous throughout football for most of the 20th Century.

by beating Sunderland 4-0 at Old Trafford on the previous Saturday afternoon. United still beat Burnley by 2-0, and it was a result which deeply upset the Burnley Chairman, Bob Lord, who always had a very strong antipathy towards Manchester United after that result. Then in October 1957, he played in a home game against Portsmouth which saw a tall, lean, long-legged Irishman make his debut for Pompey at centre-forward – his name was Derek Dougan. It was a game which would be Wilf's last in the first team before the Munich tragedy.

On Saturday, 1 February 1958, while the first team was playing in that epic match against Arsenal at Highbury, Wilf was playing in a reserve team game against Wolves at Old Trafford. On the day before, he had been told that he would be in the party to leave for Belgrade the following Monday. It was another European trip for him, and it was one which he was looking forward to. In the reserve game he suffered a bad injury when he twisted his knee, and upon medical examination, was found to have torn a cartilage. Back in those days, it was an injury which normally kept a player out of action for two months. He was saddened that it was an injury which meant that he would not be joining his young mates on the forthcoming trip.

When Thursday, February 6, arrived, Wilf was buoyed by the fact that United had drawn 3-3 in Belgrade and were into the draw for the semi-finals of the European Cup. That afternoon, as he limped along Princess Street in Manchester's city centre with his friend Joe Witherington, they noticed a small crowd gathered around a newspaper vendor. As they neared the crowd, they could hear the vendor calling; *"United in plane crash!"* Like most people that day, the first reports were very sketchy and were treated rather skeptically. However, as the minutes and hours passed, the news began filtering through of the enormity of the situation in Munich, and of the number of casualties incurred, and he knew that he had lost many of his close friends, particularly, his best friend, the impish little Eddie Colman. It was heartbreaking for him.

Wilf's career had to continue after Munich and he rose to meet the challenge. The following season he was an integral part of the team which finished runners-up in the First Division title race. He played so well that he forced his way into the England team, and also went on the international summer tour. The following season however, it was vastly different and United's early season form was poor. On 28 November 1959, United lost at Goodson Park to Everton by 2-1. Although the score line was close, it did not really reflect United's poor performance. During the following week, Busby had much to ponder. He decided to act, and for the next game against Blackpool at Old Trafford, he axed four international players from the team; Bobby Charlton, Harry Gregg, Warren Bradley ..... and Wilf McGuiness.

Playing in the Reserve team on 12 December 1959, against Stoke City Reserves, Wilf went into a tackle with one of their forwards. He heard a sharp crack and felt excruciating pain down the leg, and his worst fears were realized when after getting to the hospital, it was confirmed that he had broken both the tibia and fibula bones in his leg. His career as a professional footballer had come to an end at the young age of just 22 years.

Undeterred, he began another career as a Coach, and was Manchester United's reserve team coach for several years, as well as being an assistant coach with England during their World Cup winning campaign in the summer of 1966. As a coach, he was very highly thought of by Sir Alf Ramsey. In 1969, Sir Matt Busby decided to retire, and it was a surprise when Wilf McGuinness was nominated as his successor. The records state that he didn't hold the position for too long, but they certainly do not tell the full story. His United team reached the semi-finals of both domestic Cup competitions. Sadly though, he was never ever given the free reign to bring into the club quality players who he thought would strengthen the team. Mick Mils, from Ipswich Town, Colin Todd from Sunderland, and a young striker who was making headlines with Luton Town, a certain Malcolm MacDonald. The Manchester United Board however, never gave him the full backing which he deserved and consequently thwarted his attempts to buy the quality players who he needed.

Things at Manchester United were a hard, long slog, and although hindsight is a wonderful thing, it is interesting to note the difference in resources which afforded to the four managers who followed Wilf McGuinness's tenure. Frank O'Farrell was allocated £570,000 during his time; Tommy Docherty £830,000; Dave Sexton £1.15 million; and Ron Atkinson £3 million. Compare that to the modest £80,000 given to Wilf, and it tells its own story. In December 1970, the Board panicked and Wilf was sacked. The sacking hurt Wilf deeply and for a few years afterwards there was a little resentment. He left to coach in Greece in Salonika, and it was here where he first started to lose his hair. He was diagnosed with alopecia, a condition caused by sever loss, or trauma. He was to spend three years in Greece before returning home to manage York City which lasted for four years. He also spent considerable time in a number of positions at Bury Football club, the main one being physiotherapist. Bury holds a myriad of happy memories for him.

Wilf McGuinness (centre front) sits alongside the schoolchildren from Stretford High School as they display the 'Blue Heritage Plaques' which were later put up on the former homes of Duncan Edwards, and Tommy Taylor. In the rear sit Tom, and Cheryl Clare, Chris Hirst (Director of Learning), and School Headmaster and Principal, James Hasledine.

Today, Wilf is back at his beloved Old Trafford working in corporate hospitality on match days. He is also a very active member of the Association of Former Manchester United Players, which raises substantial sums for local charities. He is a well-known figure on the After-Dinner Speaking circuit and is in much demand. An evening spent in his company is never to be forgotten. Each year, I host a dinner in Manchester on the Friday evening before Manchester United's last home game of the season. In May 2006, Wilf was my guest at the Village Hotel, which is in Cheadle. The 200 persons attending were captivated and enthralled by him, and during his speech he said;

"I spent eighteen years at United, and I am happy to be back there now doing what I do. Anybody who has been there will tell you, it is in the blood. The main reason that I will always love the club so much is because of the 'Busby Babes.' I grew up with them. They were my true pals. We took our first pints together in the clubs, the first time we stayed in a hotel abroad we were together, the first time we won big trophies was together, we were growing up together. It was just such a wonderful, wonderful, life. Whatever happened afterwards, I still carried half of me at United wherever I went."

Watching Wilf McGuinness talk to the children and the staff at Stretford High School on that May morning in 2011, his eyes lit up brightly as once again he began to recall his times with those wonderful young boys who were his pals from more than fifty years ago. The memories still burned bright for him. He regaled the children with many stories but the funniest was when he told them, that when he was playing, the newspapers and media always used to compare him to the legendary Duncan Edwards. Pulling an old newspaper cutting from his inside pocket, he began to read out the headline......... *"Compared to Duncan Edwards, it is true say that left-half Wilf McGuinness is............... Absolutely rubbish!"* There were guffaws of laughter from the schoolchildren, and then rapturous applause for this lovely fellow for who Manchester United Football Club has dominated his life.

That is Wilf, always happy to tell a story against himself.

Wilf McGuinness played 85 games for Manchester United and scored 2 goals.

He won 2 full international caps for England, and was also capped at every international level for his country from schoolboys all the way through to the full international team.

Epilogue

On 6 February 1958, the city of Manchester woke up to a dark grey winter morning with the threat of snow coming later on in the day. For the 'Red' half of the city, the day was greeted with much excitement and chatter, as Manchester United fans eagerly discussed United's 3-3 draw with Yugoslavia's Red Star team, in Belgrade the previous afternoon. The draw for the semi-finals was looked forward to with tremendous anticipation, and almost everybody wanted United to meet Real Madrid. In the immediacy though, there was a vital First Division game to be played the following Saturday, at Old Trafford, against the League leaders, Wolverhampton Wanderers.

United were in third place in the League after they had defeated Arsenal by 5-4 at Highbury the previous Saturday. That win had left trailing Wolves by six points. However, United had hit a rich vein of form since mid-December 1957, and were unbeaten in eleven games in all competitions and they had scored thirty four goals in the process. They were buoyant, and a win against Wolves would reduce the Midlander's lead to just four points. As the United party checked in at the airport terminal in Belgrade, they were happy, and confident that they would get the job done at Old Trafford. After a slight delay due to Johnny Berry mislaying his Passport, the aircraft departed and the party had an uneventful trip to Munich, where they landed in early afternoon. The aircraft was refueled and made ready for the flight to Manchester where it was scheduled to arrive just before 6.30pm.

Back in Manchester it was late afternoon and the darkness had started to descend when the news filtered through to Manchester of the tragic happenings at the Riem Airport, in Munich. Initially the news was sketchy and blurred, and did not seem to make much sense. There were reports of a plane carrying the Manchester United team crashing, but those reports seemed to indicate that it was nothing too serious. As late afternoon turned into early evening, the gravity of the situation became much clearer. The BBC and other media bulletins became more updated with information and it became more than clear that here there was a major tragedy unfolding, and one that was affecting the whole City of Manchester, and not just followers of Manchester United. Throughout the country, even people with little or no interest in soccer were touched by the horror which was being reported.

There had been many fatalities including seven members of the Manchester United team, plus two of the club's coaches, and the club secretary. Eight of Britain's finest sporting journalists had also perished, as well as an ardent Manchester United supporter, a member of the crew, and a travel agent. Many people lay critically injured. It was a tragedy of a huge proportion. Over the next few weeks, two more people would lose the fight for their lives; one a player, one a member of the crew. The tragedy claimed a total of twenty three lives.

For many of the survivors, their injuries would impair them for the rest of their lives. The team that had been dubbed the *Busby Babes* was no more. This unique team of young men, who had set England's, and Europe's soccer fields alight, would never be seen again. Even today, fifty four years on, any mention of them in soccer circles, provokes heated debate and argument. Just how good were they? Many years later, when asked the question by the television chat show host, Michael Parkinson, Sir Matt Busby said;

"If they had even entered the Boat Race, they would have won it."

In today's modern era, people tend to forget that this was the club which had pioneered and championed the promotion of a youth policy. Eddie Colman, Duncan Edwards, Wilf McGuinness, and Bobby Charlton, all won FA Youth Cup winners medals three times in succession, something that has never been done since. The club was the holders of the FA Youth Cup for the five successive years after its inception. They were the club which blazed the trail into competitive European football for English clubs. In 1955, The Football League was so set against any English clubs taking part in European competition. Matt Busby, Harold Hardman, and Manchester United, fought the case until they prevailed and the young *Busby Babes* were the standard bearers for the years which followed. They won friends all over Europe, not only by the bright attacking style of football which they played; but also with their conduct, bearing, dignity, and personalities.

Of the players who survived the tragedy – Gregg, Wood, Foulkes, Blanchflower, Morgans, Berry, Viollet, Scanlon, and Charlton – two of them never played football again - they were Blanchflower and Berry. Wood, Morgans, Viollet and Scanlon, were to leave Manchester United within three years of the accident occurring. Only Charlton, Foulkes, Gregg, and Viollet can be said to have had any kind of first class careers afterwards. The others drifted off into lower league football, and even retirement. The club also lost key staff personnel as well. Walter Crikmer the Secretary; Tom Curry, and Bert Whalley, the Coaches. The tragedy decimated the club both on and off the field. It was going to take a massive job to rebuild the club once again and put it back at the forefront of British football.

Every year around the anniversary date of the tragedy, the question always comes up; *Munich -what if the accident had never happened?*

It is rather ironic that the preceding ten days before the Munich tragedy shaped the future and destiny of Manchester United Football Club. The decision to hire a charter aircraft for the trip to Belgrade, and the death of George Whittaker, a United director, in London, on 1 February 1958, had enormous effects on the club's future.

The Munich tragedy is like an octopus, it has so many tentacles; so many ifs and buts. I do not think that there is any doubt that given the foundations and structure of the club at that time, they would certainly have dominated English and maybe even European football, for the following decade. There was so much strength in depth at the club, and the young players that had to be thrust into the first team immediately after the accident would have had more time, under far different circumstances, to further their careers.

The England team would certainly have been far, far stronger, because although Roger Byrne, Duncan Edwards, and Tommy Taylor, were permanent first choices for England, players like Eddie Colman, Mark Jones, and David Pegg (who had already received one cap), were already knocking on the door for selection. There was also a certain young inside forward named Bobby Charlton forcing his way through. The accident cost not only Manchester United, but also the England national team a generation of the most talented players in Europe at that time.

It is my contention that had the accident not happened, England may well have won the World Cup held in Sweden that year. People tend to forget that just eighteen months earlier, Brazil, the eventual winners of the 1958 tournament, were heavily defeated by England at Wembley by 4-2, and England also missed two penalty kicks during the game.

Traveling with the United party to Belgrade on that ill-fated aircraft was a fan who was a huge friend, and very close to, Matt Busby. His name was Willie Satinoff. Willie Satinoff had become a very successful businessman and had made his money in the "rag trade" in and around city centre Manchester. Outside of his business interests and commitments, he was a devoted family man, and his main leisure pastime was following Manchester United. He was a fanatical supporter and had traveled to League games and throughout Europe with the official Manchester United party. It was well known in Manchester sporting circles and especially amongst the press boys that Willie was on the verge of becoming a Manchester United Director.

In the early hours of the morning of February 1st 1958, United director George Whittaker, who had traveled with the United party down to London for the game against Arsenal, was found dead in his bedroom at the Russell Hotel. Later that day his funeral arrangements were made and it was to take place on Wednesday, February 5th 1958 – the same day that Manchester United would be playing Red Star in Belgrade. Not one director traveled out to Munich as they chose to attend George Whittaker's funeral.

Louis Edwards was also around the scene in those days, but he was looked upon more as a 'hanger on' than anything else. George Whittaker had loathed the man and had thwarted him a number of times as he made attempts to become a Manchester united Director. It was Willie Satinoff who was flavor-of-the-month and it was he who traveled out to Belgrade with the team and the accompanying party. He was far, far, from being just a 'supporter.'

Satinoff was one of the casualties at Munich, and that opened the door for Louis Edwards to become a Manchester United Director. Had Satinoff not traveled to Belgrade, or had even survived the accident, then it is very doubtful if Louis Edwards and his family would have ever have gotten near to being a part of Manchester United. Most certainly Satinoff would have been elected to the board, and in my opinion would probably have succeeded Harold Hardman as Chairman in 1966. One thing is for certain, off the field, and under his leadership, the club would have moved with the times and would also have grown exponentially. There is no doubt that the club would have still become the commercial juggernaut that it is today. Under Satinoff's direction, that power would certainly have been used to ensure that the club never lost sight of the fact that it was a football club first and foremost.

Sir Matt Busby was just sixty one years old when he retired in 1971. There is no doubt that his injuries received at Munich eventually caught up with him and played a big part in that decision to retire. If there had been no Munich, it is more than probable that a fit Busby would have taken Manchester United through the 70s years. Young players coming through the Manchester United system would never have been allowed to progress naturally without having the pressures of being forced into service far too early. Sir Matt would have had time to groom his eventual successor. Who would that have been? My guess is that it would have been Duncan Edwards who would have been just forty four years old in 1980.

Edwards and Eddie Colman were both only twenty one years old when they died. It was a half-back pairing that would have been difficult to break up, and it is more than likely that they would have filled those positions for Manchester United and England for at least the next eight to ten years. Would Bobby Moore have played for England? I think that the answer to that is most unequivocally - yes. Moore was a great, great player, and would have forced his way into the team because of his sheer ability. However, I doubt that he would have worn the number six shirt, or would have collected the World Cup trophy from HM the Queen in 1966. Most certainly, in my opinion, it would have been Edwards.

Would we have seen Stiles and McGuinness break through into the United first team, and would they have bought Pat Crerand? Somehow I doubt it however I do think that they would still have bought Denis Law. George Best would almost certainly have forced his way in simply because of his sheer natural talent. There are so many ifs and buts. In the end it is all hypotheses.

John Arlott, whose gentle, dulcet voice tone became the voice and name of Test Match cricket in England, was also a wonderful journalist. In the years leading up to 1958, he had contributed football articles on a regular basis for the *Manchester Guardian* newspaper. The newspaper's senior correspondent was Harold Donald 'Donny' Davies, who wrote under the pen name of *An Old International*. The week before the game in Belgrade, the newspaper's Sports Editor, Larry Montague, had contacted Arlott when it became known that Davies would not be able to make the trip because he could not get the time off work - Davies was actually a full-time schoolteacher and sports writing was more of a hobby for him. The Editor offered the job to John Arlott which he accepted and looked forward to with great anticipation. He was sent to cover the famous Arsenal v Manchester United clash at Highbury, which took place on 1 February, 1958 and which produced the never to be forgotten game which culminated in a 5-4 win for Manchester United. It was to be their last ever game on English soil.

It is ironic that late on Sunday afternoon, 2 February 1958, Arlott took a telephone call from the same Sports Editor which informed him that Davies had been able to get the time off from his teaching duties and it would be he who would make the trip out to Belgrade. Arlott's services would not be required and it left him feeling more than a little deflated. In an article in *The Guardian* on February 5 1983, Arlott recalled:

The Thursday after the match in Belgrade had been played, I was still irritated by the fact that I had not been allowed to travel out there to cover the match. That afternoon I visited book shops. At the fourth there was a 'phone call. 'Ah! I was tracking you south through the book shops: you're to ring Larry Montague before the Guardian switchboard chokes. The Manchester United plane has crashed. Be ready to write a lot of obituaries — starting with Donny's.' A shudder of horror, mixed with relief, coursed through me - then came the nausea.

Arlott's piece for *The Guardian* began;

'Yesterday, on a Munich Airfield, Association Football shrank to small matter. Twenty four hours before, Manchester United had drawn with Red Star Belgrade to pass into the semi-finals of the European Cup on aggregate. It was yet another triumph for the finest club team ever produced in Britain. For the moment, that victory seems slight, at best, a memorial to young athletes now dead.'

He concluded the article with;

No club in the history of football had ever shouldered such a burden of strain as the Manchester United team of the last two seasons, which strove so mightily for the triple honour no British team has ever achieved.

Yet even under that weight, they invested the playing of a game with something near, indeed, to glory in the imaginations of hundreds of thousands who had never come within miles of Manchester. This was to have been another triumphant homecoming to Old Trafford. If their triumph has become a wreath, it is one in which many memories will never fade.

On that sad day in February 1958, at the end of a snow covered runway, the cream of English football perished. They were, as far as I am concerned, the greatest English football team that I have ever seen.

"They say that they were the best team that we have ever seen.

Well, maybe.

They say that they may have gone on to be the best team that we have ever seen.

Well again, maybe.

However, there is one thing that is for certain – they were certainly the most loved

team that there has ever been."

By kind permission of Harry Gregg MBE.

The Flowers of Manchester

One cold and bitter Thursday in Munich, Germany
Eight great football stalwarts conceded victory
Eight men will never play again, who met disaster there
The flowers of English football, the flowers of Manchester

The Busby Babes were flying home, returning from Belgrade
This great United family all masters of their trade
The pilot of the aircraft, the skipper Captain Thain
Three times tried to take off and twice turned back again.

The third time down the runway disaster followed close
There was slush upon that runway and the aircraft never rose
It ploughed into the marshy ground, it broke, it overturned
And eight of that team were killed as the blazing wreckage burned

Roger Byrne and Tommy Taylor, who were capped for England's side
And Ireland's Liam Whelan and England's Geoff Bent died

The Last Line Up –Stadion JNA – Belgrade, Yugoslavia v Red Star – 5 February 1958
From left to right; Duncan Edwards, Eddie Colman, Mark Jones, Kenny Morgans, Bobby Charlton, Dennis Viollet, Tommy Taylor, Bill Foulkes, Harry Gregg, and Roger Byrne.

Matt Busby leads out his Busby Babes at Wembley before the start of the 1957 FA Cup Final. He is followed by his Captain, Roger Byrne, and then Johnny Berry, Jackie Blanchflower, Ray Wood, Bill Foulkes, Bobby Charlton, Tommy Taylor, Liam Whelan, Duncan Edwards and David Pegg. The player who cannot be seen is Eddie Colman who was behind Duncan Edwards.

Mark Jones and Eddie Colman and David Pegg also
They all lost their lives as it ploughed on through the snow.

Big Duncan he went too, after suffering so much pain
And Ireland's Jackie Blanchflower will never play again
The great Matt Busby lying there, the father of his team
Three long months passed by before he saw his team again.

The trainer, coach and secretary, and three members of the crew
Also eight sporting journalists who with United flew
and one of them Big Swifty, who we will ne'er forget
the finest English 'keeper that ever graced the net
Oh, England's finest football team its record truly great
its proud successes mocked by a cruel turn of fate
Eight men will never play again, who met destruction there
the flowers of English football, the flowers of Manchester

Anon